12/09

Digital Media, Youth, and Credibility

D1407970

This book was made possible by grants from the John D. and Catherine T. MacArthur Foundation in connection with its grant making initiative on Digital Media and Learning. For more information on the initiative visit www.macfound.org.

The John D. and Catherine T. MacArthur Foundation Series on Digital Media and Learning

Civic Life Online: Learning How Digital Media Can Engage Youth, edited by W. Lance Bennett

Digital Media, Youth, and Credibility, edited by Miriam J. Metzger and Andrew J. Flanagin

The Ecology of Games: Connecting Youth, Games, and Learning, edited by Katie Salen

Digital Youth, Innovation, and the Unexpected, edited by Tara McPherson

Learning Race and Ethnicity: Youth and Digital Media, edited by Anna Everett

Youth, Identity, and Digital Media, edited by David Buckingham

Digital Media, Youth, and Credibility

Edited by Miriam J. Metzger and Andrew J. Flanagin

The MIT Press
Cambridge, Massachusetts
London, England

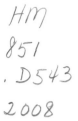
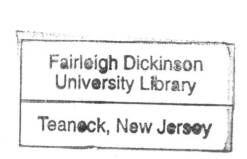
For information about special quantity discounts, please email special_sales@mitpress.mit.edu.

This book was set in Stone sans and Stone serif by Aptara, Inc.

Printed and bound in the United States of America.

Library of Congress Cataloging-in-Publication Data

Digital media, youth, and credibility / edited by Miriam J. Metzger and Andrew J. Flanagin.
       p.   cm.—(The John D. and Catherine T. Macarthur Foundation series on digital media and learning)
   Includes bibliographical references.
   ISBN 978-0-262-06273-2 (hardcover : alk. paper)—ISBN 978-0-262-56232-4 (pbk. : alk. paper)
   1. Digital media—Social aspects.   2. Electronic information resources.   3. Information behavior.
   4. Mass media and youth.   5. Mass media in education.   6. Internet in education.
   7. Truthfulness and falsehood.   I. Metzger, Miriam J.   II. Flanagin, Andrew J.
HM851.D543   2008
302.23'10835—dc22   2007029493

10 9 8 7 6 5 4 3 2 1

CONTENTS

Foreword

In recent years, digital media and networks have become embedded in our everyday lives, and are part of broad-based changes to how we engage in knowledge production, communication, and creative expression. Unlike the early years in the development of computers and computer-based media, digital media are now *commonplace* and *pervasive*, having been taken up by a wide range of individuals and institutions in all walks of life. Digital media have escaped the boundaries of professional and formal practice, and the academic, governmental, and industry homes that initially fostered their development. Now they have been taken up by diverse populations and non-institutionalized practices, including the peer activities of youth. Although specific forms of technology uptake are highly diverse, a generation is growing up in an era where digital media are part of the taken-for-granted social and cultural fabric of learning, play, and social communication.

In 2005, The John D. and Catherine T. MacArthur Foundation began a new grant-making initiative in the area of digital media and learning. An initial set of exploratory grants in the study of youth practices and the development of digital literacy programs has expanded into a major initiative spanning research, educational reform, and technology development. One component of this effort is the support of this book series. As part of the broader MacArthur Foundation initiative, this series is aimed at timely dissemination of new scholarship, fostering an interdisciplinary conversation, and archiving the best research in this emerging field. Through the course of producing the six initial volumes, the foundation convened a set of meetings to discuss the framing issues for this book series. As a result of these discussions we identified a set of shared commitments and areas of focus. Although we recognize that the terrain is being reshaped even as we seek to identify it, we see these as initial frames for the ongoing work to be put forward by this series.

This book series is founded upon the working hypothesis that those immersed in new digital tools and networks are engaged in an unprecedented exploration of language, games, social interaction, problem solving, and self-directed activity that leads to diverse forms of learning. These diverse forms of learning are reflected in expressions of identity, how individuals express independence and creativity, and in their ability to learn, exercise judgment, and think systematically.

The defining frame for this series is not a particular theoretical or disciplinary approach, nor is it a fixed set of topics. Rather, the series revolves around a constellation of topics investigated from multiple disciplinary and practical frames. The series as a whole looks at the relation between youth, learning, and digital media, but each book or essay might deal with only a subset of this constellation. Erecting strict topical boundaries can exclude some of the most important work in the field. For example, restricting the content of the series only to people of a certain age means artificially reifying an age boundary when the phenomenon demands otherwise. This becomes particularly problematic with new forms of online participation where one important outcome is the mixing of participants of different ages. The same goes for digital media, which are increasingly inseparable from analog and earlier media forms.

In the case of learning, digital media are part of the redefinition and broadening of existing boundaries of practice and our understanding of what learning means. The term *learning* was chosen rather than *education* in order to flag an interest in settings both within and outside the classroom. Many of the more radical challenges to existing learning agendas are happening in domains such as gaming, online networks, and amateur production that usually occur in informal and non-institutional settings. This does not mean we are prejudiced against learning as it happens in the classroom or other formal educational settings. Rather, we hope to initiate a dialog about learning as it spans settings that are more explicitly educational and those that are not.

The series and the MacArthur Foundation initiative respond to certain changes in our media ecology that have important implications for learning. Specifically, these are new forms of media *literacy* and changes in the modes of media *participation*. Digital media are part of a convergence between interactive media (most notably gaming), online networks, and existing media forms. Navigating this media ecology involves a palette of literacies that are being defined through practice but require more scholarly scrutiny before they can be fully incorporated pervasively into educational initiatives. Media literacy involves not only ways of understanding, interpreting, and critiquing media, but also the means for creative and social expression, online search and navigation, and a host of new technical skills. The potential gap in literacies and participation skills creates new challenges for educators who struggle to bridge media engagement inside and outside the classroom.

The shift toward interactive media, peer-to-peer forms of media communication, and many-to-many forms of distribution relate to types of participation that are more bottom-up and driven by the "user" or "consumer" of media. Audiences have always had the opportunity to "talk back" to corporate media or to create their own local media forms. However, the growing dominance of gaming as a media format, the advent of low-cost digital production tools, and online distribution means a much more dynamic range in who participates and how they participate in the production and distribution of media. Gamers expect that media are subject to player control. Add to this the fact that all forms of media are increasingly being contextualized in an online communication ecology where creative production and expression is inseparable from social communication. Finally, new low-cost digital production tools mean that amateur and casual media creators can author, edit, and distribute video and other rich media forms that were once prohibitively expensive to produce and share with others.

We value the term *participation* for the ways in which it draws attention to situated learning theory, social media literacies, and mobilized forms of media engagement. Digital media networks support existing forms of mass media distribution as well as smaller publics and collectivities that might center on peer groups or specialized niche interests. The presence of social communication, professional media, and amateur niche media in shared online spaces introduces a kind of leveling effect, where small media players gain new visibility and the position of previously authoritative media is challenged. The clash between more socially driven or niche publics and the publics defined by professional forms of media is playing out in high-profile battles in domains such as intellectual property law, journalism, entertainment, and government. For our purposes, the questions surrounding knowledge and credibility and young people's use of digital media to circumvent adult authority are particularly salient.

The emerging power shift, where smaller and edge players are gaining more visibility and voice, is particularly important to children and youth. If we look at children and youth through the lens of digital media, we have a population that has been historically subject to a high degree of systematic and institutional control in the kinds of information and social communication to which they have access. This is one reason why the alchemy between youth and digital media has been distinctive; it disrupts the existing set of power relations between adult authority and youth voice. While many studies of children, youth, and media have for decades stressed the status of young people as competent and full social subjects, digital media increasingly insist that we acknowledge this viewpoint. Not only must we see youth as legitimate social and political actors, but we must also recognize them as potential innovators and drivers of new media change.

This does not mean that we are uncritical of youth practices or that we believe that digital media necessarily hold the key to empowerment. Rather, we argue against technological determinism, stressing the need for balanced scholarship that recognizes the importance of our current moment within the context of existing structures and unfolding histories. This means placing contemporary changes within a historical context as well as working to highlight the diversity in the landscape of media and media uptake. Neither youth nor digital media are monolithic categories; documenting how specific youth take up particular forms of media with diverse learning outcomes is critical to this series as a whole. Digital media take the form they do because they are created by existing social and cultural contexts, contexts that are diverse and stratified.

As with earlier shifts in media environments, this current turn toward digital media and networks has been accompanied by fear and panic as well as elevated hopes. This is particularly true of adult perception of children and youth who are at the forefront of experimentation with new media forms, and who mobilize digital media to push back at existing structures of power and authority. While some see "digital kids" as our best hope for the future, others worry that new media are part of a generational rift and a dangerous turn away from existing standards for knowledge, literacy, and civic engagement. Careful, socially engaged, and accessible scholarship is crucial to informing this public debate and related policy decisions. Our need to understand the relation between digital media and learning is urgent because of the scale and the speed of the changes that are afoot. The shape and uses of digital media are still very much in flux, and this book series seeks to be part of the definition of our sociotechnical future.

Mizuko Ito
Cathy Davidson
Henry Jenkins
Carol Lee
Michael Eisenberg
Joanne Weiss
Series Advisors

Introduction

Miriam J. Metzger and Andrew J. Flanagin

University of California, Santa Barbara, Department of Communication

This volume addresses credibility in the digital media environment, with a particular emphasis on youth audiences, issues, and experiences. The focus is on how young people assess the objective and subjective components of the believability of sources and messages as they come to trust the veracity of what they read, see, or hear through digital media. In some cases, individuals are honing new skills, and invoking novel tools, for assessing information credibility. In other instances, the voice of the community is emerging as the coin of credibility, and self-regulation serves as evidence that the locus of knowledge ownership is moving to communities of users. In still other cases, institutional or corporate entities are emerging as arbiters of credibility. Overall, it is clear that as youth increasingly take advantage of media offering a diversity of information sources, but where the motivations, identity, and quality of those sources and information can be difficult to determine, the issue of credibility becomes crucially important to consider as we determine how best to teach children to navigate the vast ocean of information now available thorough digital technologies.

Although research on credibility and new media is burgeoning, extremely little of it focuses on youth (with the exception of college students), in spite of this population's exceptional immersion in digital technologies. To address this void, the chapters in this volume highlight the special problems and opportunities with regard to credibility that young people who have grown up with digital media face today. To do this, the authors endeavor to reach beyond the somewhat trite rhetoric that all digital information is untrustworthy, that all youth are inherently more vulnerable than adults, and that technological tools determine specific outcomes. Thus, a goal of the volume is to offer an appropriately sophisticated, balanced, and thus enduring view of youth, credibility, and digital media.

The book can be divided informally into five sections. First, Chapter 1 (Flanagin and Metzger) situates credibility by considering its intellectual heritage and its evolution in light of digital media. This discussion serves to position credibility as a contemporary topic of inquiry, particularly relevant for today's youth. Second, Chapters 2 (Eastin) and 3 (Rieh and

---

Several people were helpful in generating and discussing the ideas in this book. Most notably, we would like to acknowledge the contribution of the following, who participated in substantive online discussions with the authors and editors: Denise Agosto, Katherine Arens, Marilyn Arnone, John Bell, Michael Buckland, Erik Bucy, Jacquelyn Burkell, David Danielson, Mike Eisenberg, Robert Ennis, Sari Feldman, Linda Garcia, Yetta Goodman, Margaretha Haughwaut, Carl Heine, Jim Hirsch, Jon Ippolito, Lana Jackman, Jonathan Lazar, George Lorenzo, Kitty Lucero, Clifford Lynch, Deanna Kuhn, Ryan Lingsweiler, Mary McIlrath, Melody Pinkston, Lauren B. Resnick, Ron Rice, Ruth Small, Bob Stonehill, Amanda Toperoff, Joyce Valenza, Kate Wittenberg, and Kristina Woolsey.

Hilligoss) look specifically at two different youth populations, younger (children) and older (college students) youth. Questions about whether and how youth may differ from adult user populations are explored therein. Chapters 4 (Sundar) and 5 (Lankes) examine how digital media challenge some of our traditional assumptions about credibility assessment, including notions that credibility assessment is mostly a conscious, effortful process on the part of users, and that credibility is necessarily tied to authority and hierarchy. Chapter 6 (Eysenbach) offers an in-depth discussion of how users assess the credibility of one particularly important category of information, online health information. Finally, Chapters 7 (Harris) and 8 (Weingarten) respectively examine the educational and political issues surrounding credibility and digital media and offer recommendations for both policy and practice. Collectively, the chapters demonstrate that digital media technologies simultaneously empower and disempower youth as they strive to reach their informational goals. As a means by which to further frame the contribution of the volume overall, each chapter is next discussed in detail to highlight its particular contribution.

Chapter 1, by Andrew Flanagin and Miriam Metzger, defines credibility after situating it in relation to allied terms and concepts. Against this backdrop, the authors argue that understanding credibility is particularly complex—and consequential—in the digital media environment, especially for youth audiences, who have both advantages and disadvantages due to their relationship with contemporary technologies and their life experience. To sort out the new and emerging types of credibility and credibility assessment that are implicated in modern media tools, a categorization of credibility construction is offered that considers individuals as networked actors engaged with others, as opposed to isolated appraisers of credibility. This understanding is leveraged to explain why credibility is a worthy and important topic of inquiry, what is and is not new about credibility in the context of digital media, and the major thrusts of current credibility concerns for scholars, educators, and youth. The chapter concludes by considering the research, policy, and educational implications of credibility today and by making recommendations for practitioners of all kinds who are affected by youth, credibility, and digital media.

In Chapter 2, Matthew Eastin discusses children's cognitive development—or the evolution of their cognitive structures, abilities, and processes—and how it influences their ability to process information encountered online. By examining Piaget's stages of cognitive development, Eastin explores the information evaluations (e.g., assessment of various source cues) that children make when online. One conclusion is that the complex informational environments children must navigate online tax their cognitive capabilities in ways that are variously consequential, depending on their stage of cognitive development. In all cases, however, the Web constitutes a demanding information-processing environment that must be considered when trying to understand credibility assessment among youth audiences. Overall, Eastin argues that research needs to consider how evaluation shifts as children evolve from one developmental stage to another.

Chapter 3, by Soo Young Rieh and Brian Hilligoss, examines the relationship between information-seeking strategies and credibility judgments through an in-depth exploration of how college students identify credible information in everyday information-seeking tasks. The authors argue that credibility assessment is a process that takes place over time rather than a discrete evaluative event. Moreover, the context in which credibility assessment occurs is crucial to understand, because it affects both the level of effort as well as the strategies that people use to evaluate credibility. The authors also find that credibility assessment is best described as an iterative process whereby people make predictive judgments about the value of information resources prior to taking information-seeking actions and evaluative judgments after accessing information. In turn, information verification or reevaluation may occur after information use. The college students in their study indicated that although credibility was an important consideration during information seeking, they often compromised information credibility for speed and convenience, especially when the information sought was less consequential.

In Chapter 4, S. Shyam Sundar argues that beyond explicit, considered assessments of sources and content, Web users are heavily affected by more subtle cues as they evaluate information online. Particularly for youth audiences, heuristics such as the "surface features" of the interface are important in credibility assessment, since these users are more prone than adults to attend to such elements. Specifically, the "technological affordances" of modality, agency, interactivity, and navigability influence credibility judgments by triggering cognitive heuristics that form impressions of information quality. Thus, Sundar argues that in addition to explicitly conscious efforts, structural and technological factors can profoundly influence credibility judgments by transmitting certain cues that trigger cognitive heuristics leading to impressions of the quality of information. In this manner, the chapter demonstrates that a great deal of automaticity governs youths' assessment of the credibility of information, and that users may rely heavily on cues to make snap judgments while in the midst of online activities rather than on the effortful consideration of the totality of information on any given subject or site. Overall, this work offers important insight for developing effective educational campaigns to teach young people how to discern credible information online.

R. David Lankes, in Chapter 5, looks at how digital media technologies provide means of determining credibility that formerly were not available to individuals. He argues that increased "information self-sufficiency," where consumers are expected or required to seek and assess information critical to their everyday activities, is now normative. As a result, effective credibility assessment is crucial: because information is now disconnected from its physical origin (e.g., people now buy products online without ever inspecting them physically beforehand), accurate and reliable information is essential for sound decisions. In addition, interactions that are increasingly mediated by software—which actually make potentially consequential decisions as users perform various tasks—place users at the mercy of these tools. Both factors suggest a paradox where consumers relying on digital information are simultaneously more independent in their personal lives but also increasingly dependent on digital information and tools. In the end, the separation of credibility from authority afforded by digital media technology necessitates a "reliability" approach to credibility assessment, rather than one founded primarily on authority. In light of this, Lankes explores the opportunities to leverage the special characteristics of digital media to create new methods of credibility assessment.

In Chapter 6, Gunther Eysenbach considers the role of Web technologies on the availability and consumption of health information. He notes that, contrary to some well-publicized surveys of individuals' health information-seeking behaviors, the actual incidence of health-related searches on the Internet is much lower than most estimates. Thus, although many people have sought health information online, virtually nobody does so frequently. The implication is that people, and especially young people, are largely unfamiliar with trusted health sources online, making credibility particularly germane when considering online health information. Eysenbach argues that as information consumers use these tools to participate more in their own health choices and decisions, humans and technologies act as new intermediaries—or "apomediaries"—that "stand by" and steer consumers to high-quality information. He concludes by highlighting the credibility implications of this paradigm shift and demonstrating how it can empower health information seekers of all ages.

In Chapter 7, Frances Jacobson Harris, an educator and high school librarian, explores the many challenges that exist to teaching credibility assessment in the school environment. Challenges range from institutional barriers such as government regulation and school policies and procedures to dynamic challenges related to young people's cognitive development and the consequent difficulties of navigating a complex Web environment. The chapter also includes a critique of current practices for teaching kids credibility assessment and highlights some best practices for credibility education, including a discussion of ways to leverage what children are actually doing with digital media into an effective curriculum for training youth to assess the credibility of the information they receive via these media. A key contribution is Harris's contention that teaching youth to assess credibility effectively requires recognizing their special relationship to digital media by respecting their own experience and practices while providing appropriate instruction and guidance.

Finally, Fred Weingarten, in Chapter 8, notes that as concern about the credibility of information on the Internet grows, so do pressures for government attempts to mitigate the problem. He examines the potential roles of government in dealing with public concerns about information credibility on the Internet. Weingarten argues that public policy has been and will continue to be a political negotiation between a positive view of digital media as crucial infrastructure for education as well as the nation's economic and social well-being, and a negative view of an unregulated, hostile, and dangerous environment, especially for children. The chapter then discusses and compares "protective" policies that attempt to restrict access to content and "supportive" policies that focus on equipping users and intermediary institutions (such as schools and libraries) to meet their informational goals, arguing that more attention should be paid to developing policies that support both users and educators to find and evaluate the information they need.

By assembling a wide-ranging yet cohesive set of chapters, this volume addresses pressing research, policy, educational, and practical issues and sets an agenda for the continuation of this important work. Indeed, collectively, the chapters in this volume represent foundational pieces in a new area of inquiry that is interdisciplinary in scope, drawing from scholarship in communication, library and information science, social and cognitive psychology, sociology, education, and other fields to understand credibility issues in the digital media environment as they pertain to youth audiences. Interestingly, the chapters look backward—to glean what is known from existing and important work on credibility, information seeking, critical thinking, human cognition and development, and media literacy—as well as forward, to offer suggestions for future work in this domain.

In the end, this volume is about how those who are immersed in digital media produce, seek, share, and digest information and about the promise and perils offered in the contemporary media environment. As information is increasingly provided, assembled, filtered, and presented by sources either more removed from us personally, or that are mediated in ways not yet well understood, it is important to comprehend the effects on those most fully immersed in this environment. This volume is the first comprehensive treatment of digital media, youth, and credibility and, as such, offers an important step toward such an understanding.

Digital Media and Youth: Unparalleled Opportunity and Unprecedented Responsibility

Andrew J. Flanagin and Miriam J. Metzger

University of California, Santa Barbara, Department of Communication

With the sudden explosion of digital media content and access devices in the last generation, there is now more information available to more people from more sources than at any time in human history. Pockets of limited availability by geography or status notwithstanding, people now have ready access to almost inconceivably vast information repositories that are increasingly portable, accessible, and interactive in both delivery and formation. Basic human activities have changed as a result, and new possibilities have emerged. For instance, the process by which people locate, organize, and coordinate groups of individuals with shared interests, the number and nature of information and news sources available, and the ability to solicit and share opinions and ideas across myriad topics have all undergone dramatic change as a result of interconnected digital media.

One result of this contemporary media landscape is that there exist incredible opportunities for learning, social connection, and individual entertainment and enhancement in a wide variety of forms. Indeed, recent evidence indicates that 45 percent of users in the United States say that the Internet played a crucial or important role in at least one major decision in their lives in the last two years, such as attaining additional career training, helping themselves or someone else with a major illness or medical condition, or making a major investment or financial decision.[1] Enhanced connectivity and information availability have changed not only *what* people know, but *how* they know what they know.

However, the wide-scale access and multiplicity of sources that ensure vast information availability also make assessing the credibility of information extremely complex. The origin of information, its quality, and its veracity are now in many cases less clear than ever before, resulting in an unparalleled burden on individuals to locate appropriate information and assess its meaning and relevance accurately. Doing so is highly consequential: assessing credibility *in*accurately can have serious social, personal, educational, relational, health, and financial consequences. As a result, determining trust, believability, and information bias—key elements of credibility—become critical as individuals process the information in their lives gleaned from digital media.

Understanding credibility in this environment is also important because it is a concern that cuts across personal, social, and political domains. For instance, digital media increasingly deliver information that results (or fails to result) in an informed citizenry that, in turn, drives the pursuit of particular social agendas, the degree and nature of engagement in public discourse, and the determination of public policy.[2] In addition, in light of the prevalence of interactions with others that now routinely occur online, personal and social identity is often established and known primarily or exclusively through computer-mediated interactions.[3]

Thus, the credibility of information sources is no longer necessarily a function of sustained, face-to-face interaction, nor is it established solely through the endorsement of those whom one knows personally or directly. Nonetheless, source credibility remains a key component of persuasion, with decision-making implications ranging from consumer choices to political candidate selection.

Contemporary youth are a particularly interesting group to consider with regard to credibility today. In many ways, this generation (demarcated roughly by birth around 1980, give or take a few years) is different from any before in its relationship to information technology, and also in its relationship to information sources.[4] Known variously as "The Millenials,"[5] the "Net Generation,"[6] "Digital Natives,"[7] and "Generation Y,"[8] members of this generation share the feature of having been immersed in an environment of digital technologies (e.g., computers and the Internet) for their entire lives. They have been described, for instance, as "digital natives in a land of digital immigrants" whose experience with digital media has led them to have "new and different expectations about how to gather, work with, translate, and share information."[9] Compared to their elders, they are more likely to turn to digital media first when researching a topic for school or personal use, to read news on the Internet than in a printed newspaper; and to use online social network tools to meet friends and to find information. In other words, the primary sources of information in their world are often (although not exclusively) digital, which is quite different from any generation prior.

Their special relationship to digital media greatly influences the way they approach learning and research.[10] As the first generation to grow up with interactive digital media, millennials are comfortable with collaborating and sharing information, and do so "in ways that allow them to act quickly and without top-down direction."[11] This, of course, has profound implications for credibility construction and assessment. The interactivity afforded by digital media has set up an expectation among many young people to play roles of both information source and receiver simultaneously as they critique, alter, remix, and share content in an almost conversational manner using digital media.[12] Here again, the implications of the uses of technology that are favored by young people present new and different challenges for both discerning and learning to create credible information.

Nonetheless, despite these realities, examinations of youth and digital media have often been somewhat crude, focusing for example on the popular generation gap caricature, where youth are portrayed as technologically adept compared with adults. Such considerations fail to focus on the most important and enduring by-products of heavy reliance on digital media: The impact of "growing up digital"[13] is that more and more of the information that drives our daily lives is provided, assembled, filtered, and presented by sources that are largely unknown to us, or known to us primarily in nontraditional ways. Yet, we have only begun to explore what this means, particularly for younger users who are not only immersed in digital media now but will be for the entirety of their lives.

In terms of credibility specifically, youth are also intriguing in large part due to the tension between their technical and social immersion and skill with digital tools and their inherent limitations owing to their limited development and experience. On the one hand, those who have literally grown up in an environment saturated with digital media technologies may be highly skilled in their use of technologies to access, consume, and generate information. This view suggests that in light of their special relationship to digital tools, youth are especially well positioned to navigate the complex media environment successfully. On the other hand, youth can be viewed as inhibited, in terms of their cognitive and emotional development, life experiences, and familiarity with the media apparatus. This perspective suggests that although youth are talented and comfortable users of technology, they may lack crucial tools and abilities that enable them to seek and consume information effectively.[14]

As a way of beginning to understand the complex relationship between credibility, digital media, and youth, we proceed by first defining credibility after situating it in relation to allied terms and concepts. With this background, we consider credibility in the digital media environment, and examine the various credibility assessment strategies in use today, particularly those relying on group and social engagement. From there, we consider why credibility is worthy and important as a topic of inquiry, including what is and is not new about credibility in the context of digital media. Next, we examine the major issues with regard to credibility and, in particular, what special concerns arise for youth populations. Finally, we offer some perspectives of scholars, educators, and, most important, youth regarding credibility, and with this context we examine the research, policy, and educational implications. We conclude by considering the gaps to be filled in credibility research and providing recommendations for practitioners of all kinds who are affected by youth, credibility, and digital media.

Credibility Origins, Definitions, and Current Issues

Origins of Credibility Research

Scholarly interest in credibility dates back to Aristotle's writings on rhetoric and his notions of ethos (appeal based on the character of a speaker; e.g., reputation), pathos (appeal based on emotion; e.g., fear appeals), and logos (appeal based on logic or reason; e.g., the content of a speech). According to Aristotle, all three were necessary to be trustworthy,[15] although in his view credibility was mainly in the speaker and his or her ability to relate to different audiences. Ethos was thus "the communicator's ability to inspire confidence and belief in what was being said,"[16] and high-ethos speakers were considered fair, trustworthy, sincere, reliable, and honest.

Source credibility was addressed in earnest during the twentieth century by psychologists interested in studying persuasion, largely as a response to propaganda efforts during the World Wars. The "Yale Group," led by social psychologist Carl Hovland, defined credibility as expertise and trustworthiness and, for the first time, drew a distinction between source credibility, message credibility, and audience credulity.[17] In contrast to Aristotle's view, they suggested that credibility is a receiver-based construct and is determined by the acceptance of a speaker by the audience. The Yale group conducted numerous studies of source credibility as it pertained to persuasion and attitude change and identified the major components of what it means for a source to be perceived as credible by an audience. This work spurred a large body of research looking at both "source" and "message" credibility—characteristics of speakers and characteristics of messages or information.

The next major interest in credibility research came from professional rather than academic concerns. As television diffused widely in the 1950s, subscription rates for daily newspapers started to sag. As a result, newspaper professional organizations became interested in the perceived credibility of newspapers versus television (i.e., "media credibility"). The major finding in this domain was that the more people relied on a medium for news—television or newspapers—the more credible they believed that medium was.[18]

The study of credibility was resurrected in the late 1990s by the emergence of the Internet, the Web, and academic (psychology, communication, persuasion) and professional (news, e-commerce) concerns surrounding these technologies. In this domain, the Internet and

Web conflate notions of source, media, and message credibility, which formerly have been treated as rather distinct, or at least addressed largely separately.[19]

Defining Credibility

There exists no one, clear definition of credibility that has arisen from this heritage. Rather, the overarching view is that credibility is the *believability* of a source or message, which is made up of two primary dimensions: trustworthiness and expertise. Some secondary dimensions include source dynamism (charisma) and physical attractiveness, for example. Moreover, the two primary dimensions (trustworthiness and expertise) have both objective and subjective components. That is, trustworthiness is a receiver judgment based primarily on subjective factors. Expertise can be similarly subjectively perceived but includes relatively objective characteristics of the source or message as well (e.g., source credentials or information quality).

The study of credibility is highly interdisciplinary, and definitions are also somewhat field-specific. For example, communication and social psychology treat credibility as a perceptual variable: credibility is not an objective property of a source or a piece of information; instead, it is a subjective perception on the part of the information receiver.[20] Thus, this perspective emphasizes audience *perceptions* of credibility rather than the objective credibility of a source or piece of information. Information science perspectives, by contrast, view credibility as more of an objective property of information given that field's focus on defining credibility in terms of information "quality," which is how useful, good, relevant, reliable, accurate, and so forth some information is for a specific purpose. Thus, one key disciplinary distinction is that while psychology and communication tend to focus on *source credibility*, information science focuses instead on message or *information credibility*. Nonetheless, these distinctions are not perfectly clean. For example, source credibility is often a criterion for judging information credibility. Furthermore, researchers variously study the objective characteristics that make some source or piece of information *worthy* of being believed (e.g., a source's qualifications or how "good" a piece of information is compared to some accuracy metric), while others study what characteristics make sources or information *likely* to be believed by audience members (e.g., the attractiveness of a source or the congruence of some message with the receiver's own point of view).

Moreover, the notion of credibility is allied closely with several concepts, including trust, reliability, accuracy, reputation, quality, authority, and competence. Although several of these concepts include both of the core dimensions of credibility, some seem to more closely resemble the trustworthiness dimension (e.g., reputation, reliability, trust), while others seem to tilt toward the expertise dimension (e.g., quality, accuracy, authority, competence). It is beyond the scope of this discussion to elucidate the complex and intricate relationships between these concepts, but Rieh and Danielson[21] provide a useful discussion of this issue.

Understanding Credibility in the Digital Media Environment

Many studies of credibility of Web-based information rely in some form on the traditional distinctions of source, message, and medium credibility. *Source credibility* has conventionally considered characteristics of persuasive sources (traditionally, speakers), primarily expertise and trustworthiness, but also dynamism, composure, sociability, liking for the source, and similarity to the source.[22] Conceiving of Web sites as sources that engender greater or lesser credibility has shown that it is possible to translate several components of source credibility to the Web environment. Specifically, expertise may be communicated through the accuracy and comprehensiveness of a Web site's information, its professionalism, and its sponsor's credentials.[23] Trustworthiness is associated with a Web site's integrity as demonstrated by its policy statements, use of advertising, professionalism, and firm or author reputation.[24] Attractiveness and dynamism, or how "entertaining" a site is, may be reflected in the site's use of colorful graphics, interesting content, or interactive features.[25] Finally, differences exist across Web content "sponsors": institutional Web sites are perceived as more credible than other types, for example, commercial, advocacy, and personal Web sites.[26]

Message credibility typically examines how message or information characteristics influence perceptions of believability. Major dimensions of message credibility include message structure, content, language, and delivery.[27] Although little research has directly addressed message credibility online, Internet users report very similar criteria in judging online and offline information.[28] Aspects of message content such as accuracy, use of evidence and citations, comprehensiveness, and currency have been shown to affect perceptions of the credibility of information online.[29] Moreover, Fogg et al.[30] found that structural characteristics of online messages, such as their organization (or navigability), and message delivery elements, like the presence of typographical errors, affect credibility assessments. Looking across the literature, several message attributes appear to affect credibility perceptions of messages when they appear online.

Finally, studies of *media credibility* focus on the relative credibility or believability of various media channels through which a message is sent. Cross-media comparisons have sought to assess the credibility of digital media relative to other communication channels, with mixed results. While some studies have found that traditional mass media (e.g., newspapers) are perceived as more credible than the Internet and Web,[31] others have found the opposite results[32] or have found no differences between traditional and digital channels of information.[33] Overall, research in this area indicates that although the Web is largely considered an equally credible source of information as compared to traditional venues, it may be perceived as more credible among those who are particularly motivated to seek out specific types of information and who may rely on the Web to a large extent.[34]

While conceptually tidy, Chaffee[35] argued that various dimensions of credibility overlap, and that many information consumers do not distinguish, for example, between the source of a message and the channel through which they receive the message. This type of convergence is especially pronounced in today's media environment that offers an astonishing amount of information, across various media, from a vast array of providers. Moreover, perceptions of credibility vary from person to person and between various media; digital media venues such as Web sites are themselves moving targets, constantly changing and evolving; users are also evolving, with regard to their experiences, capabilities, and the media environment in which they mature; and, there are many levels of analysis consider. For example, it makes sense to measure the credibility of the Web as a medium of communication, various forms or tools of Internet communication separately (e.g., Web sites, blogs, e-mail), entire Web sites, particular information or messages on a Web site, a site operator (e.g., nytimes.com), or individual authors of information (e.g., former *New York Times* reporter Jayson Blair). Thus, source, message, and medium credibility are overlapping concepts in many instances, and research designs that do not always enable clear distinctions among these factors complicate our current understanding of online credibility. Overall, such factors underscore the complexity of credibility in the current media environment.

Indeed, making sense of credibility today requires accounting for the various types of digital media and forms of information currently available, in order to understand how individuals assess both information and source credibility, and how each of these influences the other. To date, however, research examining the credibility of information people obtain via digital media has primarily examined the perceived credibility of Web sites, as opposed to considering the full range of available digital information resources (e.g., e-mail, blogs, text messaging), and has tended to emphasize how individuals assess credibility in isolation, rather than considering group and social-level processes. Yet, in addition to commercial, informational, and other Web sites produced by organizations or individuals, blogs, wikis, social networking sites, and other digital media applications—linked across a wide variety of devices—constitute a significant portion of today's media environment. In fact, these tools may be especially popular among younger users.[36] It is crucial, therefore, to consider what new and emerging types of credibility and credibility assessment are implicated in these media tools.

To highlight this, we next propose a categorization of credibility construction, which is leveraged to draw attention to the range of relevant credibility assessment strategies available to information consumers today. This approach is intended to provide a way to organize and consider the diverse means by which information consumers understand, approach, and assess credibility in the contemporary digital media environment.

Contemporary Forms of Credibility and Credibility Assessment

A hallmark of the digital media environment is the ability of individuals to connect to one another more easily owing to reductions in the costs of communication and information sharing. Nonetheless, the majority of research on online credibility considers individuals largely as isolated appraisers of credibility, rather than as networked actors engaged with others. Group and social engagement, however, are crucial to credibility construction and assessment, and are likely increasingly important to younger user groups, which are the first to mature with a full appreciation of the potential of networked environments.

Processes of social endorsement—a fundamentally network phenomenon—have always been central to credibility. In communities where individuals and other entities are relatively well known to one another, a small number of endorsements can serve to effectively establish credibility. However, in large, relatively anonymous environments, personal connections become more tenuous. In these instances, credibility may be constructed by members of informally bounded groups of individuals who have some form of firsthand experience with the target under scrutiny, which can range from individuals, to products, to organizations or institutions, to which they lend their endorsement. In essence, endorsed credibility in the digital media environment compensates for the relative anonymity of tools like the Web with the sheer volume of users, at least some of whom have had private experiences that they make public via communication networks. The means of sharing these assessments can take many forms, resulting in several variants of credibility, most notably *conferred*, *tabulated*, *reputed*, and *emergent* credibility.

Credibility may be conferred on some information or its source when well-regarded entities, such as organizations, agencies, or associations, produce or recommend things like information repositories or service providers to information consumers. For example, libraries and teachers confer credibility on the information databases they make available to their patrons and students,[37] and doctors confer credibility on the sites they recommend to patients.[38] Similarly, organizations confer the credibility of their "preferred vendors," and the Better Business Bureau confers credibility on those businesses that adhere to their standards of conduct. In such instances, entities establish credibility by leveraging their expertise to approve a resource.

Of course, the effectiveness of *conferred credibility* rests on the referring entity's widely recognized, positive reputation that alleviates users' skepticism. However, if users fail to recognize relationships between sources and recipients of conferrals that might compromise credibility, conferred credibility may be earned falsely. For example, the search engine Google currently provides a number of sponsored links, for which Google has been financially compensated, that appear on each page of search results. Research shows, however, that the majority of users is unaware of the sponsored status of such links and views these resources as equivalent to the remainder of search results shown.[39] In this case, Google has conferred its credibility to the sponsored links, if not intentionally than at least functionally, in light of users' ignorance of the preexisting sponsorship model. Similarly, hyperlinks among blogs and Web pages of similar content might indicate a presumed endorsement when instead the linkage might be based simply on shared topical interest.

Tabulated credibility relies on peer rating of some dimension of an individual, organization, transaction, opinion, or product that is subsequently tallied to provide an omnibus rating score. For example, the online auction site eBay.com relies on its members to rate others with whom they have engaged in a transaction, in order to mitigate the considerable risk involved in such financial transactions by enhancing trust, or the "perception of the degree to which an exchange partner will fulfill the transactional obligations in situations characterized by risk or uncertainty."[40] Several studies have demonstrated that tabulated group-based credibility rating systems such as the one used by eBay are consequential for users: indicators of positive reputation can result in higher bid prices, more bid activity, items that are more likely to sell, and fewer problematic transactions[41] and indicators of negative reputation can result in lower bid prices or fewer bids.[42]

Tabulations may also emerge from individuals who interact with one another indirectly. For example, amazon.com provides not only a venue for users to rate their experiences with products and retailers, but also provides means by which users can assess reviews provided by fellow Amazon users. In this manner, those providing reviews earn a reputation over time as being (non)credible information sources. Importantly, such reputational ratings demonstrate the complexity of the concept of credibility: reputation differs from credibility inasmuch as one can potentially be highly credible, but yet have a negative reputation.

Tabulation procedures can also be fairly complex. The online forum slashdot.org, for instance, provides a sophisticated group-based credibility tool to rate its users, their posts, and content provided by and to members. Especially active and valued members are given "moderator" status, whereby they can edit conversational strands and rate contributions to the forum. Moderators rotate over time and are selected from among good contributors, defined by their "karma," which is assigned based on an assessment of "good" versus "bad" posts to the forum. Although complex, this system appears to be effective among slashdot's approximately 700,000 users. From the user's perspective, the ability to aggregate ratings from known or unknown others widens the range of social input that information consumers can use to judge credibility in a way that was not possible before the appearance of networked digital media.

Reputed credibility is also a form of endorsement that is perpetuated through personal and social networks.[43] A good reputation is a powerful mechanism for persuasion. Individuals may not even be able to recount the origins of their reputational credibility perceptions of various sources, relying on general recollections rather than specific information or on subtle cues conditioned over experience and time. In this manner, information consumers might widely recognize and understand differences between the *New York Times* and *New York Post*, for example, in both their print and online forms. Indeed, studies show evidence that information seekers rely on reputational cues gleaned from their social networks as a primary means of assessing credibility online.[44] Accordingly, sources strive to construct credibility by establishing a good reputation and perpetuate that reputation through social networks. In addition, there is evidence for "credibility transfer," where "recipients use the credibility of a medium or media product as a (heuristic) indicator for the credibility of a single news story or programme."[45] In this manner, credibility transfer can occur both between different media (e.g., from the *New York Times* printed version to NYTimes.com) and within a medium (e.g., from a credible Web site such as CNN.com to a story residing on that site).

Finally, *emergent credibility* also arises from group and social engagement. Several online venues including wikis, social networking sites, and many other applications now provide vast information repositories created by largely self-coordinating individuals, rather than by a central organization. The result is that credibility can sometimes be an emergent phenomenon that arises from a pool of resources, achieved through a system of open access to all. Emergent credibility is at the core of Lankes's[46] "reliability approach" to credibility and Eysenbach's[47] discussion of "apomediaries" as the new arbiters of credibility, particularly among youth who are at ease with social uses and applications of digital media.[48] Wikipedia.com, the vast online encyclopedia with over one million entries provided entirely by individual users, is a prime example of emergent credibility. Indeed, a direct comparison of the accuracy of science entries in Wikipedia and Encyclopedia Brittanica revealed very few differences.[49] Ultimately, credibility through emergence draws attention to crucial elements of credibility assessment: in such environments, users would be wise to consider issues of bias, source identity, and perspective as they navigate resources provided collectively by multiple interested parties.

Concerns about Credibility and Digital Media

Concerns about the credibility of sources and information certainly pre-date the advent of digital media. The need to teach young people to critically appraise information has long been a part of educational efforts, under various monikers such as literacy training and critical thinking.[50] In many ways, the core skills and issues in this domain are the same today as they were before the recent rise in digital technologies. As argued elsewhere, digital media have not so much changed what skills are needed to evaluate the credibility of information as they have changed the need for people to know how and when to exercise those skills.[51]

Digital media do, however, present new challenges for information consumers, and have in many ways shifted the burden of information evaluation from professional gatekeepers to individual information consumers. Accordingly, several scholars have addressed the question of what *is* new about digital media that makes the need for effective critical evaluation more pressing today.[52] This discussion focuses on why digital media present special problems with regard to credibility and credibility assessment, including the quantity and access of information afforded by digital media technologies, the lack of gatekeepers and quality control standards, source and context ambiguity, convergence of information and media channels, disintermediation, and shifting norms and expectations for information retrieval and processing. These functions are examined next.

Special Circumstances of Digital Media and Credibility

Today, few question the notion that digital, networked media have profoundly changed the information landscape, as well as the means of social interaction. Perhaps the greatest change is that digital media have provided access to an unprecedented amount of information available for public consumption. Until recently, the enormous cost and complexity involved in producing and disseminating information limited the number of information providers, who generally had substantial financial investment in the media apparatus.[53] Network and digitization technologies, however, have lowered the cost of information production and dissemination, thus increasing the sheer amount of information available. Indeed, the adage "On the Internet, anyone can be an author" is largely true, barring, of course, a few well-known caveats about cost and access to technology.

The combination of the vast quantity of and accessibility to digitally stored and transmitted information has prompted concerns about its credibility because, as Rieh and Danielson[54] argue, this combination creates greater uncertainty regarding both who is responsible for information and, consequently, whether it can be believed. Two important and related issues are the nature of gatekeeping in the digital media environment and the level of ambiguity surrounding both the source and context of information.

Several scholars have pointed out that information posted on the Web may not be subject to filtering through professional gatekeepers and, as a result, digital information may be more prone to being poorly organized, out of date, incomplete, or inaccurate.[55] Others have noted that digital media sometimes lack traditional authority indicators such as author identity or established reputation.[56]

Indeed, source information is crucial to credibility because it is the primary basis on which credibility judgments are thought to rest. At the same time, however, "source" has become muddled as media shifted from analog to digital forms.[57] There are several ways in which the source of information is problematic in the digital media environment. In some cases, source information is unavailable, masked, or entirely missing from a Web site, chat group, blog, wiki, and so on. In other cases, source information is provided, yet hard to interpret, such as when information is coproduced; re-purposed from one site, channel, or application to another; or when information aggregators display information from multiple sources in a centralized location that may itself be perceived as the source. These technological features create a kind of "context deficit" for digital information.[58] Moreover, the hyperlinked structure of the Web contributes to this deficit by making it psychologically challenging for users to follow and evaluate various sources as they move from site to site. Research by Eysenbach and Kohler,[59] for example, showed that source and message information become confused or disassociated in users' minds almost immediately after performing searches for medical information online.

Concerns about credibility within the digital media environment also stem from the fact that there are few standards for quality control and evaluation. There are no universal standards for posting information online, and digital information may be easily altered, plagiarized, misrepresented, or created anonymously under false pretenses. The malleability and dynamic nature of digital information exacerbate potential problems of information reliability, given that the alteration of digital information is difficult—if not impossible—to detect. In addition, the global nature of the Web makes it challenging to enact standards for quality control in the form of government regulation.[60] Finally, there is greater ambiguity about how to evaluate digital information owing simply to the relative newness of these channels of information that, in turn, makes the lack of standards for information presentation and evaluation more significant in comparison to traditional media.[61]

Another reason that the credibility of digital information may be suspect relative to more traditional media is due to channel convergence and conflation of content types afforded by digital technologies. Some have suggested that visual and other types of distinctions that were once clear between, for example, information and commercial content are not so easily distinguished in the digital environment.[62] Examples include sponsored and unsponsored links on search engine result pages and ads embedded in Web page content. Indeed, Burbules[63] has suggested that because information is presented in a similar format on Web sites, a psychological "leveling effect" is created that puts all information on the same level of accessibility and, thus, all sources on the same level of credibility.

In the extreme, "spam" messages (unsolicited or inappropriate messages often used for mass commercial advertising) create instances where individuals lack knowledge of the sender, although peripheral cues can serve to inform credibility evaluations. Less obvious, however, are other hybrid e-mail forms. "Phishing" techniques (e-mail messages from presumably known sources that are designed to entice individuals to visit fraudulent Web sites) are designed to appear credible in order to elicit individuals to provide personal data such as bank account information, and have been shown to be very effective, in spite of widespread knowledge of such techniques.[64] In addition, as "viral" e-mails are forwarded from one person to another, the content of the message can sometimes be so thoroughly divorced from its source as to make evaluation nearly impossible. Interestingly, spam, phishing, and viral e-mails can be viewed as attempts to construct credibility by capitalizing on users' perceptions of the credibility of the e-mail medium, which is derived in large part by its highly personal nature, as most e-mail communication takes place between parties known to one another.

Finally, digital media prompt increased concern about credibility by elevating the negative consequences of misinformation for consumers. As part of their efforts to economize, organizations are migrating more and more critical information to the Web, or making such information accessible exclusively via digital means.[65] Digital media have thus enhanced both capabilities and expectations for people to be more self-serving and self-informing. Individuals are now encouraged or expected to do everything from choose between medical treatment options, decide on retirement benefits and investment options, book airline reservations, and select and register for college courses entirely on their own, using information provided via digital media rather than interacting with live agents, experts, or customer service representatives. This trend toward "disintermediation" enabled by digital media raises the stakes for consumers to be able to locate and discern credible information online.[66]

Overall, while it is true that these characteristics and realities of digital media may not have changed the basic skills needed for credibility assessment, they certainly have changed the *need* to assess credibility, the *frequency* with which to do so, and the *strategies* that may be useful and available to assess information and its source. As Burbules[67] notes, "conventional methods for assessing credibility may not be feasible on the Web because of its speed, complex features and link structure, and lack of referencing and organizational conventions."[68]

Youth, Credibility, and Digital Media

Digital media present special credibility issues for youth. To date, however, the vast majority of research on credibility has focused on news, health/medical, and commercial information, which are often assumed to be "adult" topics, or at least topics that are of more interest to adults. Consequently, extremely little research has focused on credibility and youth, in spite of the fact that youth are avid information seekers across many domains of information, whether for class assignments or personal use.[69] It may be the case, however, that youth seek different *types* of information using digital media than do adults. For example, Eysenbach[70] points out that while adults often seek medical information about treatments or disease, youth are more likely to seek information on health (e.g., fitness, dieting) or sexuality.

The credibility of information obtained via digital media is important for youth, however, not only because they are active information seekers but also because there are some key differences between youth and adult information seekers in general, and specifically in their information-seeking goals. Compared with adults, for example, youth tend to be relatively heavily immersed in digital media by virtue of growing up in an environment saturated with these tools.[71] There is also evidence that youth access an equal or greater proportion of information via digital media than do adults, suggesting that they may find using these tools to locate information more natural compared with adults.[72]

Indeed, librarians and educators around the country have commented on a significant decline of (physical) library patronage since the appearance of the Internet and searchable databases.[73] Martell documents these trends with statistics across various university libraries, showing corresponding declines in physical library usage with increases in remote, virtual usage.[74] Beyond locating information for academic purposes, youth also rely heavily on digital media for other informational purposes on a daily basis, using a wide array of digital media technologies such as social networking Web sites, chat groups, interactive games, cellular telephones, e-mail, and text messaging to do so.[75]

Such heavy reliance on digital media could also be a consequence of the fact that youth may perceive greater social pressures to use digital media in ways consistent with their peers than do adults. Recent studies demonstrate that social and group-based applications of digital media, such as social networking sites, are extremely popular among young people,[76] and youth may feel greater desire and opportunity to expand their social connections and locate opinion leaders via these media, thus perhaps taking better advantage of opportunities for "emergent credibility" construction and assessment, as discussed earlier. At the same time, however, youth may also perceive less risk of disclosing personal information while using these applications, because they might think of themselves as having less financial and identity consequences at risk than adults. This presents complex credibility issues with regard to discerning the trustworthiness of some person with whom one is interacting via these media that are not unique to youth, but could be more pressing and widespread for this population.

Children's relative lack of life experience as compared to adults may also put them at greater risk for falsely accepting a source's self-asserted credibility, since such assessments are based on accumulated personal experience, knowledge, reputation, and examination of competing resources. As a group, youth have fewer life experiences to which they might compare information than do most adults. In addition, youth may not have the same level of experience with or knowledge about media institutions, which might make it difficult for them to understand differences in editorial standards across various media channels and outlets compared with adults who grew up in a world with fewer channels and less media convergence. As a consequence, some youth may not have the same level of skepticism toward digital media as adults do, because these media are not seen as "new" to younger users who cannot remember a time without them.

Specific instantiations of digital media technology may also pose particular credibility challenges for children, who possess less knowledge, experience, and skepticism than adults. E-mail serves as a good example. In the case of spam, younger children in particular might blindly transfer their perceptions of e-mail as a personal, credible medium and therefore not fully appreciate the sender's commercial intent. Similarly, children may not have sufficient knowledge to be appropriately skeptical of phishing techniques or viral e-mail messages that make it difficult to determine the true message source and purpose. Also, differences in life experience may affect youth's ability to appropriately understand newer forms of credibility construction and assessment discussed earlier. Specifically, both "reputed" and "conferred" credibility rest on users' familiarity with the reputation of a particular source or conferring agent, a familiarity that many children may not possess. Furthermore, it may be difficult for children to grasp the often complex relationships between sources and recipients of credibility conferrals, such as the meaning of "sponsored links" in a Google search result page.

Beyond experiential differences, children differ from adults in their cognitive development. As described by Eastin,[77] there are clear differences between children and adults, and between younger and older children, in cognitive skill acquisition that may have important credibility implications. Youth, particularly younger children, may be more susceptible to digital misinformation and less able to discern credible from *non*credible sources and information than are adults who are more cognitively advanced. Evidence shows that young children have a hard time distinguishing commercial from noncommercial information within the broadcast medium,[78] a task that can only be more difficult given trends toward channel convergence and conflation of types of information in the digital media environment discussed earlier. Other credibility "aids" that may be effective for adults may be ineffective for children who have not reached cognitive maturity. For example, a popular tool to help people negotiate unfamiliar territory online is ratings and recommender systems. The intricacies of such systems might be too difficult for younger children to grasp since these systems can actually be quite complex. To take full advantage of ratings systems, for example, users must weigh knowledge about the quality and quantity of raters, the context in which ratings are proffered, and the specific tabulation system in place. This suggests that the advantages offered by "tabulated credibility" may be lost on younger digital media users.

Differences in reliance, motivation for and patterns of use, experience, and development notwithstanding, both children and adults face serious consequences of receiving unreliable information from digital media sources. These consequences may, however, be somewhat different for the two user populations. For adults, the financial or health ramifications of making decisions based on bad or outdated information may be of primary concern, whereas for children the consequences of misinformation may be more apparent in other realms, such as in learning or physical safety. Learning and, by extension, grades are crucial concerns for youth, given their importance as determinants of opportunities later in life. Ongoing news reports of kidnappings and assault highlight the importance of children's ability to assess whether those to whom they disclose personal information via digital media really are who they claim to be. In each case, the cost of assessing credibility inaccurately is highly consequential for youth.

Although differences in experience and cognitive development suggest that there are substantial challenges for youth to assess the credibility of digital sources and information, it is simplistic to conclude that youth are inherently disadvantaged compared with adults when it comes to credibility assessment. These characteristics of youth audiences present both challenges and opportunities. On the one hand, youth may be a particularly vulnerable audience because of their special characteristics. On the other hand, forms of credibility assessment that rely on information to be spread efficiently through social networks (e.g., emergent credibility) highlight some intriguing advantages for youth populations, who are often extremely interconnected compared to adults. In such instances, younger users may actually be better equipped than adults to transmit information pertaining to an entity's credibility quickly and efficiently via their social networks.[79]

What *is* safe to conclude is that youth's high degree of immersion, coupled with areas of naïveté, differences in cognitive development, and usage of digital media elevate the importance of understanding credibility within this user population. A primary purpose of this volume is, thus, a call to arms to researchers, educators, policy makers, and others concerned with these issues to understand how youth think about credibility in the digital media environment and to devise a plan to assist youth in finding and evaluating the information that they need.

Perspectives on Credibility from Scholars, Educators, and Youth

Scholars, educators, and youth bring different perspectives about digital media and youth, each informed by different concerns and foci. Collectively, these views combine to shed light on a number of relevant issues; yet, it is worthwhile to examine each of these voices singly as well.[80]

Scholars

Many intellectuals point out that digital media have changed not only people's access to information but also the ways in which we appraise information. Traditional notions of credibility as coming from a centralized authority (e.g., a teacher, expert, or author) and individualized appraisal processes are challenged by digital technologies.[81] Electronic networks make it easier to rely on the collective to assess information. Credibility assessments constructed through collective or community efforts (e.g., wikis, text messaging via cell phones, or social networking applications) emerge as a major theme in recent discussions, and phrases like "distributed" and "decentralized" credibility, the "democratization of information," and "collectively versus institutionally derived credibility" are common. At core is the belief that digital media allow for the uncoupling of credibility and authority in a way never before possible. Digital media thus call into question our conceptions of authority as centralized, impenetrable, and singularly accurate and move information consumers from a model of single authority based on hierarchy to a model of multiple authorities based on networks of peers.

For some, this change is scary while for others it is liberating. Indeed, there are two opposing reactions to the dangers posed by noncredible digital information. One reaction calls for "protectionist measures" involving censorship and restricted access to online information (e.g., filters or restrictive policies), which necessarily rely on systems of hierarchy and authority (e.g., portals and professional vetting of sites). For others, this shift is positive and is seen as the "solution" to the credibility "problem." This view advocates allowing *greater* openness and freedom of information and is evocative of John Milton's First Amendment principle that the best way to counter bad speech is to allow more speech. In this view, all perspectives should be allowed into the marketplace of ideas and, through that process, "bad" (i.e., noncredible) ideas will ultimately be discredited and discarded.[82]

It is interesting that both views are evident in discussions of digital media and credibility. Educational efforts have more often taken the protectionist approach, and have opted for forms of censorship to shield students from potentially "bad" information online. Others argue that censorship and filtering hamper students' ability to learn to think critically about the information they receive via digital media,[83] and that collaborative filtering processes made possible by digital networked technologies will solve many of the credibility problems raised by digital technologies, as everything will be subject to unprecedented levels of peer review via digital networks.

Educators

The notion that digital media are challenging our fundamental ideas about learning and education is prevalent among teachers and librarians. Specifically, many educators argue that digital, networked media provide new opportunities for students to learn from others in a much less hierarchical and institutional way than ever before. Some go so far as to suggest that schools and teachers are no longer needed since digital media enable students to access and learn from the collective experience and intelligence of peers or communities. Of course, this type of self-directed learning carries with it a greater burden for students to critically evaluate information from these sources. The urgency with which educators speak of digital literacy is exacerbated by their feeling that digital media have changed youths' expectations about information. They say that today, young people expect information to be available at any time, instantly. Many educators feel this places greater burden on students to evaluate the information they get online, presumably because they are processing more information more quickly, and because source identity may be harder to discern online.

Some educators feel strongly that learning to assess the credibility of digital media and information requires students to participate in the online communities from which they seek information. Others feel that a critical component of digital literacy requires kids to learn credibility assessment through digital media production, thereby teaching kids to be "architects of credibility." In other words, many feel that youth need to be taught how to be "prosumers" (i.e., both producers and consumers) of digital media as a starting point for learning credibility assessment.

Another, related theme is that educators need to find ways to support what kids are naturally doing with digital media and to leverage that into opportunities to teach critical thinking. This likely involves developing new models for teaching and learning, but a problem is that most schools cast a wary eye on incorporating new forms of digital media into the curriculum. One example is that most of youths' favorite applications and uses of digital media, including social networking applications, e-mail, cell phones, and e-commerce, are banned in schools. In fact, most school policy toward digital media, as well as most media literacy curricula, is based on the assumption that children are in need of protection from vast amounts of misinformation online and other dangers lurking on the Web.[84]

Youth

In contrast to the other stakeholders, youth themselves do not seem to be terribly concerned about credibility. What few empirical studies exist find that credibility is not a primary concern to young people when using digital media,[85] although two dimensions of minor apprehension have emerged. First, youth report that they are concerned about the reliability/accuracy of information that they find and use in their schoolwork (i.e., information or message credibility). Second, youth say that they are concerned about trusting people they may meet in the virtual world. Neither of these concerns is surprising, given that academic and social motivations prompt a good proportion of young people's use of digital media. As for solutions to the credibility "problem," many youth indicate that it is up to each individual to use caution and take the necessary steps of cross-validation and background research to verify digital sources and information. Whether they will rise to that challenge in every situation is both unknown and unlikely.[86]

Perhaps the most consistent theme across all these stakeholders is that digital technologies complicate traditional notions of hierarchy and authority structures. The digital media environment offers unprecedented flexibility, allowing kids to have more authority than adults in some realms on some topics, nonexperts to be more credible than experts in certain circumstances, and unknown individuals to sometimes be more believable than the national news media. Many believe that digital media are shattering traditional models of authority and, as a result, credibility is being turned on its head. This upheaval suggests both problems and opportunities that require going beyond polemics in thinking about these issues.

Conclusions and Directions for Future Inquiry

Theoretical development provides researchers and practitioners a better understanding of the processes of credibility assessment that, in turn, aids them in devising strategies to help people become better information consumers. Although research on credibility and digital media to date has often neglected theory construction,[87] important theoretical applications and developments are currently emerging, many of which are represented in this volume. In particular, researchers are beginning to recognize the role of context and motivation in information searches and to incorporate this into models of credibility assessment.[88] In this regard, the application of dual processing theories, such as the Elaboration Likelihood Model or the Heuristic-Systematic Processing Model,[89] is particularly promising since these theories can help explain differences in credibility assessment processes across a variety of information-seeking contexts and situations.

With regard to youth specifically, theories of human development offer insight into the special problems that young people of varying ages may face when assessing the credibility of sources or information in the contemporary media environment. Eastin,[90] for instance, notes the cognitive developmental limitations that potentially inhibit youth of various ages from discerning information source, intent, and therefore credibility appropriately. In this area, the interdisciplinary nature of credibility research offers particularly exciting opportunities for innovative theoretical developments.

Credibility assessment research is also starting to profit from information-processing theories, such as the Limited Capacity Model and others, that help to understand how people evaluate and make decisions based on information they obtain from digital media.[91] Rieh and Hilligoss,[92] for example, propose that individuals make predictive evaluations of the usefulness of information sources and information-seeking strategies based on their own experiences and refine these assessments over time. In this manner, people learn to reuse or avoid information sources based on their verification of them. Similar to Sundar's[93] observation that individuals heavily invoke cognitive heuristics in their credibility assessments, rather than more laborious information-processing activities, such strategies result in increased predictability and reduced cognitive effort. In contrast to cognitive heuristics, however, predictive/evaluative strategies rely primarily on explicit and articulated social outcomes, as opposed to largely implicit evaluations of technical features and inferred social cues formed over time and experience. To gain the greatest benefit from information-processing models, future work should combine both of these perspectives.

Eysenbach similarly argues that people's evaluative strategies evolve with experience.[94] He proposes an iterative view of technology usage for credibility assessment whereby people shift from relying on information "intermediaries" (sources that stand between information consumers and pertinent information or services, such as librarians or doctors) to using "apomediaries" (sources that mediate without standing in between consumers and pertinent information or services, such as collaborative filtering via peers or technical tools) as they gain knowledge and self-efficacy. To have the greatest traction, the specific circumstances under which apomediation might occur will need to be articulated and validated. Moreover, as suggested by this view, the role of various group processes needs to be more fully expressed in credibility research as well. As it stands, most research focuses on the cognitive processes of individuals acting alone (although with tacit awareness of others) to assess the credibility of information they get via digital media. To better reflect how people are increasingly using digital media, the explicitly social, networked circumstances of credibility assessment need to be addressed.

Nonetheless, experience with digital tools appears to be a necessary, although not sufficient, condition to take full and appropriate advantage of the many sources of information accessed via digital media. For instance, the nearly automatic heuristic judgments learned through interaction with digital media are honed through experience;[95] accumulated experience can result in reliable information search results across various media;[96] and Internet experience has been shown by some to be positively related to assessments of the credibility of Web-based information and to verification behaviors.[97] Experience, however, should not be confounded with expertise, nor should experience with Web technologies be equated to life experiences. Each is consequential in its own way for youth determining the credibility of online sources and information. For instance, technological experience alone does not enable individuals to discern credible from noncredible information (although it can help),[98] nor can those without sufficient life experiences make sense of certain information dilemmas they may confront online. As Eastin[99] argues, youth are faced with rather complex cognitive tasks online, and youth at different developmental stages are equipped to different degrees to resolve these dilemmas effectively. Nonetheless, youth may enjoy certain advantages due to their relative immersion in digital media, which might not yet be readily apparent. This, of course, suggests a wealth of possibilities with regard to our understanding of credibility assessment that can only be understood as data are collected over long periods of time. Indeed, as noted earlier, we have only begun to explore what "growing up digital" means for media users who will be immersed in digital media for their entire lives.

From a practical standpoint, understanding the processes of credibility assessment among youth is critical. Credibility is a cornerstone of people's interactions, personal representation, academic and professional performance, and democratic expression and choice. As more delivery mechanisms become available, more information content migrates online, and more of the world's population is interconnected, it is crucial that individuals understand the implications of their media environment and learn to assess credibility in ways appropriate to their situational demands. This is especially significant for youth, who are uniquely and simultaneously advantaged and disadvantaged by their relation to contemporary media technologies.

Teaching youth about credibility assessment, then, must both make use of their existing knowledge of contemporary technologies and address their outstanding deficiencies. As Rainie[100] argues, research and learning among youth are increasingly self-directed, interactive with networks of peers, and reliant on group outreach and knowledge. Consequently, opportunities that use the lessons inherent in the tools that already engage youth offer strategies for teaching critical distinctions that may result in appropriate digital media literacy.[101] For example, showing students existing Web sites whose focus is to reveal published misinformation, prompting youth to examine Wikipedia's "talk pages" where collaborators discuss contested encyclopedia entries, encouraging youth to become information providers themselves, and using direct comparisons of competing news accounts all present means by which digital tools and resources can be leveraged to illustrate credibility assessment concerns and strategies.[102] These methods offer opportunities for demonstrating core credibility issues by invoking real-time and real-world instances of contested content and behaviors, via the media technologies and tools that youth naturally enjoy using. In this manner, even "managed" environments like schools can take advantage of so-called autonomous, informal learning environments and opportunities found online, which may themselves be more credible to youth.[103]

Nonetheless, in the end such strategies must overcome the "structural" challenges that are built into the political and cultural schooling environment.[104] In addition, issues of credibility and new media are subject to a range of supportive to restrictive sociopolitical interventions[105] that can alter their form and effectiveness. Ultimately, the relation among youth, digital media, and credibility today is sufficiently complex to resist simple explanations. This volume represents a first step toward mapping that complexity and providing a basis for future work that seeks to find explanations that will ultimately help scholars, educators, policy makers, and youth take advantage of the new opportunities for empowerment and learning offered by digital networked media.

Notes

1. John Horrigan and Lee Rainie, When Facing a Tough Decision, 60 Million Americans Now Seek the Internet's Help: The Internet's Growing Role in Life's Major Moments, 2006, http://pewresearch.org/obdeck/?ObDeckID=19 (retrieved October 13, 2006).

2. See Lance Bennett, ed., *Civic Life Online: Learning How Digital Media Can Engage Youth*, The MacArthur Initiative on Digital Media and Learning, 2007.

3. See David Buckingham, ed., *Youth, Identity, and Digital Media*, The MacArthur Initiative on Digital Media and Learning, 2007.

4. Matthew Grimm, . . . 'Bout your G-g-generation (Generation Y), *American Demographics* 25, no. 7 (2003): 38–41; Lee Rainie, Life Online: Teens and Technology and the World to Come (keynote address to the annual conference of the Public Library Association, Boston, MA, March 23, 2006), http://www.pewinternet.org/ppt/Teens%20and%20technology.pdf (retrieved November 7, 2006).

5. Neil Howe and William Strauss, *Millennials Rising: The Next Great Generation* (New York: Vintage Books, 2000).

6. Don Tapscott, *Growing Up Digital: The Rise of the Net Generation* (New York: McGraw-Hill, 1997).

7. Marc Prensky, Digital Natives, Digital Immigrants, *On the Horizon* 9, no. 5 (September/October, 2001): 1–6.

8. Grimm, . . . 'Bout your G-g-generation (Generation Y).

9. Rainie, Life Online; see also Prensky, Digital Natives, Digital Immigrants, 1–6.

10. Rainie, Life Online.

11. Ibid., 7.

12. Ibid.

13. Tapscott, *Growing Up Digital*.

14. Matthew Eastin, Toward a Cognitive Developmental Approach to Youth Perceptions of Credibility, this volume.

15. Gary C. Woodward and Robert E. Denton Jr., *Persuasion & Influence in American Life*, 4th ed. (Prospect Heights, IL: Waveland, 2000).

16. Charles C. Self, Credibility, in *An Integrated Approach to Communication Theory and Research*, eds. Michael B. Salwen and Don W. Stacks (Mahwah, NJ: Erlbaum, 1996), 421–41.

17. Carl I. Hovland, Irving L. Janis, and Harold H. Kelley, *Communication and Persuasion* (New Haven, CT: Yale University Press, 1953).

18. Richard F. Carter and Bradley S. Greenberg, Newspapers or Television: Which Do You Believe? *Journalism Quarterly* 42 (1965): 29–34; Bruce H. Westley and Werner J. Severin, Some Correlates of Media Credibility, *Journalism Quarterly* 41 (1964): 325–35.

19. See Miriam J. Metzger, Andrew J. Flanagin, Karen Eyal, Daisy R. Lemus, and Robert M. McCann, Credibility for the 21st Century: Integrating Perspectives on Source, Message, and Media Credibility in the Contemporary Media Environment, *Communication Yearbook* 27 (2003): 293–335, for more detail.

20. B. J. Fogg and Hsiang Tseng, The Elements of Computer Credibility, *Proceedings of CHI '99, Human Factors in Computing Systems* (1999): 80–87; Albert C. Gunther, Biased Press or Biased Public? Attitudes toward Media Coverage of Social Groups, *Public Opinion Quarterly* 56 (1992): 147–67.

21. Soo Young Rieh and David R. Danielson, Credibility: A Multidisciplinary Framework, in *Annual Review of Information Science and Technology* 41, ed. Blaise Cronin (Medford, NJ: Information Today, 2007), 307–64.

22. David Berlo, James Lemert, and Robert Mertz, Dimensions for Evaluating the Acceptability of Message Sources, *Public Opinion Quarterly* 33 (1969): 563–675; Robert H. Gass and John S. Seiter, *Persuasion, Social Influence, and Compliance Gaining* (Boston: Allyn & Bacon, 1999); Hovland, Janis, and Kelley, *Communication and Persuasion*; William E. Jurma, Evaluations of Credibility of the Source of a Message, *Psychological Reports* 49 (1981): 778; James C. McCroskey, Scales for the Measurement of Ethos, *Speech Monographs* 33 (1966): 65–72; Robert M. Perloff, *The Dynamics of Persuasion* (Hillsdale, NJ: Erlbaum, 1993).

23. B. J. Fogg, C. Soohoo, David R. Danielson, Leslie Marable, Julianne Stanford, and Ellen R. Trauber, How Do Users Evaluate the Credibility of Web Sites? A Study with Over 2,500 Participants (paper presented at the Designing for User Experiences, San Francisco, CA., 2003).

24. Janet E. Alexander and Marsha A. Tate, *Web Wisdom: How to Evaluate and Create Information Quality on the Web* (Hillsdale, NJ: Erlbaum, 1999); Mary J. Culnan and Pamela K. Armstrong, Information Privacy Concerns, Procedural Fairness, and Impersonal Trust: An Empirical Investigation, *Organization Science* 10, no. 1 (1999): 104–15; Fogg et al., *How Do Users Evaluate the Credibility of Web Sites?*

25. Qimei Chen and William D. Wells, Attitude toward the Site, *Journal of Advertising Research* 39, no. 5 (1999): 27–37; Eastin, Toward a Cognitive Developmental Approach.

26. Andrew J. Flanagin and Miriam J. Metzger, The Perceived Credibility of Web Site Information as Influenced by the Sex of the Source, *Computers in Human Behavior* 19 (2003): 683–701; Andrew J. Flanagin and Miriam J. Metzger, The Role of Site Features, User Attributes, and Information Verification Behaviors on the Perceived Credibility of Web-based Information, *New Media and Society* 9, no. 2 (2007): 319–42.

27. E.g., Gass and Seiter, *Persuasion, Social Influence, and Compliance Gaining*; M. A. Hamilton, Message Variables That Mediate and Moderate the Effect of Equivocal Language on Source Credibility, *Journal of Language and Social Psychology* 17 (1998): 109–43; James C. McCroskey, A Summary of Experimental Research on the Effects of Evidence in Persuasive Communication, *The Quarterly Journal of Speech* 55 (1969): 169–76; James C. McCroskey and R. Samuel Mehrley, The Effects of Disorganization and Nonfluency on Attitude Change and Source Credibility, *Speech Monographs* 36 (1969): 13–21; Gerald R. Miller and

Murray A. Hewgill, The Effect of Variations in Nonfluency on Audience Ratings of Source Credibility, *Quarterly Journal of Speech* 50 (1964): 36–44; Daniel J. O'Keefe, *Persuasion: Theory and Research* (Newbury Park, CA: Sage, 1990).

28. See Metzger et al., Credibility for the 21st Century, for a review.

29. Soo Young Rieh and Nicholas J. Belkin, Understanding Judgment of Information Quality and Cognitive Authority in the WWW, in *Proceedings of the 61st Annual Meeting of the American Society for Information Science* 35, ed. Cecilia M. Preston (Medford, NJ: Information Today, 1998), 279–89; S. Shyam Sundar, Effect of Source Attribution on Perception of Online News Stories, *Journalism and Mass Communication Quarterly* 75, no. 1 (1998): 55–68.

30. Fogg et al., *How Do Users Evaluate the Credibility of Web Sites?*

31. Andrew J. Flanagin and Miriam J. Metzger, Perceptions of Internet Information Credibility, *Journalism and Mass Communication Quarterly* 77, no. 3 (2000): 515–40; Spiro Kiousis, Public Trust or Mistrust? Perceptions of Media Credibility in the Information Age, *Mass Communication & Society* 4, no. 4 (2001): 381–403.

32. Thomas J. Johnson and Barbara K. Kaye, Cruising Is Believing? Comparing Internet and Traditional Sources on Media Credibility Measures, *Journalism and Mass Communication Quarterly* 75, no. 2 (1998): 325–40; Thomas J. Johnson and Barbara K. Kaye, Wag the Blog: How Reliance on Traditional Media and the Internet Influence Credibility Perceptions of Weblogs among Blog Users, *Journalism and Mass Communication Quarterly* 81, no. 3 (2004): 622–42.

33. Online News Association, Digital Journalism Credibility Survey, 2001, http://www.journalists.org/Programs/ResearchText.htm (retrieved June 25, 2001).

34. Thomas J. Johnson and Barbara K. Kaye, Using Is Believing: The Influence of Reliance on the Credibility of Online Political Information among Politically Interested Internet Users, *Journalism and Mass Communication Quarterly* 77, no. 4 (2000): 865–79; Thomas J. Johnson and Barbara K. Kaye, Webelievability: A Path Model Examining How Convenience and Reliance Predict Online Credibility, *Journalism and Mass Communication Quarterly* 79, no. 3 (2002): 619–42.

35. Steven H. Chaffee, Mass Media and Interpersonal Channels: Competitive, Convergent, or Complementary? in *Inter/Media: Interpersonal Communication in a Media World*, ed. Gary Gumpert and Robert Cathcart (New York: Oxford University Press, 1982), 57–77.

36. Amanda Lenhart, Mary Madden, and Paul Hitlin, *Teens and Technology: Youth Are Leading the Transition to a Fully Wired and Mobile Nation*, Pew Internet & American Life Report (July 2005), http://www.pewinternet.org/report_display.asp?r=162 (retrieved April 17, 2006).

37. See Soo Young Rieh and Brian Hilligoss, College Students' Credibility Judgments in the Information Seeking Process, this volume.

38. See Gunther Eysenbach, Credibility of Health Information and Digital Media: New Perspectives and Implications for Youth, this volume.

39. Deborah Fallows, *Search Engine Users: Internet Searchers Are Confident, Satisfied and Trusting—But They Are Also Unaware and Naïve*, Pew Internet & American Life report, January 2005, http://www.pewinternet.org/PPF/r/146/report_display.asp (retrieved April 17, 2006).

40. Brian P. Bailey, Laura J. Gurak, and Joseph A. Konstan, Trust in Cyberspace, in *Human Factors and Web Development*, ed. Julie Ratner (London: Erlbaum, 2003), 311–21.

41. Patrick Bajari and Ali Hortacsu, The Winner's Curse, Reserve Prices, and Endogenous Entry: Empirical Insights from eBay Auctions, *The Rand Journal of Economics* 34, no. 2 (2002): 329–55; Andrew

J. Flanagin, Commercial Markets as Communication Markets: Uncertainty Reduction through Mediated Information Exchange in Online Auctions, *New Media & Society* 9, no. 3 (2007): 401–23; Daniel Houser and John Wooders, Reputation in Auctions: Theory, and Evidence from eBay, University of Arizona, 2000, http://info-center.ccit.arizona.edu/~econ/working_papers/Internet_Auctions.pdf (retrieved October 1, 2003); Cynthia G. McDonald and V. Carlos Slawson, Reputation in an Internet Auction Market, *Economic Inquiry* 40 (2002): 633–50; Mikhail I. Melnik and James Alm, Does a Seller's ECommerce Reputation Matter? Evidence From eBay Auctions, *The Journal of Industrial Economics* 50, no. 3 (2002): 337–50; Paul Resnick and Richard Zeckhauser, Trust among Strangers in Internet Transactions: Empirical Analysis of eBay's Reputation System, in *Advances in Applied Microeconomics*, vol. 11, *The Economics of the Internet and E-Commerce*, ed. Michael R. Baye (Amsterdam: Elsevier Science, 2002); Stephen S. Standifird, Reputation and E-Commerce: eBay Auctions and the Asymmetrical Impact of Positive and Negative Ratings, *Journal of Management* 27 (2001): 279–95.

42. Bajari and Hortacsu, The Winner's Curse, Reserve Prices, and Endogenous Entry; Ulrich Brinkman and Mathias Siefert, Face-to-Interface—The Establishment of Trust in the Internet: The Case of E-Auctions, *Journal of Sociology* 30 (2001): 23–47; David Lucking-Reiley, Doug Bryan, Naghi Prasad, and Daniel Reeves, Pennies from eBay: The Determinants of Price in Online Auctions, Vanderbilt University working paper, 2000, http://eller.arizona.edu/%7Ereiley/papers/PenniesFromEBay.pdf (retrieved August 5, 2006); Standifird, Reputation and E-Commerce.

43. See Shawn Tseng and B. J. Fogg, Credibility and Computing Technology, *Communications of the ACM* 42, no. 5 (1999): 39–44.

44. See Rieh and Hilligoss, College Students' Credibility Judgments, and S. Shyam Sundar, The MAIN Model: A Heuristic Approach to Understanding Technology Effects on Credibility, this volume.

45. Wolfgang Schweiger, Media Credibility—Experience or Image? A Survey on the Credibility of the World Wide Web in Germany in Comparison to Other Media, *European Journal of Communication* 15, no. 1 (2000): 41.

46. R. David Lankes, Trusting the Internet: New Approaches to Credibility Tools, this volume.

47. Eysenbach, this volume.

48. Frances Jacobson Harris, Challenges to Teaching Credibility Assessment in Contemporary Schooling, this volume.

49. Jim Giles, Internet Encyclopedias Go Head to Head, *Nature* 438 (December 15, 2005): 900–901.

50. See Harris, this volume.

51. Miriam J. Metzger, Making Sense of Credibility on the Web: Models for Evaluating Online Information and Recommendations for Future Research, *Journal of the American Society for Information Science and Technology* 58, no. 10 (2007); Metzger et al., Credibility for the 21st Century.

52. David R. Danielson, Web Credibility, in *Encyclopedia of Human-Computer Interaction*, ed. Claude Ghaoui (Hersey, PA: Idea Group, 2005), 713–21; B. J. Fogg, *Persuasive Technology: Using Computers to Change What We Think and Do* (San Francisco: Morgan Johnson, 2003); Metzger et al., Credibility for the 21st Century; Rieh and Danielson, Credibility: A Multidisciplinary Framework.

53. It is interesting to note, though, that high cost certainly does not ensure credibility. For instance, "yellow journalism" of the late 1800s relied on partisanism, strong editorial opinions mixed with "news," and tactics of sensationalism. Similarly, contemporary publications like the *National Enquirer* remain wildly successful, in spite of (and partially because of) the nature of their stories and reportage, which are commonly understood not to be credible.

54. Rieh and Danielson, Credibility: A Multidisciplinary Framework.

55. Danielson, Web Credibility; Flanagin and Metzger, Perceptions of Internet information credibility; Flanagin and Metzger, The Role of Site Features; Joseph W. Janes and Louis B. Rosenfeld, Networked Information Retrieval and Organization: Issues and questions, *Journal of the American Society for Information Science and Technology* 47, no. 9 (1996): 711–15; Metzger et al., Credibility for the 21st Century; Rieh and Danielson, Credibility: A Multidisciplinary Framework.

56. Danielson, Web Credibility; John W. Fritch and Robert L. Cromwell, Delving Deeper into Evaluation: Exploring Cognitive Authority on the Internet, *Reference Services Review* 30, no. 3 (2002): 242–54; Metzger, Making Sense of Credibility on the Web.

57. See Sundar, The MAIN Model, this volume.

58. See Eysenbach, this volume.

59. Gunther Eysenbach and Christian Kohler, How Do Consumers Search for and Appraise Health Information on the World Wide Web? Qualitative Study Using Focus Groups, Usability Tests, and In-depth Interviews, *British Medical Journal* 324 (March 9, 2002): 573–77.

60. See Fred W. Weingarten, Credibility, Politics, and Public Policy, this volume, for a discussion of policy issues related to credibility.

61. Danielson, Web Credibility; Flanagin and Metzger, Perceptions of Internet Information Credibility; Rieh and Danielson, Credibility: A Multidisciplinary Framework.

62. Alexander and Tate, *Web Wisdom*.

63. Nicholas C. Burbules, Digital Texts and Future of Scholarly Writing and Publication, *Journal of Curriculum Studies* 30, no. 1 (1998): 105–24.

64. Rachna Dhamija, J. D. Tygar, and Marti Hearst, Why Phishing Works, *Proceedings of CHI 2006 Human Factors in Computing Systems*, Montreal, Quebec, 2006, 581–90.

65. See Lankes, this volume.

66. See both Lankes and Eysenbach, this volume, for discussions of these and related issues.

67. Nicholas C. Burbules, Paradoxes of the Web: The Ethical Dimensions of Credibility, *Library Trends* 49 (2001): 441–53.

68. As cited in Rieh and Danielson, Credibility: A Multidisciplinary Framework, 311.

69. Lenhart, Madden, and Hitlin, *Teens and Technology*.

70. Eysenbach, this volume.

71. Lenhart, Madden, and Hitlin, *Teens and Technology*.

72. Ibid.

73. E.g., Scott Carlson, The Deserted Library: As Students Work Online, Reading Rooms Empty, Leading Some Campuses to Add Starbucks, *Chronicle of Higher Education*, 2001, http://chronicle.com/free/v48/i12/12a03501.htm (retrieved August 5, 2005).

74. Charles R. Martell, The Ubiquitous User: A Reexamination of Carlson's Deserted Library, *Portal: Libraries and the Academy* 5, no. 4 (2005): 441–53.

75. Lenhart, Madden, and Hitlin, *Teens and Technology*; Susannah Fox and Mary Madden, *Generations Online*, Pew Internet & American Life, 2005, http://www.pewinternet.org/PPF/r/170/report_display.asp (retrieved July 24, 2006); Rieh and Hilligoss, College Students' Credibility Judgments; Teenage Research Unlimited, *Teen Internet Safety Survey*, National Center for Missing and Exploited Children and Cox Communications, 2006, http://www.netsmartz.org/safety/statistics.htm (retrieved July 24, 2006).

76. Lenhart, Madden, and Hitlin, *Teens and Technology*.

77. Eastin, this volume.

78. See ibid.

79. See Lankes, this volume, and Eysenbach, this volume, for similar arguments.

80. The following section was informed by online dialogues with researchers, educators, and interested members of the public, as well as by youth participants in the Global Kids Digital Media Essay Contest. Over thirty people participated in the online dialogues, which were held in the fall of 2006 and were sponsored by the MacArthur Foundation as part of the Digital Media and Learning initiative. Excerpts of the online discussions may be found at http://spotlight.macfound.org/main/category/c/Credibility/. For information about the Global Kids Digital Media Essay Contest, including the winning essays, see http://www.globalkids.org/.

81. See Lankes, this volume.

82. See Weingarten, this volume, for a similar discussion with regard to policy.

83. See Harris, this volume.

84. See ibid., for a full discussion of these educational issues.

85. Denise E. Agosto, A Model of Young People's Decision-Making in Using the Web, *Library & Information Science Research* 24 (2002): 311–41; Denise E. Agosto, Bounded Rationality and Satisficing in Young People's Web-based Decision Making, *Journal of the American Society of Information Science and Technology* 53 (2002): 16–27; Raya Fidel, Rachel K. Davies, Mary H. Douglass, Jenny K. Holder, Carla J. Hopkins, Elisabeth J. Kushner, Bryan K. Miyagishima, and Christina D. Toney, A Visit to the Information Mall: Web Searching Behavior of High School Students, *Journal of the American Society of Information Science* 50 (1999): 24–37; Sandra Hirsh, Domain Knowledge and Children's Search Behavior, in *Youth Information-seeking Behavior: Theories, Models, and Issues*, eds. Mary K. Chelton and Colleen Cool (Lanham, MD: Scarecrow Press, 2004): 241–70; Andrew Large, Information Seeking on the Web by Elementary School Students, in *Youth Information-Seeking Behavior*, 293–320.

86. See Rieh and Hilligoss, College Students' Credibility Judgments, this volume, for a discussion of when youth are more likely to invest effort in assessing credibility.

87. Metzger et al., Credibility for the 21st Century.

88. E.g., Metzger, Making Sense of Credibility on the Web; Rieh and Hilligoss, College Students' Credibility Judgments, this volume.

89. See Sundar and Eysenbach chapters, this volume.

90. Eastin, this volume.

91. See ibid.

92. Rieh and Hilligoss, College Students' Credibility Judgments, this volume.

93. Sundar, The MAIN Model.

94. Eysenbach, this volume

95. Sundar, The MAIN Model.

96. Rieh and Hilligoss, College Students' Credibility Judgments, this volume.

97. Flanagin and Metzger, Perceptions of Internet Information Credibility; J. Ha, Questioning Internet Credibility: A Test on the Cyber Marketplace (paper presented at the Annual Meetings of the

International Communication Association, Washington DC, May 2001); Johnson and Kaye, Cruising Is Believing?

98. See Lankes, Trusting the Internet, this volume.

99. Eastin, this volume.

100. Rainie, Life Online.

101. Harris, Challenges to Teaching Credibility Assessment in Contemporary Schooling.

102. H. Jenkins, Confronting the Challenges of Participatory Culture: Media Education for the 21st Century (white paper produced for the MacArthur Foundation's Digital Media and Learning initiative, November 13, 2006), http://www.digitallearning.macfound.org (retrieved November 14, 2006).

103. Bennett, *Civic Life Online*.

104. Harris, Challenges to Teaching Credibility Assessment in Contemporary Schooling.

105. Weingarten, Credibility, Politics, and Public Policy.

Toward a Cognitive Developmental Approach to Youth Perceptions of Credibility

Matthew S. Eastin

The University of Texas at Austin, Department of Advertising

Recently, while my son, now four years old, was playing on the computer, he asked me to spell his name on the screen. So, like any parent who enjoys seeing their child engage in learning, I proceeded to spell out his name: J-o-h-n-a-t-h-a-n. After I was finished he told me that I had misspelled his name. "Why?" I asked. He told me that the red line under his name indicated that it was not spelled correctly. I spent the next five minutes explaining to him that the computer is not always right and that I, his father, would not misspell his name. After all, it was my idea to spell it that way in the first place. He proceeded to let me know that computers are smart and know how to spell. Although correct, as with many things he will eventually experience during his life, this is not a hard-and-fast rule by which to live. Before computers, digital-based education, and spell-check programs, this sort of issue would not have been a topic of discussion between a father and his son. I present this as one basic example of how credibility in digital environments is being determined by youth through their increasingly different life experiences.

This chapter examines how children see and perceive information in the digital world, and how interactions with contemporary media are dynamically different than those with previous media. Through examples, descriptive data, and, at times even conjecture, this chapter will offer something for a variety of readers—parents, researchers, politicians, and media designers—to better understand issues surrounding youth, credibility, and digital media today.

Setting the Digital Stage

Because digital information has a growing importance in our lives, researchers have begun to explain how information found online is accessed, evaluated, and utilized. This work indicates that certain Internet applications are playing a significant role in human behavior, which makes understanding the uses of digital media of considerable societal importance. For example, based on data provided by researchers studying health information seeking and by the American Medical Association,[1] more people go online for medical advice on a given day than actually visit health professionals. If you don't believe the research, just ask children how important the Internet is, or how much time they spend on it, or when the last time was that they used digital media technology.

Usage estimates over the past several years suggest the number of young people using the Internet has increased dramatically. For instance, approximately 23 percent of nursery school children are online, 32 percent of kindergartners, 50 percent of children in grades

1–5, 70 percent of children in grades 6–8, and 80 percent of children in grades 9–12.[2] Beyond usage estimates, researchers have developed an understanding of young people's motivations to use digital media. Broadly speaking, entertainment, information (sought and provided), and social motivations are all found to significantly predict older adolescent Internet use.[3] That said, while much is understood about how and why children use online resources, very little is currently known regarding how these resources are perceived.

As discussed later, the challenge of identifying credible information on the Internet is great among young users, who face perhaps even greater difficulty than adults. Because they are less cognitively developed than adults, children may struggle when evaluating the legitimacy of Internet content and, especially, when comparing the information to their limited life experiences. Further complicating the issue, younger children may not be able to easily evaluate multiple pieces of information at once and may get distracted by extraneous information.[4] As a result, children's understanding of the evaluative process may not be comprehensive, reflecting both developmental differences and information-processing difficulties and challenges specific to this population of Internet users. Simply put, there is some evidence to believe that children's ability to efficaciously evaluate online content may be weak, which is unsettling given the importance of digital media in their lives.

To better understand how children process and judge online information, it is necessary to understand how children develop cognitively and process information throughout childhood. Thus, this chapter will begin with a brief overview of Piaget's approach to cognitive development.[5] Over the past several years, and despite some criticism, Piaget's work has remained an influential theory of cognitive development and has provided a foundation for discussion of the developmental changes that occur throughout childhood. A discussion of information processing within online environments will follow, with a particular focus on how children's cognitive processing limitations may influence their credibility judgments. Finally, suggestions are offered on how to educate young users of digital media more effectively.

Cognitive Development

According to cognitive development scholars, sensory input or information is required to think, and information is gained through life experiences.[6] While children are born with some innate knowledge, most knowledge is acquired through learning that occurs through accumulated experience. Life experiences are processed and transferred into memory, becoming what is known as knowledge. When assessing a new situation, people draw on knowledge to interpret new information.

Interpreting sensory input requires the ability to organize information as it is processed. To bring coherence to incoming sensory stimuli, people must develop the ability to cognitively organize information. Thus, interpreting sensory input requires the ability to organize information as it is processed against past experiences and/or existing knowledge. Lacking a reference base can create confusion and lead to inaccurate interpretations. Thus, people need the ability to categorize, identify, and recognize information inputs as being new, different, similar, or the same as preexisting information. Without this level of cognitive development, effective processing of complex information cannot occur. Moreover, the more complex a person's environment becomes, the greater capacity that person must have to organize, formulate, and synthesize information.

Since cognition is gained through life experiences, age can be used to understand cognitive development and its role in information evaluation. Piaget and his followers believe that while the mind is complex in its organization, the most basic level of organization consists of schemata. Schemata are the mental representations of some physical or mental experience, including objects, events, and so on and thus serve as the foundation for cognitive organization. As cognitive development progresses through life experiences, new schema develop, and predefined schemata are reorganized to better adapt to current and future experiences. Thus, cognitive development is a process that occurs over time as schemata develop and change to accommodate new experiences.

Although there are many cognitive development theories that focus on the mental processes that occur during life experiences,[7] Piaget has produced the most extensive body of research on cognitive development throughout childhood.[8] In fact, Piaget's work remains the benchmark for discussion on children and cognitive development, despite the fact that his theory has received some criticism and has, consequently, evolved over the years.[9] Although Piaget's research includes everything from biological intelligence to intellectual aptitude, this chapter focuses on his general explication of the successive cognitive developmental changes that occur throughout childhood.

Piaget outlined four stages of cognitive development from birth through adolescence that he called sensorimotor, preoperational, concrete operational, and formal operational. As children progress during childhood they move through the four stages, eventually overcoming various cognitive limitations associated with each stage. These limitations present special challenges to children as they process and evaluate information. Consequently, it is important to bring a developmental perspective to bear on children's abilities in order to understand how they are able to reliably evaluate the credibility of information they encounter either on- or offline. Applying a developmental perspective offers several opportunities to move work in this area forward: (1) it recognizes that there is likely to be great variation in credibility perceptions and evaluative processes among children at different developmental stages, (2) it offers theoretically based and testable hypotheses for explaining credibility judgments at each stage of development, and (3) it can help educators and policy makers create developmentally appropriate educational and policy interventions to assist children possessing varying cognitive skill levels to evaluate information effectively. Given the potential benefits of incorporating a cognitive developmental perspective to credibility research, it is surprising that no studies have done so to date. Thus, one aim of this chapter is to provide a framework for future research in this area.

That said, it must be noted that the use of developmental stages has been criticized for being globally defined and not containing enough stages. However, Piaget's stages do represent accepted benchmarks or milestones by many research psychologists. Thus, for the purposes of this chapter, the stages that are relevant to children's assessments of the credibility of digital information will be discussed. Because children in the sensorimotor stage (ages 0–2 years) are not concerned with credibility and digital media, the chapter will begin with a discussion of the preoperational stage, which is when many children first encounter digital information at home and in school. Descriptions of the concrete operational and formal operational stages will follow, and the particular challenges that each stage presents for children in terms of credibility assessment will be highlighted.

Preoperational

The preoperational stage occurs from ages 2–7, coinciding with the time when most children are introduced to digital media, and/or learn to use them independent of adults. It is during the preoperational stage that children begin to use symbols to represent thoughts.

For example, it is early in the preoperational stage (ages 2–4) that children begin to use language and to engage in make-believe play. Thought is still generally somewhat illogical at this stage of development, and most children in the early preoperational stage have difficulty understanding any perspective other than their own. As a result, preoperational children tend to be "egocentric," meaning that they do not understand that other people may have different perspectives or viewpoints than their own. Such thoughts obviously color children's understanding, and Piaget argued that one result of egocentric thinking is that it is often difficult for children in this stage of development to modify schemata in response to new information, and to revise their faulty reasoning in response to life experiences.[10] Another difficulty that early preoperational children encounter is distinguishing between fantasy and reality, and it is only during the latter part of the preoperational stage (ages 4–7) that children's differentiation skills are honed, which is also the time when logical thought begins to develop.

Concrete Operational

Children in the concrete operational stage are typically between seven and eleven years old. Through their growing ability to organize thoughts, logical reasoning is further developed during this stage. Children's reasoning is still largely constrained to physical or tangible objects, leaving abstract reasoning to develop later, in the final developmental stage. As logical thinking develops, children begin to think of others, allowing them to move beyond egocentric thought. Signs of true complex thinking also develop during the later part of the concrete operational stage. For instance, by the end of this stage children are able to sequence information, classify beyond simple groupings like size or color, and understand dimensionality. While tremendous gains in children's ability to solve problems are observed during this stage of development, children in the concrete operational stage still have difficulty with abstractions. In particular, children tend to work out the logic of each problem they encounter separately, rather than drawing general logical principles that they then apply to all relevant situations.[11]

Formal Operational

The last stage of development in Piaget's theory is the formal operational stage, which begins at approximately eleven years of age and continues throughout adolescence (and adulthood). During this stage, children learn to conceptualize, understand, and test hypothesized relationships and thus develop the capacity for abstract, scientific thinking.[12] They are able to fully understand the causes and effects of behavior, and to position logical arguments based on available concrete or abstract information. In other words, abstract thought allows children to reason beyond the information presented and, as a result, to formulate general rules of logic that are applicable across specific contexts.

Contextualizing Developmental Change

Underlying these developmental stages are the concepts of adaptation and organization. Piaget[13] argues that people hold mental structures that help them understand experienced stimuli. Throughout life, people adapt to new information by integrating it into existing mental structures, a process that requires assimilation and accommodation. Assimilation refers to the process of incorporating experiences into existing mental structures (i.e., schemata), while accommodation refers to the adaptation that must occur within the mind when new information is encountered, and specifically to the process by which new mental structures are created or existing structures are altered to interpret new information that does not fit within preexisting structures. Organization generally refers to the rearrangement and linking of mental structures, which occur over time as children move through the developmental stages. Furthermore, according to Piaget, physical and psychological maturation, accumulated experience, and social interaction allow movement from stage to stage, because as children accumulate experiences and information that either fits in their existing mental schemata or forces them to refine those schemata (a process he calls "equilibration"), they form a cognitive system that enables complex thought to develop.

Since Piaget's seminal work, many have suggested that modifications be made to his original theory.[14] For example, some researchers emphasize that at each stage there is a specific number of structural steps that occur in sequential progression.[15] This suggests that although breaking stages out into broad age categories for comparison is useful, there are also logical structures that can be compared within each stage. Within the context of this chapter, this suggests that both basic and complex credibility assessments will logically progress within as well as between developmental stages. It further suggests that failure to examine *both* children's between- and within-stage cognitive development could miss important differences among groups of children that may be critical in designing effective curriculum for teaching credibility assessment skills.

Despite the criticism, most researchers agree with the notion that children process world experiences into active cognitive structures, and they agree that development occurs in a cumulative fashion whereby cognitive skills build on each other. For instance, it is generally accepted that early development includes rather simplistic cognition, such as sensory and motor skills, followed by later stages that progressively include complex, logical, and abstract thinking. There is also agreement that, if provided with a typical learning environment, age ranges can in fact be used to help classify children within broad cognitive skill levels.

Implications of Cognitive Developmental Stages for Credibility Assessment

Developmental stages allow researchers to describe age-based cognitive changes. In doing so, stage models provide a way to understand the cognitive limitations and capabilities that children of varying ages are likely to face when they are confronted with cognitively complex situations, such as making decisions about the credibility of information they encounter online. Indeed, each stage of development has specific implications for children's ability to evaluate the credibility of online information.

Piaget's theory suggests that children in the preoperational stage will have a very difficult time evaluating source bias, and thus credibility, since many children in this stage cannot understand that others (e.g., online advertisers) may have perspectives and motivations that differ from their own. Preoperational children who cannot distinguish fact from fiction will have a hard time determining the accuracy and trustworthiness of some message or source, which are key components of credibility. Further, the confusion between fantasy and reality suggests that children in this stage would have a difficult time making accurate judgments pertaining to information authorship within applications like YouTube, blogs, MySpace, and other consumer-driven content where authorship is sometimes vague at best. Indeed, the general idea of other is itself challenging for children at this stage, and as content such as sophisticated digital animation begins to blur real and virtual characters, this could potentially delay a child's ability to distinguish fantasy from reality. Also, children in this stage of cognitive development likely won't be able to self-correct faulty reasoning to use in future information-evaluation tasks, and so intervention programs designed to assist young children in credibility assessment will need to consider this cognitive limitation.

Children in the concrete operational stage who have not yet mastered de-centered thought and perspective-taking skills will similarly struggle with understanding, and thus recognizing, bias in the information and sources they find online. In addition, children in the concrete operational stage may be likely to focus on rather superficial indicators of credibility (e.g., site attractiveness or design) given their propensity to reason based on physically tangible information. Intervention programs targeting this age group will also need to understand that early concrete operational children have difficulty with abstractions and often cannot transfer logical principles from situation to situation, making credibility assessment a difficult and piecemeal process.

The most effective credibility judgments will be made as youth advance through the formal operational stage, when they have the ability to reason beyond the information presented (i.e., as they develop the ability to examine implicit and explicit credibility cues) and to make logical arguments based on the totality of information available. Thus, credibility assessment curricula are likely to be most effective for children in the formal operational stage, given their ability to engage in abstract thought and to generalize logical principles across information-seeking contexts.

Information Processing and Credibility Judgments

The descriptive stages thus offer some insight into how children at various ages may excel at and struggle with reaching accurate credibility decisions. Inherent in children's ability to assess credibility in digital media environments is their capacity for processing information. Research in information processing may be particularly helpful in understanding the challenges that children face when evaluating information. Researchers studying cognitive development from an information-processing perspective recognize that there is great variability in human cognition both within and between developmental stages, and one way in which they conceptualize cognitive development is through over-time changes in the strategies that children employ to solve problems and perform tasks.[16] More specifically, as children develop they tend to move from using less- to more-efficient strategies. Researchers have described four strategy-based dimensions, including repertoire, distribution, efficiency, and selection, that influence children's task performance as they mature.[17]

First, for any task it is important to consider what strategies or *repertoire* a child uses or has at his or her disposal to use for a given task. Repertoire varies by task, child, age, and, of course, cognitive ability.[18] This not only implies that younger children typically have fewer strategies cognitively available to them than do older children, but also that two children of the same age may successfully (or unsuccessfully) make credibility decisions using different strategies. Strategy *distribution* focuses on the frequency with which each strategy is used for specific tasks, and thus acknowledges that strategy employment is an evolving and summative process.[19] For example, a particular strategy for credibility assessment may be most relevant when a child is in the later concrete operational developmental stage. However, a short time later, as the child moves into formal operation, that strategy will have evolved through experience and may now include more informed strategies. As such, our ability to make decisions like credibility judgments is an accumulative process, where previous strategies are replaced by or incorporated with newly acquired strategies. Third, *efficiency* explains how strategies are executed. Effective strategies are applied quickly and accurately as children age and gain experience performing cognitive tasks. This suggests that children's abilities to use credibility assessment strategies will improve (or at least become more efficient in terms of execution speed) over time, as they mature. Finally, *selection* explains how children at different maturity levels choose which strategy to select, as well as how children adjust their strategy use to perform specific tasks. Selection is thus influenced by situational constraints, such as speed and accuracy, and individual differences, such as experience or expertise on a given task. To this end, cognitive development gradually occurs as preexisting and existing strategies for task performance evolve with experience and use. This perspective highlights that as children develop cognitively, how and how effectively they make online credibility judgments will change, making the understanding of credibility a moving target throughout childhood.

A related perspective also examines the role of cognitive development in children's abilities to process information. Case's[20] neo-Piagetian developmental theory of information processing views movement both within and between Piaget's stages as resulting from increases in children's information-processing capacity. More specifically, as children mature their ability to store information in working memory improves. As children form and practice using mental schemata or strategies for problem-solving repeatedly, they become automatic, which allows working memory to focus on other tasks, such as combining existing and generating new schemata and strategies (i.e., Piaget's notion of accommodation). Eventually, children consolidate schemata into networks of related concepts that enable them to think in more advanced ways. When this occurs, children move on to the next stage of development.

Media researchers also consider information processing by looking at how and how much information is acquired, stored, and recalled within mediated environments. For example, applying Lang's[21] Limited Capacity Model (LCM), scholars have examined how informational resources are allocated when processing media content. The LCM, developed through years of research on how humans perceive, store, and access information, presents a framework through which one can understand how complex informational environments containing multiple information objects are processed. Originally designed to examine traditional media such as television, its relevance to processing Internet-based information has been asserted by several researchers in recent years.[22] The LCM states that "processing messages requires mental resources, and people have a limited (and perhaps fixed) pool of mental resources. You can think about one thing, or two, or maybe even seven at the same time, but eventually all your resources are being used, and the system cannot think yet another thing without letting a previous thought go."[23] Thus, regardless of factors such as age, all people are limited by their level of cognitive development. The LCM suggests that encoding, storage, and retrieval are all engaged when evaluating information. The encoding process determines what message information will be attended to and remembered. Once encoded, information is associated and stored with previously held memory that can be retrieved at a later time. According to the LCM, the mental resources available to the user are finite and independently allocated to each of the three processes. Thus, when the mental resources allocated to encoding increase, storage and retrieval resource allocation decreases.

Cognitively, young children (ages 2–7) are different from older children (ages 7–11), and older children are different from adults.[24] Thus, consistent with Piaget's discussion on information organization and complex thinking, the processing limitations described within the LCM should be greater for younger users. Over the past several years, developmental differences have been found in children's attention, comprehension, and retention of mediated information. For instance, Fisch, McCann-Brown, and Cohen[25] found that comprehension of television content was greatest for five-year-olds, followed by four- and three-year-olds. Children who are less cognitively developed tend to focus on the perceptually salient aspects of media stimuli and struggle to simultaneously attend to multiple information objects,[26] due to a presumed decreased cognitive capacity to organize multiple information objects existing within the same message. Colors, pictures, animation, and other message attributes that need processing make identifying central content in media messages difficult for children. For instance, preoperational (or preschool) children's attention to a television program is negatively influenced by the appearance of bright colors and music compared with program content lacking these features.[27] Others have similarly found that the inclusion of such production features distract children's attention away from central message content.[28]

Consistent with Piaget's preoperational stage suggesting that younger children lack the cognitive complexity to logically organize multiple information inputs, research indicates that younger children lack the skills needed to properly integrate television scenes together and to understand how they are related in time.[29] Confusion, or feelings that programming is incomprehensible for any reason, increases the likelihood that children will tune-out or misinterpret content. And television is a rather simplistic technology to comprehend compared to newer digital media forms. For example, in television, commercials appear at relatively predefined intervals, and generally do not run simultaneously during program content, making them time-distinct from the programs in which they are embedded. By contrast, Web pages often feature content, advertisements, animation, and video simultaneously, which may cause young children to have trouble identifying and organizing relevant content. Indeed, some preliminary research recently found that only about 60 percent of five- to seven-year-olds, and 80 percent of ten to twelve-year-olds could correctly identify either pop-up or banner ads located on a Web site.[30] Moreover, users need to both understand and remember the relationships among different Web pages and to continually assess the relevance of information to their initial search goals. In this way, the challenges that television present to processing and evaluating information are likely magnified in the Internet context. The inability to logically organize information that is characteristic of the preoperational and beginning concrete operational stages could challenge younger children's effectiveness in evaluating information within complex online environments. Simply put, young children who have difficulty storing information and inferring relationships among pieces of information will likely have difficulty evaluating Web pages and the information contained therein.

The developmental challenges and resulting information-processing difficulties suggest that programs to teach children how to evaluate Internet-based information may be best suited for children in the later concrete or formal operational stages of cognitive development. Digital media, with all of their opportunities for complex presentation, such as nonlinearity, animation, interactivity, and so on,[31] may create an experience that is beyond the life experiences and cognitive abilities of young children.

Interestingly, however, children are being introduced to online experiences earlier now than in previous years. The applications available through Internet and other digital technologies have grown dramatically[32] and altered usage patterns[33] in recent years, resulting in a new "digital generation" of sorts. Indeed, those who have not lived in a time without digital media technology are sometimes referred to as the Net-generation, the "digital generation," or most notably, "digital natives."[34] Social, entertainment, education, and other components of digital media use are now integrated and fully consumed within nearly all aspects of interaction. Today's advanced media technologies combine both old (newspapers, radio, books) and new (multiuser games, streaming video and audio, cellular telephony, and so on) media, and to process such complex information, children need sophisticated organizational skills well beyond those required for reading simple text. As but one example, basic structured online learning environments such as WebCT, Blackboard, and CARMEN allow students to communicate synchronously and asynchronously, incorporate outside Web applications like YouTube and personal blogs, as well as present course content.

Of course a possible consequence of this is that school-aged children are developing the cognitive schemata necessary to handle the informational complexities required by multimedia presentations. New presentational forms may bring new cognitive representation, or at least new thinking patterns,[35] and youth may be becoming more cognitively advanced with regard to digital media, as compared to those born before the online era. Thus, one possibility is that youth's cognitive development is actually improved through intense media integration and use.

From a problem-solving perspective, the strategies discussed earlier that are employed by youth, including repertoire, distribution, efficiency, and selection, will likely change among youth who mature as digital natives, perhaps significantly altering current understanding of human attitude and behavioral development. Because understanding human attitudes and behavior with regard to the media is based on people's media schemata and patterns of use in the past sixty or seventy years, conclusions from this work may not be reflective of current trends. As multimedia platforms increase the amount and type of media exposure, recalibration of our understanding of the processing and skills used today may be required.

Consider, for example, the availability, acquisition, and use of health information. Repertoire, strategy, and selection could all differ from the perspective of a digital native. Today, there is no single way to obtain, examine, and understand a given health issue; thus, the repertoire available to those seeking health information has increased. Strategy distribution and selection has evolved to include self-experiences as well as experiences of others who share their experiences online.[36] Experience as a selection factor, then, must include self, social network, and virtual experience. When a person seeks health information online, they often also seek information directly from others who have also been afflicted with a similar ailment. How these sources of information influence attitude and behavior such as anxiety and self-treatment will need to be reevaluated as digital natives potentially redefine the roles played by individuals and technology in health care decisions.

Thus, at this point there is some reason to believe that processing Internet-based information is more cognitively demanding than traditional media content, which may increase the likelihood that children and adults alike will make poor information-based decisions, including judgments about the credibility of online information. Over the past several years, many researchers have started to look at how information is judged online.[37] Little of this research, however, has considered children specifically.

Of the few studies that have investigated how children evaluate online information, most suggest that many children do not recognize that some information posted on the Web might be incorrect and should be questioned. For instance, Watson found that eleven- and twelve-year-old students never talk about the accuracy of the information they find, nor do they criticize the accessed content.[38] Qualitative analyses of interviews with nine- and ten-year-old students similarly suggest that when selecting information online, children rarely question its accuracy,[39] and only a small number of students showed any skepticism toward the accuracy or credibility of the information they found. Hirsh also found that seven- and eight-year-old children generally trusted the information they found online and did not question the credibility of the source or the accuracy of the information.[40] Although some data indicate teens with a great deal of Web experience critically evaluate online information,[41] Agosto found that adolescents have a tendency to equate information quantity with information quality.[42] Most recently, when examining children in the concrete operational stage of development (i.e., third-, fourth-, and fifth-graders), Eastin et al.[43] found that children have difficulty recognizing differences between different types of content (e.g., commercial versus noncommercial content) when making source and information evaluations. Supporting work on early concrete operational cognitive limitations, as well as the LCM, this study also found that children's judgments of the credibility of a Web site were higher, whereas recall of content was lower, when subjects were faced with multiple information objects appearing on a Web site, including advertising and dynamic content (colors, animation, etc.). Together, this work suggests that while young children are cognitively unprepared to critically assess Internet-based information in sophisticated ways, adolescents, both young and old, may also have trouble judging the credibility of online content.

Credibility in the Digital Media Environment

Effective evaluation of Internet sites and sources involves attending to both explicit and implicit cues that produce attitude judgments.[44] Perceived credibility of the source and message is an initial and important step in message evaluation. Tseng and Fogg explicated four categories of credibility that are particularly applicable to the Web: presumed, reputed, surface, and experienced.[45] Presumed credibility perceptions are based on culturally based assumptions or stereotypes held by the receiver toward a source; reputed credibility is determined through third-party accounts of a source's trustworthiness and expertise; surface credibility is based on initial reactions to external source or message characteristics such as appearance or design; and experienced credibility is derived from personal interaction with a source over time. Applying these categories to online information evaluation, Wathen and Burkell suggest that surface credibility perceptions are established first, whereby users evaluate a Web page's design, appearance, and organization.[46] Second, source and message credibility perceptions are made based on the source's apparent expertise and credentials, as well as on message content, relevancy, and currency.

While Wathen and Burkell present a clear model of Web site evaluation, the actual sequence and recurrence of presumed, surface, and reputed evaluation are unclear.[47] Specifically, the order and recurrence in which cues are evaluated is unspecified. For example, if, say, the source is the first cue utilized, does a user come back to source once the message has been processed, or does this cue only matter when the user encounters unknown or counterintuitive information within the message? As advertisements rotate on and off the page, are users continually rechecking for credibility? And, if such recurring and complex processes do occur, does this create more difficulties for younger children? The research on cognitive development and information processing presented earlier would suggest so. The fact that more information is required to be processed in the online environment suggests that evaluating digital information may be particularly problematic for younger, less cognitively developed users. Finally, does the order of evaluation influence judgment? If presumed, surface, and reputed evaluations are necessary to accurately judge Web site content, is it plausible that children, and especially young children, possess the level of cognitive skill needed to organize and process all this information? Furthermore, such evaluations assume that users have the appropriate experience to make such judgments and, since each judgment requires users to logically categorize and interpret, the sum volume of required cognitive skill could be overwhelming for children in the preoperational and concrete operational stages of development.

To be sure, there are many criteria that people, including youth, apply to make credibility decisions.[48] While factors such as the medium itself, perceived source bias and expertise, and so on are certainly relevant, attributes that influence processing from a developmental and information-load perspective are of particular interest when considering young users' credibility assessments. Three key informational message cues to credibility perceptions that have been identified within an online context are source information, dynamic presentation, and advertising. Each of these cues requires a need for information organization, logical thinking, and abstract reasoning and, thus, each directly links to developmental changes in cognition and points to potential information-processing difficulty for young children in determining the credibility of digital information.

Source Information

Credibility research suggests that source information such as the presence (vs. absence) of an author, as well as source credentials and expertise affect perceptions of credibility in online contexts.[49] Unfortunately, very little work has examined how youth specifically incorporate source attributes into their credibility assessments. One recent study using a population of youth in the concrete operational stage (eight- to eleven-year-olds) found that a Web site lacking an explicit source resulted in *higher* author credibility perceptions than when an explicit source was included.[50] As an explanation, the researchers speculated that children may have relied on their credibility perceptions of the Internet as a medium of communication when lacking information about the source. Defaulting to a medium-based judgment is perhaps cognitively less demanding than other strategies, but potentially a worst-case scenario in an online context. Assessments at the level of the medium are crude, and while they may be appropriate for government- or industry-regulated content such as that offered through television and newspapers, they may not be appropriate for online content that is freely offered, altered by anyone with technological access and skill, and subjected to no or very little government regulation.

Dynamic Presentation

Also presenting potential cognitive difficulties for children is the dynamic nature of content that is presented online. Dynamism is a factor that has been shown to affect people's credibility judgments across a variety of contexts.[51] In an online context, dynamism is defined as the presence of colorful borders and pictures, animation, and interactive content.[52] Research on adults has found that dynamic Web sites are perceived as more credible.[53] A study by Eastin et al. of preadolescents found that dynamic content increased source credibility ratings.[54] Furthermore, considering both source and dynamism together, when a source was presented on a nondynamic site, the source's credibility was judged to be low.

Research results offer both good and bad news to parents and educators.[55] It is good that children are considering cues to determine credibility, but basing assessments solely on an author's use of dynamic content such as pictures and animation is too simplistic for accurate credibility assessments. From a cognitive developmental perspective, however, this finding makes sense. Since most children in the concrete operational stage are not able to organize multiple information objects very efficiently, and because their reasoning still tends to be limited to more tangible objects, it is understandable that they attend to cues that are more visually appealing. In addition, many children in this stage lack both on- and offline life experiences to make judgments about a source based on attributes such as source expertise and qualifications with subject matter. The study's further finding that as dynamic content increases, children's ability to recall central message elements decreases further supports cognitive developmental models advanced by Piaget and Case, as well as Lang's Limited Capacity Model. Of course, Eastin and colleagues' research is only one study that examined children within a single developmental stage and, thus, it is not clear yet how generalizable the findings are to children across developmental levels. At minimum, however, it argues that much more research is needed in the area of cognitive development and children's credibility assessment processes.

Advertising

Another area that may present special problems for younger digital media users with regard to credibility is advertising. Much research has been conducted on how children perceive and process televised advertising, which is instructive for the Internet context. Early research suggested that younger children have difficulty making inferences from and understanding the relationships among various scenes in a television program. Collins found that younger children have trouble integrating scenes prior to and immediately after commercial breaks, thereby skewing their interpretation of programs as a whole.[56] That said, as children move through the concrete operational stage, they are better able to recognize and understand content differences between programming and advertising.[57] Children who are in the late preoperational and early concrete operational stages make distinctions between programming and advertising on the basis of characteristics such as the limited time allocated to a single commercial. As children mature cognitively, and as their understanding of others develops to include the perspective and motivations of others, the persuasive component of advertising is understood, thus allowing children to distinguish commercial from noncommercial content based on motivation rather than structural features.[58]

Recently, the presence of advertising has been found to influence Internet users' perceptions of online information, including credibility. However, as with other online message investigations, research in this realm focuses on adults and findings are mixed. Not surprisingly, online ads from companies perceived as credible are generally associated with more credible information.[59] However, while Choi and Rifon found a positive relationship between attitude toward the advertiser and site credibility, there is a growing body of literature suggesting that advertising either does not influence credibility judgments or negatively affects perceptions of credibility among adult Internet users.[60] Research specifically indicates that the presence and number of advertisements encountered negatively influence credibility perceptions,[61] and that advertising that is difficult to distinguish from page content negatively influences adults' judgments of site credibility.[62]

Focusing on younger users, Eastin and colleagues found that while online advertising can increase cognitive load (and therefore decrease recall), it does not ultimately influence credibility perceptions.[63] One explanation for this finding is that children between the ages of 7 and 11 are still developing the cognitive ability to organize and logically process multiple information objects and, thus, source confusion may be a potential reason for the null effects. Supporting this interpretation, 71 percent of the children in the study between ages 8 and 10 who saw an ad on a Web site that had no source thought that the source of the page was the advertiser. This demonstrates that many children may be easily confused or have a poor understanding of the dynamic relationship between noncommercial content and advertising in online environments.

In sum, while the research discussed earlier[64] shows that adults may become confused and judge information as less credible when large amounts of advertising are presented alongside other content, both developmental theory and research suggest that these perceptions are likely to be magnified for children who are cognitively less equipped to organize complex information and, in many cases, even to identify advertising as advertising. Moreover, consistent with Fogg's rationale, the cognitive overload created by multiple advertisements on a Web page could further confuse children as to the source of some information, thus negatively influencing content recall and, more important, creating inaccurate or unpredictable credibility assessments.

How to Educate Young Users

Any discussion of developmental differences with regard to credibility perceptions in the online environment would be incomplete without considering how we can educate young users to use digital media more effectively. To answer this question, it is useful to examine how researchers have approached similar issues with other media, for example, television. Work in this area typically comes under the heading of media and information literacy.[65]

According to Anderson, media literacy is the "skillful collection, interpretation, testing and application of information regardless of medium or presentation for some purposeful action."[66] Most media literacy curricula share a number of goals. For example, most programs are designed to increase children's understanding of the technical elements (e.g., camera techniques, special effects) and literary devices (e.g., plot and character development) used in the mass media.[67] By focusing primarily on television, many media literacy programs contain lessons that emphasize the interpretation of media advertising, stereotypes, violence, and the news.

Potter suggests that media literacy requires mastery of both rudimentary and advanced skills.[68] Rudimentary skills include gaining exposure to relevant content, recognizing symbols and patterns, and attaching meanings to identified symbols and patterns. According to Potter's framework, most children should achieve some level of rudimentary media literacy at a fairly young age. On the other hand, owing to increased cognitive demands, advanced literacy skills, including competencies such as analyzing, comparing, and evaluating mediated messages, take more time to develop. Children with advanced skills are able to "take control" of television through critical viewing and derive their own interpretation of content. In doing so, the child exhibits the ability to recognize and organize symbols, patterns, and attached meanings to message attributes such as characters' feelings. In short, these children, who are typically in the late concrete or formal operational stages, are able to think beyond the information presented.

While research on literacy within the realm of traditional media (i.e., television) can inform development of programs to teach newer media literacy, it is important to remember the unique challenges that digital media, and particularly the Internet, pose. First, skills that are considered rudimentary to traditional media literacy may be more difficult to achieve in the new media context, where the process of searching for content may be more complex online. Children using general search engines such as Google or Yahoo must be able to read, interpret, and understand search technology to make good content decisions, and they must remember search paths and relationships between different Web pages as they navigate through a sea of hyperlinks. Given their limited life experience, such complex navigation and interpretive tasks may be more difficult for young digital media users. Furthermore, once a selection of some content has been made, the Web is arguably a more demanding environment: users are simultaneously confronted with both visual and audio stimuli, including static and interactive text, video, and graphics,[69] and content is arranged nonlinearly and nonhierarchically. Younger children may simply lack the capacity and skill necessary to make good sense of such cognitively "noisy" environments.

Although scattered, research on new media literacy is starting to take shape. Terms that have been used to describe general competence in both using the Internet and evaluating its content include information literacy, digital literacy, new media literacy, and computer literacy.[70] In addition to labeling inconsistencies, the specific skills that are believed to comprise this type of literacy also vary across researchers and disciplines. A comprehensive assessment of electronic literacy presented by Swan suggests standards for using nonprint and electronic media in elementary, middle, and high school classrooms.[71] Swan outlines three kinds of Internet-based literacy that should be taught in school: tool, critical, and construction literacy. Tool literacy includes using various electronic technologies and the ability "to access, decode, encode, and locate" information.[72] Critical literacy focuses on interpreting, criticizing, evaluating, and applying information to solve problems. Finally, construction skills focus on "capabilities for composing, developing, integrating, presenting" content.[73] Although helpful, Swan's approach does not integrate a cognitive developmental perspective, which would help to highlight that elementary, middle, and high school-age children possess different cognitive skills and capabilities that are relevant to the various type of "literacies" he advocates teaching. The implication, of course, is that different programs may need to be developed for children in different stages of development, or across different points in time within each developmental stage.

It seems that, just as with traditional media literacy, access and content evaluation are the primary constructs that discriminate between low and high digitally literate individuals. Using the cognitive development stages as a guide, research now needs to document how information evaluation evolves during the preoperational, concrete operational, and formal operational stages. The opportunities for such an inquiry are wide open, and should go beyond how children's perceptions of information credibility change between and within developmental stages to include studies of cognitive demand in online environments that present a great deal of message-related as well as extra message information to young users.

Conclusion

Understanding how information within mediated messages is evaluated is not a new concern. In fact, understanding message construction and assessment in mediated environments has been a topic of interest since media began pushing information into homes. In that time, researchers have found that audience interpretation and evaluation of media messages are complex and varied, and are often difficult for children. More recent findings suggest that, in the digital environment, information that is peripheral to the main message, such as that offered through dynamic presentation and advertising, is also troublesome for younger children trying to make credibility assessments. Yet, dynamic content and advertising are a central part of the digital culture. Thus, the job of researchers now is to better understand how we can teach children to identify and interpret such message elements. Simply put, rather than the typical highbrow ranting about commercial exploitation of children, researchers, parents, politicians, and digital media content providers should tackle these concerns through education. This point becomes even more important as we increasingly realize that much of the new media content now and in the future,[74] including commercially oriented content, is and will be created by the youth of today.

This chapter has attempted to present credibility decisions in digital media environments as complex, especially for young children who have not yet developed full cognitive maturity. Narrowly defined and strictly theoretical views of online information perceptions are not adequate in today's digital media environment when investigating concepts such as credibility. Researchers must be willing to venture outside the comfort zone of their discipline's theoretical base, whether it is psychology, communication, information science, education, computer science, or media. Parents and teachers should also try to better understand how their children and students are developing, interpreting, and adapting to the information they encounter via digital media.

A recent report by the Pew Internet & American Life Project suggests that as many as 57 percent of online teens are now content creators.[75] Many of these teens are producing digital information through personal blogs, social networking sites, and YouTube. Such sites are designed to present "living" content, which is defined as information that updates through linked sites that change content regularly. This could also include content that gets altered by users. Without question, this raises important credibility issues and concerns. For example, fundamental questions such as source identity, which is traditionally the first cue for determining credibility,[76] may be virtually impossible to establish with certainty in these environments. Users must make many layers of credibility judgments, including an initial judgment about the site host, and then further judgments as they link off the site.

In addition to understanding how credibility judgments are formed, it is important to understand how credibility perceptions impact youth both on- and offline. Research indicates that many children readily offer personal information to people and organizations they encounter online,[77] but what leads to this information provision is unknown. Clearly, young people's credibility perceptions of online sources and content would help to understand such decisions. Digital literacy efforts that include credibility evaluation may help children make better decisions and, consequently, protect themselves from potential exploitation. Thus, it is recommended that researchers examine both the attitudinal and behavioral effects of Web sites that are perceived by children as credible or not. In doing so, we will better understand the social and behavioral consequences of credibility assessment.

When it comes to "digital natives," nothing should be taken for granted—the digital environment is a complex, changing entity with which children of all ages struggle when searching for and evaluating information. The more parents, politicians, teachers, and researchers work to understand and appreciate the cognitive skills, abilities, and challenges children face in this environment, the easier it will be to help them navigate the digital world of today and tomorrow.

Notes

1. Pew Research Foundation, *Vital Decisions*, 2002, http://www.pewinternet.org (retrieved March 24, 2003).

2. National Center for Education, Rates of Computer and Internet Use by Children in Nursery School and Students in Kindergarten through Twelfth Grad: 2003, (2005), http://nces.ed.gov/pubsearch/pubsinfo.asp?pubid=2005111 (retrieved May 9, 2006).

3. Matthew S. Eastin, Teen Internet Use: Relating Social Perceptions and Cognitive Models to Behavior, *CyberPsychology & Behavior* 8 (2005): 62–75.

4. Matthew S. Eastin, Mong-Shan Yang, and Amy Nathanson, Children of the Net: An Empirical Exploration into the Evaluation of Internet Content, *Journal of Broadcasting & Electronic Media* 50 (2006): 211–30.

5. Jean Piaget, *Science of Education and the Psychology of the Child* (New York: Orion Press, 1970); Jean Piaget, Piaget's Theory, in *Carmichael's Manual of Child Psychology*, Vol. 1, 3rd ed., ed. Paul Henry Mussen (New York: Wiley, 1970), 703–32.

6. Laura M. Taylor, *Introducing Cognitive Development* (New York: Psychology Press, 2005).

7. Robbie Case, Intellectual Development from Birth to Adulthood: A Neo-Piagetian Interpretation, in *Children's Thinking: What Develops?* ed. Robert S. Siegler (Hillsdale, NJ: Erlbaum, 1998); Kurt W. Fischer, A Theory of Cognitive Development, *Psychological Review* 48 (1980): 477–525.

8. Piaget, *Science of Education*; Piaget, Piaget's Theory.

9. Taylor, *Introducing Cognitive Development*.

10. Laura E. Berk, *Child Development*, 6th ed. (Boston: Allyn & Bacon, 2003).

11. Ibid.

12. Ibid.

13. Jean Piaget, *The Equilibrium of Cognitive Structures: The Central Problem of Intellectual Development* (Chicago: University of Chicago Press, 1985).

14. See Harry Beilin and Peter B. Pufall, *Piaget's Theory: Prospects and Possibilities* (Hillsdale, NJ: Erlbaum, 1992), and Taylor, *Introducing Cognitive Development*, for a detailed overview.

15. Robbie Case, *Intellectual Development: Birth to Adulthood* (Orlando, FL: Academic Press, 1985); Fischer, A Theory of Cognitive Development; Pierre Mounoud, Similarities between Developmental Sequences at Different Age Periods, in *Stage and Structure: Reopening the Debate*, ed. Iris Levin (Norwood, NJ: Ablex, 1986).

16. Case, Intellectual Development from Birth to Adulthood; Robert S. Seigler, *Emerging Minds* (New York: Oxford University Press, 1996).

17. Joke Torbeyns, Laurence Arnaud, Patrick Lemaire, and Lieven Verschaffel, Cognitive Changes as Strategy Changes, in *Cognitive Development Changes*, eds. Andreas Demetriou and Athanassios Raftopoulos (Cambridge: Cambridge University Press, 2004).

18. Ibid.

19. Siegler, *Emerging Minds*.

20. Case, Intellectual Development from Birth to Adulthood.

21. Annie Lang, The Limited Capacity Model of Mediated Message Processing, *Journal of Communication* 50 (2000): 46–70.

22. Fangfang Diao and S. Shyam Sundar, Orienting Responses and Memory for Web Advertisements: Exploring Effects of Pop-up Windows and Animation, *Communication Research* 31 (2004): 537–67; Eastin, Yang, and Nathanson, Children of the Net; Annie Lang, Jennifer Borse, Kevin Wise, and Prabu David, Captured by the World Wide Web: Orienting to Structural and Content Features of Computer-Presented Information, *Communication Research* 29 (2002): 215–45; S. Shyam Sundar, Multimedia Effects on Processing and Perceptions of Online News: A Study of Picture, Audio, and Video Downloads, *Journalism and Mass Communication Quarterly* 77 (2000): 480–99.

23. Lang, The Limited Capacity Model of Mediated Message Processing, 47.

24. Case, Intellectual Development from Birth to Adulthood; Jean Piaget, *The Child and Reality: Problems of Genetic Psychology* (New York: Penguin, 1976).

25. For instance, Shalom M. Fisch, Susan K. McCann-Brown, and David I. Cohen, Young Children's Comprehension of Educational Television: The Role of Visual Information and Intonation, *Media Psychology* 3 (2001): 365–78.

26. Eastin, Yang, and Nathanson, Children of the Net.

27. Linda F. Alwitt, Daniel R. Anderson, Elizabeth P. Lorch, and Stephen R. Levin, Preschool Children's Visual Attention to Attributes of Television, *Human Communication Research* 7 (1980): 52–67.

28. W. Andrew Collins, Interpretation and Inference in Children's Television Viewing, in *Children's Understanding of Television: Research on Attention and Comprehension*, eds. Jennings Bryant and Daniel R. Anderson (New York: Academic Press, 1983), 125–50.

29. W. Andrew Collins, Children's Comprehension of Television Content, in *Children Communicating: Media and Development of Thought, Speech, and Understanding*, ed. Ellen Wartella (Beverly Hills, CA: Sage, 1979), 21–52.

30. M. McIlrath, Children's Cognitive Processing of Internet Advertising (doctoral dissertation, University of California at Santa Barbara, Department of Communication, 2006).

31. S. Shyam Sundar, The MAIN Model: A Heuristic Approach to Understanding Technology Effects on Credibility, this volume.

32. Frank Biocca, New Media Technology and Youth: Trends in the Evolution of New Media, *Journal of Adolescent Health* 27, no. 2 (2000): 22–29; Marc Prensky, Digital Native, Digital Immigrants, *On the Horizon* 9, no. 5 (2001): 1–6.

33. Ulla Foehr, Media Multitasking Among American Youth: Prevalence, Predictors, and Pairings, A Report Prepared for the Kiaser Family Foundation, 2006, http://www.kff.org/entmedia/entmedia121206pkg.cfm (retrieved February 26, 2006).

34. Prensky, Digital Native, Digital Immigrants.

35. Sven Birkerts, *The Gutenberg Elegies: The Fate of Reading in an Electronic Age* (Boston: Faber and Faber, 1994); Prensky, Digital Native, Digital Immigrants.

36. See also Eysenbach, this volume.

37. Matthew S. Eastin, Credibility Assessments of Online Health Information: The Effects of Source Expertise and Knowledge of Content, *Journal of Computer-Mediated Communication* 6, no. 4 (2001), http://www.ascusc.org/jcmc/ (retrieved April 28, 2004); Andrew J. Flanagin and Miriam J. Metzger, Digital Media and Youth: Unparalleled Opportunity and Unprecedented Responsibility, this volume; Elaine Toms and Adam Taves, Measuring User Perceptions of Web Site Reputation, *Information Processing and Management* 40, no. 2 (2004): 291–317.

38. Jinx S. Watson, If You Don't Have It, You Can't Find It, A Close Look at Students' Perceptions of Using Technology, *Journal of the American Society for Information Science* 49 (1998): 1024–36.

39. Andrew Large and Jamshid Beheshti, The Web as a Classroom Resource: Reactions from the Users, *Journal of the American Society for Information Science* 51 (2000): 1069–80.

40. Sandra G. Hirsh, Children's Relevance Criteria and Information Seeking on Electronic Resources, *Journal of the American Society for Information Science* 50 (1999): 1265–83.

41. Jérôme Dinet, Pascal Marquet, and Elke Nissen, An Exploratory Study of Adolescents' Perceptions of the Web, *Journal of Computer Assisted Learning* 19 (2003): 538–45.

42. Denise E. Agosto, A Model of Young People's Decision-Making in Using the Web, *Library Information Science Research* 24 (2002): 311–41.

43. Eastin, Yang, and Nathanson, Children of the Net.

44. Richard Petty and John Cacioppo, Elaboration Likelihood Model, in *Advances in Experimental Social Psychology 19*, ed. Leonard Berkowitz (San Diego, CA: Academic Press, 1986), 123–205.

45. Shawn Tseng and B. J. Fogg, Credibility and Computing Technology, *Communications of the ACM* 42 (1999): 39–44.

46. C. Nadine Wathen and Jacquelyn Burkell, Believe It or Not: Factors Influencing Credibility on the Web, *Journal of the American Society for Information and Technology* 53, no. 2 (2002): 134–44.

47. Ibid.

48. See, e.g., Miriam J. Metzger, Andrew J. Flanagin, Keren Eyal, Daisy R. Lemus, and Robert M. McCann, Bringing the Concept of Credibility into the 21st Century: Integrating Perspectives on Source, Message, and Media Credibility in the Contemporary Media Environment, *Communication Yearbook 27* (Mahwah, NJ: Erlbaum, 2003), 293–335, for a review.

49. Eastin, Credibility Assessments of Online Health Information; Metzger et al., Bringing the Concept of Credibility into the 21st Century; B. J. Fogg, Jonathan Marshall, Othman Laraki, Alex Osipovich, Chris Varma, Nicholas Fang, Jyoti Paul, Akshay Rangnekar, John Shon, Preeti Swani, and Marissa Treinen, What Makes a Web Site Credible? A Report on a Large Quantitative Study, in *Proceedings of ACM CHI 2001 Conference on Human Factors in Computing Systems* (New York: ACM Press, 2001), 61–68, http://www.acm.org/pubs/articles/proceedings/chi/365024/p61-fogg/p61-fogg.pdf (retrieved October 27, 2003).

50. Eastin, Yang, and Nathanson, Children of the Net.

51. See Metzger et al., Bringing the Concept of Credibility into the 21st Century.

52. Eastin, Yang, and Nathanson, Children of the Net; B. J. Fogg and Shawn Tseng, The Elements of Computer Credibility, in *Proceedings of the CHI99 Conference on Human Factors and Computing Systems* (Pittsburgh, PA: ACM Press, 1999).

53. Jinwoo Kim and Jae Yun Moon, Designing towards Emotional Usability in Customer Interfaces: Trustworthiness of Cyber-Banking System Interfaces, *Interacting with Computers* 10 (1997): 1–29; Joseph B. Walther, Zuoming Wang, and Tracy Loh, The Effect of Top-level Domains and Advertisements on Health Web Site Credibility, *Journal of Medical Internet Research* 6 (2004), http://www.jmir.org (retrieved March 24, 2005).

54. Eastin, Yang, and Nathanson, Children of the Net.

55. Ibid.

56. W. Andrew Collins, Effect of Temporal Separation between Motivation, Aggression, and Consequences: A Developmental Study, *Developmental Psychology* 8 (1973): 215–21.

57. John H. Flavell, *Cognitive Development* (Englewood Cliffs, NJ: Prentice-Hall, 1977); Dale Kunkel, Children and Host-Selling Television Commercials, *Communication Research* 15, no. 1 (1988): 71–92.

58. Carolyn Shantz, The Development of Social Cognition, in *Review of Child Development Research 5*, ed. E. Hetherington (Chicago: University of Chicago Press, 1975), 257–323.

59. Sejung Marina Choi and Nora J. Rifon, Antecedents and Consequences of Web Advertising Credibility: A Study of Consumer Response to Banner Ads, *Journal of Interactive Advertising* 13 (2002), http://www.jiad.org/vol3/no1/ (retrieved July 14, 2004).

60. B. J. Fogg, Jonathan Marshall, Tami Kameda, Joshua Solomon, Akshay Rangnekar, John Boyd, and Bonny Brown, Web Credibility Research: A Method for Online Experiments and Some Early Study Results, in *Proceedings of ACM CHI 2001 Conference on Human Factors in Computing Systems* (New York: ACM Press, 2001), 295–96, http://www.webcredibility.org (retrieved October 27, 2003).

61. Ibid.; Walther, Wang, and Loh, The Effect of Top-level Domains and Advertisements on Health Web Site Credibility.

62. Fogg et al., Web Credibility Research.

63. Eastin, Yang, and Nathanson, Children of the Net.

64. Fogg et al., Web Credibility Research.

65. See Frances J. Harris, Challenges to Teaching Credibility Assessment in Contemporary Schooling, this volume, for a detailed discussion of efforts to teach digital literacy.

66. James A. Anderson, Receivership Skills: An Educational Response, in *Education for the Television Age*, eds. Milton E. Ploghoft and James A. Anderson (Springfield, IL: Charles C. Thomas, 1981), 22.

67. Dorothy G. Singer and Jerome L. Singer, Developing Critical Viewing Skills and Media Literacy in Children, *Annals of the American Academy of Political and Social Science 557* (Thousand Oaks, CA: Sage, 1998), 164–79.

68. W. James Potter, *Media Literacy* (Thousand Oaks, CA: Sage, 1998); W. J. Potter, *Theory of Media Literacy: A Cognitive Approach* (Thousand Oaks, CA: Sage, 2004).

69. See Sundar, The MAIN Model, this volume, for a discussion of multimodality in the digital media environment.

70. See Harris, Challenges to Teaching Credibility Assessment in Contemporary Schooling, this volume.

71. Karen Swan, Non Print Media and Technology Literacy Standards for Assessing Technology Integration, *Journal of Educational Computing Research* 23 (2000): 85–100.

72. Ibid., 9.

73. Ibid., 13.

74. E.g., MySpace and YouTube.

75. Pew Research Foundation, Content Creation Online: 44% of U.S. Internet Users Have Contributed Their Thoughts and Their Files to the Online World, 2004, http://www.pewinternet.org (retrieved March 31, 2004).

76. See Flanagin and Metzger, this volume; and Sundar, The MAIN Model, this volume.

77. Joseph Turow and Lilach Nir, The Internet and the Family 2000, A report from the Annenberg Public Policy Center, 2000, http://www.appcpenn.org/02_reports_releases/report_2000.htm (retrieved January 1, 2001).

College Students' Credibility Judgments in the Information-Seeking Process

Soo Young Rieh and Brian Hilligoss

University of Michigan, School of Information

Information seeking is an important part of people's everyday lives. To obtain information, people use Web search engines, consult authorities, ask questions of friends, go to libraries, read newspapers, and watch television, among other methods. Through such activities, people continually make judgments about how useful information is to their particular needs, actively construct meaning, and form judgments about the relevance of the information to their goal based on various attributes or criteria.[1]

When people assess information, however, they may notice that the characteristics and value of some information are not always consistent.[2] That is, people may find texts that seem to be clearly written but are inaccurate, that are easy to obtain but out-of-date, that are current but not sufficiently comprehensive, and so on. In such cases, how do they make judgments about information? According to Wilson, people tend to ask whether they can believe what the text says or, if not, whether they can at least take it seriously.[3] Wilson thus notes that credibility is a chief aspect of information quality and states that what and who people believe to be credible constitutes the potential pool of "cognitive authorities," or those that influence people's thoughts because they are perceived as "worthy of belief."[4]

Selecting credible information from among the various available resources is a challenge for anyone. The kinds of challenges may, however, differ for adults and for young people. For instance, adult information seekers are likely to select information when they think it is accurate, current, novel, objective, reliable, authoritative, trustworthy, understandable, well-written, comprehensive, easy to obtain, and on topic.[5] Young people, on the other hand, often mainly consider whether information is related to the topic and whether it is new, interesting, and convenient, while showing less interest in authority, the readability of the language, and recency.[6]

Moreover, most adults possessed knowledge of how to evaluate information in traditional print media before newer digital media, especially the Internet, were introduced. Consequently, they had to learn how to apply the old rules and criteria for evaluating information to the relatively newer digital media.[7] Their experiences differ from those of today's youth, who have used digital media since a very young age. Indeed, survey reports show that 20 percent of college students began using computers between the ages of 5 and 8, and by the time they reached 16–18 years, virtually all of today's college students were using computers.[8] Thus, today's college students represent the first generation to "grow up digital."[9] They have experienced life in which personal computers were commonplace from the time they were born, and where the Internet has been available since their elementary school years.

College students constitute an interesting population occupying the middle ground between childhood and adulthood. While the characteristics of college students closely approximate those of children and teenagers in terms of technology adoption and immersion, the information tasks they must perform in their daily lives are more like those of adults given that they often must strike a balance among school, work, and social life. This means that the kinds of information tasks in which college students engage are potentially much more diverse and complex than those of younger children and teenagers, and may be equally or even more complex as those of many adults.[10]

Although a number of empirical studies have examined college students' credibility assessments,[11] little research to date has examined the credibility judgments that young people make with respect to their information-seeking goals and strategies. We believe that examining young people's credibility assessments and concerns is best achieved by looking at their decision making and judgments in the process of information seeking because judgments, as guides for decision making, are always made internally and can be observed only through choice and its outcomes.[12]

This chapter examines how young people's credibility judgments are embedded in the process of everyday-life information seeking and identifies the relationship between credibility judgments and information-seeking strategies. The significance of information-seeking goals, information use contexts, and their effects on credibility assessments are also discussed. Specifically, the chapter seeks to answer a number of research questions. For instance, what kinds of information do young people pursue in their daily lives? What kinds of information resources do they use to accomplish their tasks? What strategies do they take in the process of information seeking? How do they evaluate the information they find? How do their credibility concerns relate to their information-seeking goals? And how do their credibility judgments differ, depending on the phases of information seeking? To address these questions, examples are drawn from empirical data collected as part of a qualitative study of college students' credibility judgments in the context of their everyday-life information seeking.

Youth Information Seeking, Perceptions of Digital Media, and Credibility

Information seeking refers to the "purposive seeking for information as a consequence of a need to satisfy some goal."[13] In the course of information seeking, an individual may interact with people, printed materials, and digital media such as the Internet. Previous studies on youth information seeking first focused on information searching in the use of CD-ROMs[14] and online library catalogs.[15] Work in this area has more recently turned to Web search engines.[16] Considerably less attention, however, has been given to identifying characteristics of information seeking with respect to a wider variety of information resources. Dresang presents a meta-analysis of youth information-seeking behavior and points out that research in this area generally overlooks newer behaviors emerging in the digital environment.[17] She proposes interactivity, connectivity, and access as primary principles to better understand youth information-seeking behavior. Large, in reviewing a number of previous studies about children and adolescent information seeking behavior on the Web, found that young users of digital media often fail to express their information needs as queries required by Web-based search engines and experience difficulty making judgments about the relevance and, thus, credibility of the information they find.[18] They also tend to spend relatively little time reading or digesting information found on the Web.

In the field of information seeking, children, adolescents, and college students are typically considered distinct user groups. Researchers tend to study young people's information behaviors within narrowly defined age groups as they believe that different ages are characterized by both different mental models of information systems and different cognitive capabilities relevant to information seeking.[19] Only a few researchers have investigated young people's information seeking within broader age groups. Shenton and Dixon's participants, for instance, ranged from four to eighteen years of age.[20] Interestingly, their informants tended to assess the value of a source on the basis of the quantity rather than the quality of information. According to the authors, the young people in their study often used the most accessible information sources first and were very concerned with finding information as quickly and effortlessly as possible. As a result, they ended up using only a few sources and relied heavily on the same Web site or successive issues of a magazine over a prolonged period of time. Shenton and Dixon concluded that the most fundamental pattern of young peoples' information behaviors was an attempt to simplify the search process and ignore more thorough and conscientious approaches. However, as mentioned earlier, because there is so little research that compares young people's behavior across the range of children, teenagers, and college students, we do not yet have a good understanding of the similarities and differences that may exist between groups of young people from elementary school through collegiate life.

Literature reviews in the field of youth information-seeking behavior[21] indicate that little research has focused on credibility assessments in the process of information seeking. If any, researchers have looked at credibility concerns of young people on the Web. For example, Agosto's study of high school students indicated that credibility was not a factor that students used in evaluating information.[22] Agosto's participants paid greater attention to the amount of graphic and multimedia content than they did to information quality. Agosto's findings are consistent with those of Fidel et al.[23] in demonstrating that high school students relied on design and graphics of a Web site to determine its relevance and quality, while rarely mentioning credibility as an important factor for consideration. As these two studies did not look further than identifying whether credibility was discussed extensively by high school students when they evaluated information on the Web, it is difficult to conclude that young people simply ignore the importance of information credibility. Credibility assessments may be embedded implicitly in the selection of Web sites or strategies that young people take in Web searching. Young people, especially children and teenagers, may find it difficult to articulate their credibility judgments explicitly in the information-seeking process.

Several studies have examined college students' perceptions of digital media and their information-seeking behaviors on the Web. An early study by Lubans found that 20 percent of respondents believed that the Web had a positive influence on the quality of their written schoolwork, whereas 40 percent believed that the Web made no difference.[24] More recently, however, Metzger, Flanagin, and Zwarun showed that college students rely very heavily on the Web for both general and academic information, and that they expect this usage to increase over time.[25] Moreover, the Pew Internet & American Life Project reported that 79 percent of college students agreed that the Internet had a positive impact on their college academic experience.[26] While Dilevko and Gottlieb noticed that students tend to start the research process with print books, because they believe that books provide a more general overview than Internet resources and are more reputable, reliable, and, balanced,[27] the Pew study revealed that 73 percent of college students said they used the Internet more than the library, whereas only 9 percent said that they used the library more than the Internet for information searching.[28] Finally, D'Esposito and Gardner reported that students are keenly aware of the importance of discerning reliable information on the Internet.[29] Although research has also shown that college students find information to be more credible than do those from a more general adult population, they verify the information they find online significantly less.[30]

Most credibility studies of college students have taken approaches comparing young people's perceptions of the information on the Web with their perceptions of information from other media. Mashek, McGill, and Powell found that users rated traditional media as more fair and unbiased than their Internet equivalents,[31] which is similar to Metzger, Flanagin, and Zwarun's finding that college students found the Internet to be less credible than newspapers, yet equally credible as television, magazines, and radio.[32] By contrast, Johnson and Kaye reported that online newspapers and political issue-oriented Web sites were rated as more believable than their traditional counterparts.[33] Sundar's study revealed a similarity between the factor structures underlying readers' perceptions of the credibility of print news and those of online news.[34] It was noted that the findings from previous studies failed to show consistent trends in college students' perception of digital media in terms of credibility. This may be because the type of Web site (e.g., news, commercial, personal, entertainment) and type of information within a Web site may influence credibility perceptions.[35] This suggests that it is essential to examine young people's perceptions of online information and judgments of credibility across a diverse set of information tasks, information-seeking motivations, and information-use contexts.

A Study of College Students' Everyday-Life Information Seeking

To understand how college students conceptualize credibility, as well as when and why they are concerned about it and how they go about evaluating it, this chapter will discuss a qualitative study examining college students' credibility assessments in the context of everyday-life information seeking. The goal of the study was to develop a more complete understanding of credibility as it relates to information seeking by examining college students' credibility assessments in a wide variety of activities, using many different sources and media. School, work, and personal-interest information-seeking activities were studied, including those in which Web sites, libraries, books, newspapers, and other media, as well as person-to-person interactions, were used by participants to find desired information. The result is a rich set of data that provides insight into the ways that credibility assessments are shaped by, embedded within, and exert an influence on young people's information seeking processes.

Data were collected during 2005–2006, and twenty-four male and female undergraduate students took part in the study. Several efforts were made to ensure the diversity of the college students within the sample. First, participants represented a variety of majors including nursing, business, film and video, engineering, special education, social work, pre-medicine, and several others. Second, participants were recruited from three different institutions located in the U.S. Midwest, including a large research university, a middle-sized state university, and a community college. As is typical for qualitative research, the sample size was relatively small in order that detailed information could be collected and analyzed from each participant. Thus, this study should be considered exploratory until further work with larger samples can ensure that its results are generalizable to the entire college student population.

For this study, collection of the data through the students' own, natural information-seeking activities was critical because it enabled examination of how credibility judgments vary depending on the types of information activities in which students engage. Each day for ten consecutive days, participating students were asked to use a password-protected Web site to record one information-seeking activity they had engaged in that day. These Web site entries served as information-seeking diaries, capturing the details of the processes undertaken. After the ten-day period, each student was interviewed individually about his or her entries.

The data were analyzed to identify the factors that influenced the college students' credibility assessments. The roles of information-seeking goals and tasks in the credibility assessment process were examined, as was the effect of credibility assessments on the selection of information-seeking strategies. The students' thoughts about credibility as they pertained to sources and media provided insight into the similarities and differences in their level of trust or distrust of various kinds of information sources and media. In other words, the data were examined to understand how credibility assessments fit into and shape the information-seeking process.

Information Seeking Goals and Credibility Concerns

User goals are the essential factor in information seeking given that they motivate the individual to engage in information-related activities. There are several levels of user goals ranging from long-term goals (a personal goal over a long time) and leading search goals (a current information task–related goal), to current search goals (specific search results sought), and interactive intentions (subgoals to be achieved during the seeking process).[36] For instance, a typical information-seeking goal of a college student might be composed of (1) academic achievement (long-term), (2) preparing for an exam (leading), (3) looking for papers (current), and (4) reading and evaluating papers (intention). Another example might be (1) entertainment (long-term), (2) keeping up with movies (leading), (3) looking for latest releases (current), and (4) comparing movie reviews (intention). In such an information-seeking process, today's college students use a wide array of media to achieve their search goals and intentions. Furthermore, they may switch their search goals and intentions during the process while their long-term goals and leading goals remain the same.[37] The study described in this chapter sought to examine the extent to which user goals influence credibility concerns and which levels of user goals matter the most in making credibility judgments.

The data indicate that long-term goals such as academic achievement, problem solving, personal information needs, entertainment, and routine work appear to be most directly related to the extent of credibility concerns. Participants in our study were more concerned with credibility when they were looking for information on academic achievement and problem solving. In addition, their concern for credibility increased when they were dealing with goals related to personal information needs such as health and finances. On the other hand, participants appeared not to be greatly concerned about credibility while seeking information for the purpose of entertainment.

These differential concerns for credibility are related to participants' perceptions about the consequences of information use. For instance, one student was considering a method of contraception involving a device that would be placed in her uterus. She indicated she was extremely interested in getting credible information about the procedure because it would "mess" with her body. The perceived effect on her long-term health increased her desire to find trustworthy information, making credibility a higher priority than it might otherwise have been. These findings are consistent with a previous study of scholars that found participants were more concerned with credibility and authority during health-related information search tasks than during product-related or travel-related information tasks,[38] and with the results of a previous study of college students' credibility assessments by Flanagin and Metzger,[39] who found that credibility is less important for entertainment information than it is for other kinds of Web-based information, including factual and news information. The findings are also in line with theoretical predictions of dual-processing models of persuasion and social judgment, such as the elaboration likelihood model.[40]

Another well-known fact of information seeking is that people sometimes seek information for other people.[41] There are two common information-seeking situations in which this occurs. The first entails people looking for information on behalf of family members, friends, and so on; in this situation, the information obtained will be used by someone else. The second involves information seekers using the information for themselves, but where the information will eventually affect others. The participants in our study were aware of such social impacts of information seeking and often expressed a sense of responsibility. As one student put it, "If it's your own personal [use], that's not so important. But when other people are involved, and other people are going to use that information, you definitely have to have good sources of credibility." Apparently, like this student, participants were more concerned about information credibility when the use of information had the potential to affect others directly. One participant wanted to buy a video game as a birthday gift for a disadvantaged teenager for whom he served as a mentor. Before making a purchase, he researched several options. He explained that he was concerned about the credibility of the information he found given that the teenager had a tough life and would not likely be receiving any other gifts. That is, the fact that the information was to be used by a person he cared about increased his concern for finding credible information.

Another important element in the information-seeking process is context. People pursue their goals with respect to the context of information seeking. Context can serve as a framework of meaning, thus bringing the world into focus.[42] Just as with information-seeking goals, various contexts can also influence the range and nature of credibility judgments. The next section discusses how the information-seeking context is an important element in the credibility assessment process.

Credibility Judgments in Social Context

The individual can be conceptualized as a social actor,[43] and information-seeking activities take place within a social community whose knowledge, characteristics, expectations, and norms are internalized within the individual.[44] This may be especially relevant for young people, whose information seeking and learning is inherently social given the importance of social ties and networks during adolescence and early adulthood.[45] Credibility judgments themselves are also inherently social in that these judgments usually involve the relationship of at least two people.[46] For example, with regard to the "expertise" dimension of credibility[47] even if a source of some information has expertise on a certain topic, this alone may not make that source automatically credible in the eyes of the information seeker: ideally, there should be others who also recognize the source as credible.[48]

As a case in point for the students in our study, being a professor or a teaching assistant does not necessarily guarantee that students will believe their instructor to be a credible source, though many still do. Some participants were more explicit about this, as seen in the following example in which a participant was discussing her graduate student instructor

(GSI): "They're credible. They become GSIs, you know, you study something so hard and therefore you get that position, you don't just get it out of nowhere. You have to have credibility in order to become a GSI." This is evidence that students use a type of "authority" or "expertise" heuristic to judge credibility.[49] On the other hand, we found some students made credibility judgments using the standards of other people (in many cases professors and teaching assistants) as a guide for their own. One student, for example, said that he prefers using books to Internet resources for his school work because he is "pretty nervous about just using the Internet just because professors usually don't like that, and it's good to include some actual books." Said another student, "Well, I just assume that the textbook was credible because the teacher wouldn't make us buy a book that didn't have all the information she would be teaching in there" and she knows it is her professor's opinion that "this is the best book." Thus, participants sometimes used other people's credibility assessments in making their own judgments, most frequently when seeking information related to their schoolwork.

Awareness of the boundaries of the information-seeking context may help students determine the selection of resources by filtering out stimuli in the information-seeking process. For instance, as a rule of thumb, most students place a lot of trust in their textbooks. However, this general rule of thumb may not apply in certain contexts. For example, one participant from our study told us about an experience that led her to distrust her art textbook. Her professor had disagreed with some parts of the textbook and said that the theory had changed since the textbook was written. The participant said, "So for that class I know at least not to look in the book for everything. You have to go to lecture."

Another way in which contextual factors influence credibility judgments is by "bounding" or otherwise limiting the information-use environments. We found numerous instances in which certain contexts led participants to make particular credibility judgments that prevented them from extending their judgments to other contexts. In our study, such cases were most frequently found when participants made credibility judgments in the context of a particular class. Several participants talked about the credibility of the information they acquired from their instructors, acknowledging that some information might not be credible in the world outside of the classroom. As one participant expressed it, "It's reliable in the context of the class. It may or may not be reliable in the real world." Another said, "I would assume it's credible, but I also know it's completely credible within the class because the class is designed around it. So even if it's false, it's true within the bounds of the classroom."

The comments above highlight the fact that credibility is not always viewed as absolute but rather may be seen as relative with respect to the social context in which information seeking is pursued and credibility judgments are made. In other words, many of the students in the study demonstrate "cognitive flexibility"[50] in their credibility assessments. The following student clearly articulated how credibility judgments are closely related to the contexts of information seeking. In this example, credibility assessment was limited to a particular class. For questions falling within the class context, a professor is perceived to be credible, but on questions outside of it the professor may have no credibility at all:

I think I would be more easily swayed in believing something from a professor if it were on the subject of the class he was teaching, rather than on some completely random subject that he decided to talk about, just because you would think he would have the qualifications to be a professor of that subject. But on a different subject he could have nothing, no knowledge of that subject you know to answer your question.

Credibility Judgments as Process

Credibility assessment in the information-seeking process is not entirely dichotomous, nor does it occur only at one point in time. Rather, it is a consideration that people make throughout the entire process of information seeking. Based on Hogarth's judgment theory,[51] Rieh found that people (especially scholars) tend to make two distinct kinds of judgments on the Web: predictive judgments and evaluative judgments.[52] First they make predictions that reflect what they can expect when they access certain information resources. Then, once they encounter some information, they make evaluative judgments in which they express values and preferences about the information that they just have found. Occasionally, people make a third kind of credibility-related judgment, verification, at some later point when they encounter contradictory information or begin to use the information.

Predictive Judgments

As people identify their goals and initiate the information-seeking process, the first decision they make is where to start. At this point people make predictions that reflect what they expect to happen.[53] Their predictions guide them in deciding what actions they will take when given a number of different choices among information-seeking paths and resources. For instance, they consider how long it will take to access different resources, how long it will take to read a book, how someone might react to what they say or do, how likely certain actions are to be successful, and other similar factors. In addition, they make predictive judgments about how good and useful the information from a particular resource will be. According to Rieh, in the prediction stage, scholars (faculty members and doctoral students) are more likely to turn to resources they have used before, have heard of directly from someone, or have read about somewhere.[54] Thus, they begin the information-seeking process where they think they are most likely to find the best information.

The students who participated in our study seemed to make such predictive judgments before they took any actions in information seeking. Credibility is an aspect that the students in our sample took into consideration when making predictive judgments. These credibility judgments helped them determine where to start by identifying trustworthy resources. While Google was often the first place for students to begin on the Web, as also found in other studies,[55] most students were able to articulate why they decided to start at a certain point, such as with the Web, a book, a person, or some other medium. Such decisions based on predictive judgments were closely related to the type of information task, context, and perception of credibility that students might have with regard to a certain medium or source. For example, the following three cases from our study resulted in the use of three different media: (1) One student was looking for some Halloween costume ideas. He decided to go first to Google because "When I'm looking for a general thing, like, Google is generally the place to be, and it's likely to give me an answer." (2) Another student wanted some background information on the Gulf War and said that he would not use Google for information on such a topic because it was an "encyclopedia topic" and expected that he would find information about it "quickest and best in the encyclopedia." Based on this prediction, he decided to use Wikipedia. (3) Yet another student had questions about doing business on eBay. For advice she turned to her father because she knew he has had several successful experiences selling items on eBay. These three examples indicate that the college students in our sample were capable of making predictive judgments by paying attention to particular dimensions of successful past experiences or other knowledge that could inform them about various media or source options.

Even though to some extent credibility assessments occur in predictive judgments, as just discussed, credibility is not necessarily always a determining factor influencing predictive judgments. In our study there were some situations in which credibility concerns had to be balanced with or subordinated to other factors, including the nature of the task, time, convenience, access, familiarity with resources/systems, and so on. For instance, one student who majored in film and video was looking for a list of the movies directed by a particular film director. He knew that the Internet Movie Database (IMDb) Web site would have details about exactly which movies the director had worked on and in what capacity. The student said that IMDb was more trustworthy than Wikipedia since the latter is prone to human error by virtue of being editable by the general public. He admitted that IMDb could also suffer from human error but believed those errors to be much less likely considering that the content on IMDb is controlled by professional editors. Of Wikipedia, he added that anyone could "intentionally put wrong information there." But despite his awareness of the difference in trustworthiness between these two resources in the prediction stage, he chose Wikipedia over IMDb because all he needed was "a little information about the person himself" rather than a complete listing of the director's work as offered on the IMDb site. Type of information needed, rather than credibility, was a more important reason for choosing Wikipedia in this context. Furthermore, while in this particular example the student chose Wikipedia for explicit reasons, there might be cases in which students simply decide not to choose the most credible sources because they have insufficient time, do not care much about credibility, or are unwilling to invest extra effort, among other reasons.[56]

Evaluative Judgments

Once an individual has accessed an information resource as the result of a predictive judgment, that individual may then make evaluations of the information. These evaluations are value judgments by which preferences are expressed.[57] Evaluative judgments may include, for example, whether a book is interesting, whether a paper is relevant to an assignment, whether what they hear from a friend sounds reliable, or how good some information from the Web appears to be. Some evaluative questions are directly related to credibility judgments, for example, by addressing whether some information is trustworthy and/or appears to be reliable, whether the author looks to be authoritative, whether the text is written in a scholarly way, and whether the Web site is official.[58] If an individual finds that the evaluative judgments do not match the expectations of the predictive judgments, he or she might decide to start over using a new strategy. When making such a decision, the individual makes another predictive judgment, seeks more information, and then makes one or more evaluative judgments. The process tends to be iterative, repeating until the evaluative judgments meet the expectations of the predictive judgments.[59]

Most studies examining credibility assessments and digital media tend to focus on evaluative credibility judgments of information and sources, and have identified a common set of factors that either do or should influence people's evaluative credibility judgments and perceptions of online information.[60] Metzger notes that although there are myriad factors suggested by researchers that may play into credibility assessments, there are relatively few factors found in empirical studies to be criteria that people actually employ.[61] The criteria commonly appearing in various domains and research methods include the information itself (e.g., its organization, content, breadth, depth, type), source (e.g., its reputation, type), and presentation/design (e.g., its design, layout, graphics, navigability, functionality, readability).[62] In terms of the significance of each criterion, findings from earlier research are mixed. While Fogg and colleagues' respondents, who consisted of the general public, mentioned site/presentation elements most frequently,[63] Rieh's academic participants put much more emphasis on content and source reputation than on presentation, graphics, and functionality. Hong's college student study participants reported that messages were more important than structural features (e.g., navigation tools, site ownership, site contact information).[64] And, as mentioned earlier, studies of high school students seem to indicate that this group considers graphics and design more important than authority of sources in undertaking Web searching.[65]

The credibility criteria identified in previous studies were also frequently mentioned by the participants in our study when they made evaluative judgments. Although we were not able to determine which criteria—information, source, or presentation—played the most important role in determining credibility judgments, we could identify some patterns of credibility assessments in evaluative judgments based on participants' behavior and experience.

First, participants said that their current knowledge on the topic mattered considerably in the process of making evaluative judgments. If a student has little knowledge of a topic, it will be difficult for him/her to make a decision on the credibility of the information. For example, one student who ran marathons needed more information on nutrition, a topic about which he had little knowledge. He first went to a local art fair where he encountered a woman from a company that sells sports nutrition products. He did not trust her because he thought she would just recommend products to make a sale. Furthermore, she was able to provide only general information, whereas he wanted more specific and detailed information. He then turned to his coach, whom he trusted because he knew the coach was a runner. The coach talked to him about the benefits and problems of sports nutrition but ultimately did not tell him what he should do. This student said he did not find the coach's advice useful because the coach "didn't say 'don't do it' or 'just forget about it.'" This student next turned to the Web and found that there was a sports nutrition store nearby. He went to the store and talked with a salesperson who was also a weightlifter. The student said that at that point he was able to make an "informed credibility judgment" because by then he "already knew a little bit, like, that a particular ingredient is for endurance athletes." In this case, the student began the information-seeking process where the information was most accessible (art fair), then turned to a trusted source (coach). Because he was not quite satisfied with his coach's advice, he used the Web to find a local store where he finally found the information that he could trust. During this process, he gathered and evaluated information piece by piece. As illustrated in Bates's "berry-picking" model of information search,[66] he moved through a variety of sources. Each piece of information gave him new ideas and directions to follow, allowing him to learn little by little. At the end of his information-seeking process, he could make a credibility judgment with confidence.

The second interesting finding is that college students in our sample made evaluative judgments based on their perceptions of the quality control mechanisms in digital media. Most of our study participants were able to distinguish general Web resources from scholarly information published in journals and could point out the lack of quality control mechanisms on the Internet. As one participant put it: "People can just make up sites and stuff online, but with a book you have to go through publishing companies and getting that whole book process." The participants generally showed high levels of respect and trust toward peer-reviewed scholarly journals. One student said that she used Google Scholar for her homework because "it's [Google Scholar] only looking for journal articles and peer reviewed information so I think that's a really nice part about Google. You know it's coming from a better source. You're not going to get a .com or .net where their ultimate goal is to get you to buy something." When she got two articles from Google Scholar, one from *American Psychologist* and another from the *Journal of Public Health*, she knew that "they're peer reviewed and the articles were of good quality." Indeed, there were a number of other examples in which our participants relied not only on the source itself but also on the process of publishing and dissemination mechanisms when making evaluative judgments. College students in general are likely more aware of publishing standards and the meaning of peer review than are younger students (e.g., primary through secondary school students). This indicates that life experience, in this case a college education, shapes and influences the credibility criteria that people use.[67]

The third point based on the data analysis of our study is that not all participants were confident in evaluating the credibility of information. Some of them would simply say that credibility could not be known for certain. Others would say that they would know the credibility of some source or information only when actually using the information. As one student put it, "I personally cannot know if they're telling the truth unless I try some." One student relayed the experience of injuring her ankle while dancing. Her dance teacher told her to rest her ankle and apply heat; however, she eventually realized the heat was causing additional inflammation. As she was aware that her ankle was not healing, she went to a physical therapist, who informed her that the heat was indeed making the injury worse and that she should instead be applying ice. This experience considerably changed her level of trust in her dance teacher. Subsequently, she has tended to "second guess" everything her teacher tells her. This example indicates that once the credibility of a source is questioned, all information from the source may be suspect from that point forward. It also raises an important question about verification in the process of information seeking and credibility judgments. Had she doubted the teacher's recommendations in the first place, she could have tried to verify them early on. The judgments that young people make to verify information are discussed in the next section.

Verification

Young people sometimes need to verify or reevaluate information after they have made evaluative judgments. There are at least two kinds of information-seeking situations in which young people attempt to verify information. One involves initially accepting information without questioning its credibility, but later being prompted to doubt the credibility of that information as a result of encountering contradictory information from another source or due to finding that the information is incorrect when it is used. This creates the need to verify information that may then be accomplished by continuing to look for information either to confirm or refute the initial information. The other situation arises when people are uncertain about the credibility of information when first encountered. These doubts prompt them to engage in the verification process to decide whether or not they should believe the information and thus whether or not to use it.

The following example aptly illustrates the first situation involving information reevaluation. When one student we interviewed heard her friends speaking negatively of a particular political action campus group that was planning a local protest, she did not doubt the credibility of what her friends said. As she put it, "I didn't really question at the time whether what they were saying was true or not. I just assumed [it was]." Later, while reading about the group on its Web site, she encountered information that contradicted many of the things her friends had said. She explained that she "questioned [whether] what [my friends] were talking about was true." To further complicate the picture, she found other Web sites that gave negative information about the man whom the group had invited to speak at the protest, and "these awful things that happened as a result of his speaking." She felt that she could not tell what was true "because people probably blow things out of proportion, and then write about it on the sites. I don't know, you just have to make your own judgment on whether it's credible or not." After reading "both sides" of the story, she decided to go to the protest, see for herself, and make her own judgment. This example indicates that people's credibility judgments are enacted over time, often in an iterative process. It is possible for young people to change their judgments when they encounter additional contradictory information.

The second information-seeking situation that may call for verification arises when individuals have doubts or uncertainties upon first encountering new information. One participant, a transfer student, had to engage in a series of information-seeking activities to verify that information she'd originally gotten from "random people on campus" was reliable. In the process, she met several other students registered for the same Linguistics course. They told her there was a homework assignment due on the first day of class. When she questioned them for details, she realized that none of them had actually seen a syllabus for the course but were simply repeating what they had heard from others. In an attempt to verify the "rumors" and gather details, she went to a university Web site that lists syllabi for all courses but only found that it did not display the syllabus for her course. Next, she went to the linguistics department office. The individual with whom she spoke there instructed her to check her e-mail as the instructor had just sent out a notification. Later when she checked her e-mail, the student found a message from her instructor with a link to the online course syllabus that included the due date for the first assignment.

This example also indicates that credibility judgments are a continuous and iterative process from prediction and evaluation through verification. In addition, the story reveals there is a close relationship between motivation and credibility judgments.[68] In this case, the student's uncertainties regarding the credibility of information motivated her to engage actively in information seeking by using multiple resources and strategies until she solved her problem. Motivation appears to be key, however, to verification efforts, as some work shows that college students verify information only occasionally and do so significantly less than adults.[69] The next section discusses how people's concerns about credibility influence the strategies they employ in the information-seeking process.

Influence of Credibility Assessment on Information-Seeking Strategies

Concerns about credibility as it influences information-seeking behaviors in general and information-seeking strategies in particular are discussed in this section. A strategy is a plan for an entire information-seeking episode and contains various kinds of "stratagems" or repetitive sequences of information-seeking activities.[70] Young people's credibility assessments can be embedded in the ways in which they plan their information seeking, often without their conscious realization that selection of stratagems is closely related to the notion of credibility. Our data revealed a number of different information-seeking strategies that students employ to accomplish information seeking. At least three strategies emerged as significant and closely related to young people's credibility judgments: (1) starting information seeking at a trusted place, (2) using multiple resources and cross-referencing, and

(3) compromising information credibility for speed and convenience. Each of these strategies is discussed in detail below.

Starting Information Seeking at a Trusted Place

Although today's youth live in a digital environment, they do not necessarily always begin their information-seeking process on the Internet. In many cases, the participants in our study turned to a person they knew for information, just as young people always did prior to the advent of the Internet.[71] Sometimes they talked to a professor, a teaching assistant, a coach, a mother, a father, or a friend in expectation of obtaining information directly. In other cases, they approached these people looking only for advice on where to start their information seeking. That is, students may consult other trusted individuals for help when choosing the best place to go for credible information, which is similar to the idea of "reputed credibility" discussed by Flanagin and Metzger.[72] When doing this, students preferred e-mail over face-to-face communication because it seemed not only to be convenient but also effective in receiving the information anticipated when that entailed links, book titles, journal names, individuals' names, and so on.

There appear to be at least two compelling reasons behind our participants' strategy of turning to human resources first. On the one hand, the students understood that they would get the best answers or the most credible information by asking knowledgeable people. On the basis of personal experience with an individual, a student might know that person to be a "diligent researcher" or to have considerable knowledge on the subject. The participants also felt that asking people is easier and more time-efficient than finding information online. For instance, one person stated, "It has to do with accessing. It has to do with: are you asking the correct person, the person who has that specific piece of knowledge? However, they're much easier to get knowledge out of than to get such knowledge out of Google. Google can't understand what you say. It can just guess and [you] hope [it's correct]," while another said: "Okay, time is like a real big thing to me, so I always go to the most credible people. So I usually don't get wrong answers."

On the other hand, the participants tend to have a few "favorite" Web sites to which they turn on a regular basis for routine tasks such as news, technology, cooking, movies, sports, and so forth. As with trusted human resources, these students show a great deal of loyalty and trust for their favorite Web sites. One student talked about a movie Web site he regularly visits that gives information about movie tickets and show times. Of it, he said "it's a very well-known site and one that I knew would probably have most, if not all, the information I was looking for." Another student talked about a technology site that he visited "just about everyday [to] check stuff out." He explained the reason for his regular visits by stating that the information there is "generally pretty good." He also described this site as "a very good springboard" and added, "it's where you start . . . if you want to look at electronics or something."

Google is a place where many participants like to begin when looking for information. When asked why they would start with Google, many students in our study said that Google is much more accessible, easy, fast, quick, and convenient than any other resource they could rely on. These students displayed considerable trust in Google, asserting that "Google is generally the place to be and it's likely to give me an answer," "It was excellent quality," "Google seems to be more legitimate," and "Google appears to be more credible because it does not have any of the other stuff." They also said that they are most comfortable with using it compared to other search engines, so now going to Google is their "habit." Thus, whether they turn first to another human or to the Web, one strategy many young people use to begin their information seeking is turning to a trusted source that has served them well in the past. This is quite similar to Tseng and Fogg's notion of "earned credibility,"[73] which is defined as credibility based on first-hand experience that extends over time. According to Fogg, earned credibility is difficult for an online information source to gain in the eyes of users, and yet is the most effective in terms of influencing users' attitude and behavior owing to users' perceptions of the reliability and usefulness of the information resource.[74]

Using Multiple Resources and Cross-Referencing

Cross-referencing multiple resources was one of the most common information-seeking strategies employed by our participants. A number of the students said that it would be too risky to judge the credibility of the information they found by merely examining the information or its source. Rather than making a credibility judgment of information retrieved from a single source, they often attempted to find other sources of information for comparison and verification. In general, participants seemed to use a type of "bandwagon" credibility heuristic[75] in their perception that "information is more credible, more trustworthy if it comes from different sources, and all the sources agree," as one of the students said in our study.

Many students appeared to use what Meola terms a "contextual approach" to credibility assessment.[76] For example, another student believed that a source was "probably correct because it was very similar information. Two separate sources have similar information. So that's kind of where I got the idea that it's probably credible." One student took news as an example. She asserted that she did not trust everything she read because, "You tell one side of the story, they tell another side, and I tell a different story." She said that she also did not trust everything she found on the Web. If she goes to Google and types in "diabetes," she would then go to at least three sites from the results to see if the information "matches." She explained that when she is uncertain as to whether or not a story is true, she would like to have the story from "another Web site." According to her, "If you read something on a news Web site, you hear it on the TV news, and then see it in the local newspaper, it reassures you." Another student working on a research paper for his history class needed information regarding the different types of space missions undertaken by the United States and the Soviet Union. He went to a local bookstore and scanned two books. He trusted the information in them when he realized that "both of them were consistent with one another—both the books had the same type of information and exact same information." Therefore, he found them to be "really useful" for his paper.

All of these examples indicate that college students in our sample often use multiple information sources as a way of assessing the credibility of the information they find. If they discovered that the information from multiple sources was inconsistent, they were likely to engage in the verification process as described in the preceding section. One student initially believed without questioning the information she received from her friends about a politically active campus group. When she encountered contradictory information on the Web site, she engaged in the verification process to settle the matter in her own mind. In this case, the strategy she employed was to turn to the third source—attending the protest to listen directly to the speech.

Although students in our study sometimes used this strategy for nondigital materials, such as books, television, and magazines, it seemed that they most frequently used it when seeking information on the Web. In part, this is because the Web tends to heighten concerns about information credibility in the first place given the ease with which anyone can publish information there. Furthermore, the structure of the Web also makes it easy for people to cross-check information and thus may encourage them to use the cross-reference strategy.

Compromising Information Credibility for Speed and Convenience

Although the strategy of using the most accessible resource to get the most credible information seems to work, there are situations in which the young people in our study had to decide between two kinds of information resources: one that is quickly accessible and one that is more credible but also more time-consuming to access. We found that the participants, when faced with this dilemma, were willing to compromise credibility, that is, to give it less priority, in favor of other considerations that most frequently involved speed and convenience. One participant expressed this information behavior pattern: "If it's a question of how fast I'll find it over how trustworthy it is, I will generally go with fast, as long as I have a good deal of trust in it." Another participant, whose major was special education, was looking for information on how to teach probability to a learning-disabled student. Not knowing a good way to approach the topic, he chose Google because he "always" uses it. He considered other ways of finding information, such as e-mailing people who were in the teaching program, but did not pursue this strategy because "It might be two, three, four days before I hear back from somebody" or "They might blow me off." Therefore, rather than risking a significant loss of time by relying on his network of people, he used Google, which he considered "faster," "very immediate," "the quickest way," and most of all, because "There's not a human being that's going to be involved in the process."

These cases occurred often when participants perceived that the consequences of using the information were not critical enough to warrant the additional time needed to obtain more credible information. That is, the degree to which they were willing to "satisfice" was closely related to the goals and motivations of information seeking. For example, one student in our study wanted to know when an aerobics or kickboxing class would be offered at her gym. She checked the flyers on her gym's wall and visited their Web site from her home. She noted that she could have called the gym to ask about classes, but felt that using the Web was "more convenient" because "You don't have to actually talk on your phone." She said that if she had received inaccurate information from the Web, she might have shown up at the wrong time, but eventually someone would have informed her of the correct date and time. While it may be important to have accurate information, she added that "it's not [a] life or death situation." Therefore, she chose the most convenient method, which was looking at the flyer on the wall and checking the Web site.

Thus, college students are not necessarily ignorant of information credibility concerns nor do they necessarily lack the knowledge and skills required to evaluate credibility. Rather, they often feel the need to balance credibility concerns with other demands. In practice, this means that they sometimes decide where to begin their information seeking based not on credibility per se but on speed or convenience. However, the concerns of speed and convenience sometimes conflict with credibility concerns. Students want to start their searches at trustworthy places and often turn to trustworthy sources to verify the information they find. In some cases, doing so actually saves them time. Their reasons for relying on human resources and Google are the same: quick and easy access. Assessing credibility is not something with which students are explicitly concerned every time they select information resources; rather, their concerns about information credibility are incorporated into their existing information-seeking strategies. In fact, students may not even realize the extent to which they actually assess credibility in the process of information seeking.

Conclusions and Future Directions

As mentioned earlier, the research reported in this chapter was an exploratory study in which only twenty-four college students were interviewed; consequently, further work is needed to verify our findings among a larger population of college students and other young people. Nevertheless, the results provide a fruitful basis for a number of interesting discussion points. First, our study findings imply that young people, or at least college students, may not be as naïve in assessing credibility with digital media as some prior work suggests. In general, most students we interviewed did not seem to believe that information can be considered trustworthy simply because they "saw it on the Internet."[77] They were aware of the potential problems of information credibility in digital media and employed several information-seeking strategies to deal with it. For instance, they often begin their information seeking at a place recommended by knowledgeable (e.g., professors and teaching assistants) or trusted (e.g., parents, coach, friends) individuals. They sometimes report verifying the information obtained by checking it out using multiple sources.

This chapter demonstrates the importance of examining young people's credibility assessments within the context of everyday-life information seeking by identifying a number of interesting patterns of youth information-seeking strategies related to their credibility concerns and judgments. It was found that depending on the long-term goals young people pursue (e.g., academic achievement, personal needs, entertainment) and consequences of information use (e.g., health, finances, impact on other persons), the participants in our study were more or less motivated to pay greater attention to credibility issues. At the same time, it was found that young people's credibility judgments were socially directed. If the use of information had the potential to affect others, they were more likely to take credibility issues seriously. They also made credibility judgments by "bounding" or limiting their assessment within certain social contexts.

As we investigated credibility judgments with respect to the information-seeking process, we also found that credibility assessment was an ongoing and iterative process rather than a discrete evaluation event, as the participants made three distinctive kinds of judgments: predictive judgments, evaluative judgments, and verification. In this process, credibility judgments are deeply influenced by students' accumulated knowledge and prior experiences. The participants in our study made predictions about information and accessed sources based on their prior experiences, and thus were more likely to trust those sources. The rationale for these strategies was related to their preference for obtaining "the best information in the quickest way." Rather than wandering around the digital world randomly, they want to begin their information-seeking process at a place that they predicted would be most trustworthy, which then becomes their "shortcut." Sometimes their initial predictions about trusted sources might not meet their expectations. In such cases, the students faced situations in which they needed to decide whether they would accept the information that was easily accessible, even though they were uncertain about its credibility. Again, depending on the types of information-seeking goals and motivations, the students were either willing to compromise credibility concerns for speed and convenience, or they invested further effort into information seeking until they were assured about information credibility.

Digital media make it easy to collaborate, relay, and clarify information with other students.[78] The study presented here also has implications for teaching young people to improve their credibility assessment capabilities. One of the major findings of the study is that participants tended to consult individuals whom they felt were likely to have knowledge and expertise on a topic. Often these individuals were professors, teaching assistants, coaches, or parents. However, participants also turned to their classmates, roommates, and friends when they believed their friends might have some knowledge on the topic. Indeed, it is well known in the field of information seeking that information exchange between two parties works best when they share similar beliefs, values, educational levels, and social statuses.[79] This means that young people's strategies for seeking information and deciding whether to use certain information is deeply influenced by others with whom they feel socially close and with whom they share common ground. This is likely especially true with college students, who often voluntarily belong to study groups or need to work as a group to meet class requirements. Thus, when developing an intervention program to help young people, it is critical that the social aspects of credibility assessments be considered, a point echoed by Flanagin and Metzger.[80]

This chapter has implications as well for methodology in future investigations of credibility. In general, there seem to be two prevailing research methods in this field. One is to produce a list of terms and conceptual dimensions that are related to credibility by eliciting verbal reports from study participants.[81] The other approach is to assemble a list of candidate terms based on literature reviews of past empirical research and present it to the study participants, asking them to select, rate, or rank the terms based on exposure to experimental stimuli or survey questions.[82]

With the former method, it proves quite difficult to design a study that allows researchers to generate comprehensive credibility-related terms from the study participants.[83] This is because credibility assessments are made internally, and not everyone is capable of articulating cognitively processed judgments. The second method, using predetermined credibility factors and Likert-type scales, might make study participants merely passive recipients of information. This method also makes it difficult to collect rich qualitative data about people's goals, intentions, knowledge, and other information problems. Given the limitations of previous credibility study methods, the study presented in this chapter took a more naturalistic approach in which students kept records of their information-seeking activities in Web-based diary form and did not necessarily pay special attention to credibility issues. Even in the interviews, questions were mostly asked about participants' information-seeking strategies and experiences, while minimizing use of the terminologies of credibility, trust, and believability. The purpose of this design was to identify the implicit values of credibility often embedded in the information-seeking process. This method seemed to work well because it identified a number of information-seeking patterns and strategies employed by the participants without obviously leading them toward credibility. In the future, more discussion is needed on the topic of methodological approaches to credibility research. As credibility judgments are not something that researchers can easily observe, it is important that credibility researchers develop research methods that can accommodate the complex nature of the credibility concept.

Finally, the findings of this study imply that research on young people's credibility assessments can progress by taking into consideration the broader contexts of information seeking and use. Previous credibility studies involving college students have looked at credibility assessments within a limited domain: news and political information,[84] scholarly information,[85] and health information.[86] This appears to be a reasonable approach to the study of young people's credibility assessments because the types of information with which young people are interacting have been shown to influence their assessments.[87] On the other hand, young people are using digital media for diverse purposes as was illustrated by the examples and quotes in this chapter. It is important to note that young people can carry over to one domain the perceptions and judgments that they have acquired from another.[88] Furthermore, the students in our study did not use the Internet as an isolated medium. While the participants relied heavily on the Internet for information and communication purposes, they used the Internet along with other more traditional resources such as people, books, newspapers, and online library materials. In addition, because of the mobility of digital media, the borderline between tasks for schoolwork and tasks for everyday life is much less clear than ever before.[89] Therefore, it is important for credibility researchers to include a variety of information tasks, information-seeking activities, and information resources and media encompassing various contexts, including school, personal life, news, and entertainment, in order to better understand young people's credibility assessments in the digital environment.

Notes

1. Nicholas J. Belkin, Interaction with Texts: Information Retrieval as Information-Seeking Behavior, in *Information Retrieval'93, Von der Modellierung zur Anwendung* (Konstanz: Universitaetsverlag Konstanz, 1993), 55–66.

2. Soo Young Rieh and David R. Danielson, Credibility: A Multidisciplinary Framework, in *Annual Review of Information Science and Technology 41*, ed. Blaise Cronin (Medford, NJ: Information Today, 2007), 307–64.

3. Patrick Wilson, *Second-hand Knowledge: An Inquiry into Cognitive Authority* (Westport, CT: Greenwood, 1983).

4. Ibid., 15.

5. Judy Bateman, Modeling the Importance of End-user Relevance Criteria, *Proceedings of the 62nd Annual Meeting of the American Society for Information Science* 36 (1999): 396–406; Carol L. Barry and Linda Schamber, Users' Criteria for Relevance Evaluation: A Cross-situational Comparison, *Information Processing and Management* 34, no. 2–3 (1998): 219–36; Kelly L. Maglaughlin and Diane H. Sonnenwald, User Perspectives on Relevance Criteria: A Comparison Among Relevant, Partially Relevant, and Not-Relevant Judgments, *Journal of the American Society for Information Science and Technology* 53, no. 5 (2002): 327–42; Peiling Wang, The Design of Document Retrieval Systems for Academic Users: Implications of Studies on Users' Relevance Criteria, *Proceedings of the 60th Annual Meeting of the American Society for Information Science* 34 (1997): 162–73.

6. Sandra Hirsh, Children's Relevance Criteria and Information Seeking on Electronic Resources, *Journal of the American Society for Information Science* 50 (1999): 1265–83.

7. Soo Young Rieh, Judgment of Information Quality and Cognitive Authority in the Web, *Journal of the American Society for Information Science and Technology* 53, no. 2 (2002): 145–61; Soo Young Rieh and Nicholas J. Belkin, Understanding Judgment of Information Quality and Cognitive Authority in the WWW, *Proceedings of the 61st Annual Meeting of the American Society for Information Science* 35 (1998): 279–89.

8. Steve Jones, *The Internet Goes to College: How Students Are Living in the Future with Today's Technology* (Washington, D.C.: Pew Internet and American Life Project, 2002). http://www.pewinternet.org/pdfs/PIP_College_Report.pdf (accessed January 10, 2007).

9. Don Tapscott, *Growing Up Digital: The Rise of the Net Generation* (New York: McGraw-Hill, 1997).

10. Lisa M. Given, The Academic and the Everyday: Investigating the Overlap in Mature Undergraduates' Information-Seeking Behaviors, *Library and Information Science Research* 24, no. 1 (2002): 17–29.

11. E.g., Andrew J. Flanagin and Miriam J. Metzger, The Perceived Credibility of Personal Web Page Information as Influenced by the Sex of the Source, *Computers in Human Behavior* 19, no. 6 (2003): 683–701; Thomas J. Johnson and Barbara K. Kaye, Webelievability: A Path Model Examining How Convenience and Reliance Predict Online Credibility, *Journalism and Mass Communication Quarterly* 79, no. 3 (2002): 619–42; Ziming Liu, Perceptions of Credibility of Scholarly Information on the Web, *Information Processing and Management* 40, no. 6 (2004): 1027–38; Miriam J. Metzger, Andrew J. Flanagin, and Lara Zwarun, College Student Web Use, Perceptions of Information Credibility, and Verification Behavior, *Computers and Education* 41 (2003): 271–90; S. Shyam Sundar, Exploring Receivers' Criteria for Perception of Print and Online News, *Journalism and Mass Communication Quarterly* 76, no. 2 (Summer 1999): 373–86.

12. Howard Rachlin, *Judgment, Decision, and Choice: A Cognitive/Behavioral Synthesis* (New York: Freeman, 1989).

13. Thomas D. Wilson, Human Information Behavior, *Informing Science* 3, no. 2 (2000): 49–56. http://inform.nu/Articles/Vol3/v3n2p49-56.pdf (accessed January 10, 2007).

14. Andrew Large, Jamshid Beheshti, and Alain Breuleux, Information Seeking in a Multimedia Environment by Primary School Students. *Library and Information Science Research* 20, no. 4 (1998): 343–75; Gary Marchionini, Information-Seeking Strategies of Novices Using a Full Text Electronic Encyclopedia, *Journal of the American Society for Information Science* 40, no. 1 (1989): 52–66.

15. Sandra Hirsh, How Do Children Find Information on Different Types of Tasks? Children's Use of the Science Library Catalog, *Library Trends* 45 (1997): 725–45; Paul Solomon, Children's Information Retrieval Behavior: A Case Analysis of an OPAC, *Journal of the American Society for Information Science* 44 (1993): 245–64; Christine L. Borgman, Why Are Online Catalogs Still Hard to Use? *Journal of the American Society for Information Science* 47, no. 7 (1996): 493–503.

16. Dania Bilal, Children's Use of the Yahooligans! Web Search Engine. I. Cognitive, Physical, and Affective Behaviors on Fact-Based Tasks, *Journal of the American Society for Information Science* 51, no. 7 (2000): 646–65; Dania Bilal, Children's Use of the Yahooligans! Web Search Engine. II. Cognitive and Physical Behaviors on Research Tasks, *Journal of the American Society for Information Science and Technology* 52, no. 2 (2001): 118–37.

17. Eliza T. Dresang, The Information-Seeking Behavior of Youth in the Digital Environment, *Library Trends* 54, no. 2 (2005): 178–96.

18. Andrew Large, Children, Teenagers, and the Web, in *Annual Review of Information Science and Technology* 39, ed. Blaise Cronin (Medford, NJ: Information Today, 2005), 374–92.

19. Matthew S. Eastin, Toward a Cognitive Developmental Approach to Youth Perceptions of Credibility, this volume; Gary Marchionini, Information-Seeking Strategies of Novices Using a Full Text Electronic Encyclopedia.

20. Andrew K. Shenton and Pat Dixon, Issues Arising from Youngsters' Information-Seeking Behavior, *Library and Information Science Research* 26 (2004): 177–200.

21. E.g., Mary K. Chelton and Colleen Cool, eds., *Youth Information-Seeking Behavior: Theories, Models, and Issues* (Lanham, MD: Scarecrow, 2004).

22. Denise E. Agosto, A Model of Young People's Decision-Making in the Web. *Library and Information Science Research* 24 (2002): 311–41; Denise E. Agosto, Bounded Rationality and Satisficing in Young People's Web-Based Decision Making, *Journal of the American Society of Information Science and Technology* 53 (2002): 16–27.

23. Raya Fidel, Rachel K. Davies, Mary H. Douglass, Jenny K. Holder, Carla J. Hopkins, Elisabeth J. Kushner, Bryan K. Miyagishima, and Christina D. Toney, A Visit to the Information Mall: Web Searching

Behavior of High School Students, *Journal of the American Society for Information Science* 50, no. 1 (1999): 24–37.

24. John Lubans Jr., *How First-Year University Students Use and Regard Internet Resources (Report)* (Durham, NC: Duke University Library, 1998).

25. Miriam J. Metzger, Andrew J. Flanagin, and Lara Zwarun, College Student Web Use.

26. Steve Jones, *The Internet Goes to College*.

27. Juris Dilevko and Lisa Gottlieb, Print Sources in an Electronic Age: A Vital Part of the Research Process for Undergraduate Students, *Journal of Academic Librarianship* 28, no. 6 (2002): 381–92.

28. Steve Jones, *The Internet Goes to College*.

29. Joann E. D'Esposito and Rachel M. Gardner, University Students' Perceptions of the Internet, *Journal of Academic Librarianship* 25 (1999): 456–61.

30. Miriam J. Metzger, Andrew J. Flanagin, and Lara Zwarun, College Student Web Use.

31. John W. Mashek, Lawrence T. McGill, and Adam C. Powell, *Lethargy '96: How the Media Covered a Listless Campaign* (Arlington, VA: The Freedom Forum, 1997).

32. Miriam J. Metzger, Andrew J. Flanagin, and Lara Zwarun, College Student Web Use.

33. Thomas J. Johnson and Barbara K. Kaye, Cruising Is Believing?: Comparing Internet and Traditional Sources on Media Credibility Measures, *Journalism and Mass Communication Quarterly* 75, no. 2 (1998): 325–40.

34. S. Shyam Sundar, Exploring Receivers' Criteria.

35. Andrew J. Flanagin and Miriam J. Metzger, Perceptions of Internet Information Credibility, *Journalism and Mass Communication Quarterly* 77, no. 3 (2000): 515–40; Miriam J. Metzger, Andrew J. Flanagin, Keren Eyal, Daisy R. Lemus, and Robert M. McCann, Credibility for the 21st Century: Integrating Perspectives on Source, Message, and Media Credibility in the Contemporary Media Environment, in *Communication Yearbook 27*, ed. Pamela J. Kalbfleisch (Mahwah, NJ: Erlbaum, 2003), 293–335; Miriam J. Metzger, Andrew J. Flanagin, and Lara Zwarun, College Student Web Use.

36. Hong Xie, Shifts of Interactive Intentions and Information-Seeking Strategies in Interactive Information Retrieval, *Journal of the American Society for Information Science* 51 (2000): 841–57.

37. Soo Young Rieh, On the Web at Home: Information Seeking and Web Searching in the Home Environment, *Journal of the American Society for Information Science and Technology* 55 (2004): 743–53.

38. Soo Young Rieh, Judgment of Information Quality.

39. Andrew J. Flanagin and Miriam J. Metzger, Perceptions of Internet Information Credibility.

40. See Miriam J. Metzger, Making Sense of Credibility on the Web: Models for Evaluating Online Information and Recommendations for Future Research, *Journal of the American Society for Information Science and Technology* (in press); Harris, Challenges to Teaching Credibility Assessment in Contemporary Schooling, this volume.

41. Sanda Erdelez and Kevin Rioux, Sharing Information Encountered for Others on the Web, *The New Review of Information Behaviour Research* 1 (2000): 219–33; Melissa Gross and Matthew L. Saxton, Who Wants to Know? Imposed Queries in the Public Libraries, *Public Libraries* 40, no. 3 (2001): 170–76.

42. Colleen Cool, The Concept of Situation in Information Science, in *Annual Review of Information Science and Technology* 35, ed. Martha E. Williams (Medford, NJ: Information Today, 2001), 5–42; Rieh, On the Web at Home.

43. Roberta Lamb and Rob Kling, Reconceptualizing Users as Social Actors in Information Systems Research, *MIS Quarterly* 27 (2003): 197–235.

44. Christina Courtright, Context in Information Behavior Research, in *Annual Review of Information Science and Technology 41*, ed. Blaise Cronin (Medford, NJ: Information Today, 2007): 273–306.

45. Amercian Psychological Association, Developing adolescents: A Reference for Professionals, 2002. http://www.apa.org/pi/cyf/develop.pdf (accessed January 10, 2007).

46. Patrick Wilson, *Second-Hand Knowledge*.

47. See Andrew J. Flanagin and Miriam J. Metzger, Digital Media and Youth: Unparalleled Opportunity and Unprecedented Responsibility, this volume.

48. See, e.g., S. Shyam Sundar, The MAIN Model: A Heuristic Approach to Understanding Technology Effects on Credibility, this volume, for a discussion of the bandwagon credibility heuristic.

49. Ibid.

50. Frances J. Harris, Challenges to Teaching Credibility Assessment in Contemporary Schooling, this volume.

51. Robin M. Hogarth, *Judgment and Choice: The Psychology of Decision*, 2nd ed. (New York: Wiley, 1987).

52. Soo Young Rieh, Judgment of Information Quality.

53. Robin M.Hogarth, *Judgment and Choice*.

54. Soo Young Rieh, Judgment of Information Quality; Soo Young Rieh and Nicholas J. Belkin, Understanding Judgment of Information Quality.

55. Karl V. Fast and D. Grant Campbell, "I Still Like Google": University Student Perceptions of Searching OPACs and the Web, *Proceedings of the 67th Annual Meeting of the American Society for Information Science and Technology* 41 (2004): 138–46; Yong-Mi Kim and Soo Young Rieh, Dual-Task Performance as a Measure for Mental Effort in Library Searching and Web Searching, *Proceedings of the 68th Annual Meeting of the American Society for Information Science and Technology* 42 (2005). http://www.asis.org/AM05Proceedings/openpage.html (accessed January 10, 2007).

56. Soo Young Rieh, Is Web Searching Easier Than Library Searching? Differential Expectation, Perceived Difficulty, and Effort (paper presented at the Annual Conference of Association for Library and Information Science Education, Boston, MA, January 2005).

57. Robin M. Hogarth, *Judgment and Choice*.

58. Soo Young Rieh, Judgment of Information Quality.

59. Soo Young Rieh and Nicholas J. Belkin, Interaction on the Web: Scholars' Judgment of Information Quality and Cognitive Authority, *Proceedings of the 63rd Annual Meeting of the American Society for Information Science* 37 (2000): 25–38.

60. See Soo Young Rieh and David R. Danielson, Credibility: A Multidisciplinary Framework, and Miriam J. Metzger, Making Sense of Credibility on the Web, for a comprehensive list.

61. Miriam J. Metzger, Making Sense of Credibility on the Web.

62. Gunther Eysenbach and Christian Köhler, How Do Consumers Search for and Appraise Health Information on the World Wide Web? Qualitative Study Using Focus Groups, Usability Tests, and In-depth Interviews, *British Medical Journal* 324 (2002): 573–77; Andrew J. Flanagin and Miriam J. Metzger, The Role of Site Features, User Attributes, and Information Verification Behaviors on the Perceived Credibility of Web-Based Information, *New Media and Society* 9, no. 2 (2007): 319–42; B. J. Fogg, Cathy

Soohoo, David R. Danielson, Leslie Marable, Julie Stanford, and Ellen R. Tauber, How Do Users Evaluate the Credibility of Web Sites? A Study with Over 2,500 Participants, *Proceedings of DUX2003, Designing for User Experiences Conference*, 2003; Soo Young Rieh, Judgment of Information Quality.

63. See also Andrew J. Flanagin and Miriam J. Metzger, Digital Media and Youth.

64. Traci Hong, The Influence of Structural and Message Features on Web Site Credibility, *Journal of the American Society for Information Science and Technology* 57, no. 1 (2006): 114–27.

65. Denise E. Agosto, A Model of Young People's Decision-Making in the Web; Denise E. Agosto, Bounded Rationality and Satisficing in Young People's Web-Based Decision Making; Raya Fidel et al., A Visit to the Information Mall.

66. Marcia J. Bates, The Design of Browsing and Berrypicking Techniques for the Online Search Interface, *Online Review* 13 (1989): 407–24.

67. See also Miriam J. Metzger, Andrew J. Flanagin, and Lara Zwarun, College Student Web Use.

68. Miriam J. Metzger, Making Sense of Credibility on the Web.

69. Miriam J. Metzger, Andrew J. Flanagin and Lara Zwarun, College Student Web Use.

70. Marcia J. Bates, Where Should the Person Stop and the Information Search Interface Start? *Information Processing and Management* 26, no. 5 (1990): 575–591.

71. Carol C. Kuhlthau, *Seeking Meaning: A Process Approach to Library and Information Services*, 2nd ed. (Westport, CT: Libraries Unlimited, 2003).

72. Andrew J. Flanagin and Miriam J. Metzger, this volume; see also Shawn Tseng and B. J. Fogg, Credibility and Computing Technology, *Communications of the ACM* 42, no. 5 (1999): 39–44.

73. Shawn Tseng and B. J. Fogg, Credibility and Computing Technology.

74. B. J. Fogg, *Persuasive Technology: Using Computers to Change What We Think and Do* (San Francisco: Morgan Johnson, 2003).

75. Sundar, The MAIN Model.

76. Marc Meola, Chucking the Checklist: A Contextual Approach to Teaching Undergraduates Web-site Evaluation, *Portal: Libraries and the Academy* 4, no. 3 (2004): 331–44.

77. Leah Graham and Panagiotis T. Metaxas, "Of Course It's True: I Saw It on the Internet!" Critical Thinking in the Internet Era, *Communications of the ACM* 46, no. 5 (2003): 71–75.

78. Steve Jones, *The Internet Goes to College*.

79. Roma M. Harris and Patricia Dewdney, *Barriers to Information: How Formal Help Systems Fail Battered Women* (Westport, CT: Greenwood, 1994).

80. Andrew J. Flanagin and Miriam J. Metzger, Digital Media and Youth.

81. Soo Young Rieh, Judgment of Information Quality; Soo Young Rieh and Nicholas J. Belkin, Understanding Judgment of Information Quality.

82. Andrew J. Flanagin and Miriam J. Metzger, The Role of Site Features; B. J. Fogg et al., How Do Users Evaluate the Credibility of Web Sites?; Ziming Liu, Perceptions of Credibility; S. Shyam Sundar, Exploring Receivers' Criteria.

83. Soo Young Rieh and David R. Danielson, Credibility: A Multidisciplinary Framework.

84. Thomas J. Johnson and Barbara K. Kaye, 1998, Webelievability: A Path Model Examining How Convenience and Reliance Predict Online Credibility; John W. Mashek et al., *Lethargy '96: How the*

Media Covered a Listless Campaign; S. Shyam Sundar, Exploring Receivers' Criteria; Thomas J. Johnson and Barbara K. Kaye, Cruising Is Believing?

85.   Ziming Liu, Perceptions of Credibility; Ziming Liu and Xiaobin Huang, Evaluating the Credibility of Scholarly Information on the Web: A Cross Cultural Study, *International Information and Library Review* 37, no. 2 (2005): 99–106; Ethelene Whitmire, The Relationship between Undergraduates' Epistemological Beliefs, Reflective Judgment, and Their Information-Seeking Behavior, *Information Processing and Management* 40 (2004): 97–111.

86.   Gunther Eysenbach and Christian Köhler, How Do Consumers Search for and Appraise Health Information on the World Wide Web?

87.   Andrew J. Flanagin and Miriam J. Metzger, Perceptions of Internet Information Credibility.

88.   Soo Young Rieh and David R. Danielson, Credibility: A Multidisciplinary Framework.

89.   Soo Young Rieh, On the Web at Home.

The MAIN Model: A Heuristic Approach to Understanding Technology Effects on Credibility

S. Shyam Sundar

The Pennsylvania State University, College of Communications

The media world of today's youth is almost completely digital. With newspapers going online and television becoming increasingly digital, the current generation of youth has little reason to consume analog media. Music, movies, and all other forms of mass-mediated content can be obtained via a wide array of digital devices, ranging from CDs to DVDs, from iPods to PDAs.

Even their nonmedia experiences are often characterized by a reliance on digital devices. Most young people communicate with most of their acquaintances through cell phones and computer-mediated communication tools such as instant messengers and e-mail systems.[1] And, with the arrival of personal broadcasting technologies such as blogs and social networking sites, many youngsters experience the world through their own self-expression and the expressions of their peers. This serves to blur the traditional boundary between interpersonal and mass communication, leading to an idiosyncratic construction of one's media world. Customization in the digital age—be it in the form of Web sites such as customizable portals that allow users to shape content or devices such as iPods that allow for customized playlists—enables the user to serve as the gatekeeper of content. As media get highly interactive, multimodal, and navigable, the receiver tends to become the source of communication.[2]

While this leads naturally to egocentric construals of one's information environment, it also raises questions about the veracity of all the material that is consumed. The ease of digital publishing has made authors out of us all, leading to a dramatic profusion of information available for personal as well as public consumption. Much of this information, however, is free-floating and does not follow any universally accepted gatekeeping standards, let alone a professional process of writing and editing. Therefore, the veridicality of information accessed on the Web and other digital media is often suspect.[3] This makes credibility a supremely key concern in the new media environment, necessitating the constant need to critically assess information while consuming it.

Credibility is classically ascertained by considering the source of information. If the attributed source of a piece of information is a credible person or organization, then, according to conventional wisdom, that information is probably reliable. However, in Internet-based media, source is a murky entity because there are often multiple layers of sources in online transmission of information (e.g., e-mail from a friend giving you a piece of information that he or she found on a newsgroup, posted there by another member of the group, who obtained it from a newspaper Web site that picked this up from a wire report) leading to a confusing multiplicity of sources of varying levels of perceived credibility.[4] Some have suggested that in addition to considering credibility of sources, information receivers also consider message credibility as well as the credibility of the medium as a whole.[5]

Cues and Heuristics in the Digital Age

Ultimately though, source, message, and medium credibility serve as *nominal* cues—a given source is perceived as credible or not, a given message element is perceived as credible or not, and likewise a given medium or media vehicle or channel is perceived as credible or not—that provide mental shortcuts for effortlessly assessing the believability of information being received. While an assessment of these simple cues was feasible in traditional media, it is next to impossible for an average Internet user to have a well-defined sense of the credibility of various sources and message categories on the Web because of the multiplicity of sources embedded in the numerous layers of online dissemination of content. This has motivated researchers[6] to suggest the inclusion of so-called credibility markers on Web sites, for instance, to indicate the relative expertise and trustworthiness of an online source. These markers serve as cues to the consumer about the relative merits and demerits of the information being retrieved from the Web. Security seals on e-commerce sites and relevance ranking of search-engine results are examples of such markers.

What do these cues or markers do? Social psychologists have long argued that cues in a persuasion context can lead message receivers to make loose associations between the cue and the message. For example, advertisers often use an attractive source to promote a positive, even if somewhat superficial, association between the source and the product. The elaboration likelihood model (ELM) labels such cues as peripheral cues and the resulting attitude formation as having taken the peripheral route. This is contrasted with the more cognitively effortful central route, which is characterized by attention to and evaluation of message content rather than peripheral aspects such as the attractiveness of the source and font color.[7] The heuristic-systematic model (HSM) makes a similar distinction, with systematic processing referring to a detailed analytical consideration of judgment-relevant information, and heuristic processing relying on mental shortcuts to judgmental rules (or heuristics) that are already stored in memory.[8] For instance, a long message carries with it the length cue, which at a glance can trigger the "length implies strength" heuristic, leading to the conclusion that the message is strong—a conclusion drawn without taking into consideration the actual content of the message. Another judgmental rule relevant to credibility evaluations is the expertise heuristic ("experts' statements can be trusted") which is often invoked simply by using an expert source in the presentation of the message. The presence of the expert is the cue that serves to trigger the expertise heuristic in receivers' minds. For example, a message on a Web site about particular safe-sex practices may be more likely to be taken on face value (i.e., without much scrutiny or counterargumentation) by some youth if they see that it is endorsed by a seemingly expert source such as the American Medical Association (AMA) or the popular radio and television host "Dr. Drew" Pinsky. The expertise = credibility equation is a generalization that people make based on their prior experience and use it whenever possible given our natural tendency to be frugal with our mental resources.

So, what predicts the use of heuristics such as the expertise heuristic? Researchers[9] have identified three criteria. First of all, the cue (e.g., AMA as information provider) has to be cognitively available at the time of making a decision about the credibility of the content. Second, the heuristic or judgment rule (e.g., expertise implies accuracy) should be accessible (if it is a rule that is used often to judge content, then it is likely to be more easily accessed by our brain) at the time of decision making. Third, the heuristic should be applicable or relevant to the situation at hand (i.e., judging accuracy of medical information is an important aspect of digesting health information).

A heuristic thus invoked can either directly lead to a snap judgment as in heuristic processing (e.g., the safe-sex practices are good) or serve to frame, bias, or otherwise guide more systematic processing of content (e.g., experts such as AMA are recommending safe-sex practices, so prevalence of casual sex must be quite high). It is important to note that the use of heuristics does not automatically mean heuristic processing. Heuristics are, after all, evolved generalizations stored in one's knowledge base that often get refined with experience. So, they can certainly be very helpful as analytical tools while processing systematically as well. If the perceiver is willfully applying the heuristic to arrive at a conclusion (as in the example above of estimating prevalence of casual sex in society), then the processing is said to be conscious or controlled.[10] More often, the perceiver is unaware of the operation of the heuristic and, thus, its role in influencing judgment, in which case the process is said to be unconscious or automatic.[11] This often results in the direct acceptance of a message (e.g., the safe-sex message on the Web site) whereby users can seldom attribute the reason for their acceptance; they simply say that they feel that the message is credible. Cues that trigger heuristics could be either embedded within a message (e.g., message length) or appear in the context of message presentation (e.g., message source). They might even be internally located within the perceiver (e.g., attitudes, mood states).[12]

One could argue that the more fundamental source of all these types of heuristic-cue information is the technology of the medium used for communication. Each technology brings with it a set of affordances or capabilities[13] that can shape the nature of content in a given medium. In addition to dictating content, these affordances also determine the way the content is typically presented via the medium[14] and receivers' states of mind while using it.[15] For example, the affordance of interactivity on a Web site suggests "action possibilities"[16] such as clicking on hyperlinks or typing in a chatroom. These possibilities suggest openness of information access and the participatory nature of the forum, among other things. If this were a political candidate's Web site, open flow of information and invitation to participate can immediately translate into higher credibility for the candidate because these are desirable qualities in a politician.[17] Therefore, each affordance could be seen as a repository of cues, some of which may aid judgments of credibility of the device or site by triggering heuristics about the typical nature of underlying content.

Credibility Assessment: What Youth Notice First and Foremost

Cues embedded in—and transmitted by—the structure (rather than content) of digital technologies are likely to be particularly salient to today's youth. As is evident with the success of each new technology, youth are eager to try out new structures and formats. While the previous generation took a relatively long time to switch from vinyl records to audiocassettes and from videocassettes to DVDs, the current generation has been swift in its adoption of digital audiovisual technologies. Their basic message needs from mass media remain the same, however, and the content of their mediated communications is largely similar across technologies (e.g., from telephone to instant messaging). What has really changed is the nature of their interactions with and through digital media. This clearly privileges the formal features of these new technologies over their content characteristics.

In fact, in one of the earliest surveys of Web site credibility involving over 2,500 respondents, nearly half the open-ended comments mentioned the "design look" of the site. This was indeed the most commented upon aspect of the site when it came to self-reports of credibility considerations. The second most-commented aspect was "information design/structure," appearing in nearly 30 percent of the comments.[18] Both of these clearly signal the importance of the structure of the medium in the context of credibility evaluations.

Furthermore, among the four types of credibility identified by Tseng and Fogg,[19] the two that depend on site scrutiny (the other two pertain to individual expectations and experiences) refer directly to superficial aspects of the site: *reputed credibility* refers to the ascribed source labels seen on the site (markers of the source's expertise and trustworthiness), while *surface credibility* relies on a simple global inspection of the site. In the multistage model proposed by Wathen and Burkell,[20] the first stage that a user goes through for judging the credibility of online information is an evaluation of surface credibility, which involves a consideration of such surface characteristics as appearance/presentation and information organization, as well as interface design elements such as interactivity, navigability, and download speed. This is true even for highly motivated users of primarily informational sites such as health sites. Users are known to not only reject or ignore Web sites that have poor design appeal, but also to mistrust them.[21] As Metzger concludes in her review of research, people rely most heavily on design/presentational elements for judging information credibility and quality even though this is not one of the "five critical evaluation skills recommended" for judging credibility.[22]

So, whether we like it or not, the so-called surface features of the interface likely have a profound influence on youths' assessment of credibility. The general tendency among researchers appears to be to find ways to focus youth on the content and away from these structural features so that they can make "real" and "accurate" credibility assessments. The truth, however, is that these surface features are what hold youth's interest and what attract them to these technologies in the first place. So, it would probably be a wasteful endeavor to devise ways of getting them to ignore the very thing they are attracted to; if anything, it is likely to be counterproductive. Instead, a more inclusive strategy would be to seek methods for harnessing these technological features for leading youth toward making accurate credibility evaluations.

To do so, we must first gain a fundamental understanding of the psychology of technological elements present in digital media. If we gain insights into how young people process different technological aspects of digital media, we will not only be able to deliver content to them in a way that better positions them to scrutinize the central, nonsurface aspects for judging credibility, but also help spark design and marketing innovations that eventually serve to improve users' ability to scrutinize information in digital media.

Technological Hope ≠ Psychological Reality

Research on technological affordances reveals that a chasm exists between our expectations about and the effects of digital media, and between our perceived needs and actual use of their offerings. The operating principle behind the introduction and use of these structural features is to enhance the range and scope of communication by enriching the experience of content, emerging from the assumption that more affordances result in higher credibility. For example, a Web site with more interactivity would be considered higher in credibility than one with less interactivity because, after all, it makes retrieving additional information easy and efficient, implying a generally benevolent intention on the part of the communicator.

As it turns out, such predictions of the monolithically positive effects of technological affordances are largely unfounded. They are more reflective of technological hope than the psychological reality of digital media. In the rush to capture the imagination and fascination of our youth, software and other digital media designers go to great lengths to build affordances that dazzle them initially, but fail to sustain long-term interest and use. A case in point is the use of digital media to enhance education, especially at a distance. Despite enormous expenditure of vision, expertise, and money on a large scale, technological affordances have not resulted in a noticeable, let alone commensurate, improvement in the quality of education or learning among our youth.[23] The literature on the status of informational content on the Web bemoans the lack of completeness of information[24] even though the Web is unparalleled in its ability to provide comprehensive and timely information on virtually any topic. New technologies such as blogs are criticized as being too partisan or too narrow or both. News organizations are chided for following the shovelware approach whereby they slap print content directly onto their Web sites without fully utilizing the unique capabilities of the digital medium. Paid services on the net that do make good use of the medium's features are seldom successful as business ventures. As for entertainment content, digital technologies are similarly underutilized. Most users do not take advantage of most of the advanced features designed to enable better gatekeeping of content and access to deeper layers of information. Ultimately, the Web and many other digital technologies carry content that is truly gargantuan in scope, but much of it is, as Clifford Stoll once put it, "unedited, unreviewed gunk." As a result, youth are likely to be overwhelmed both by the technology itself and the enormous amount of content that it delivers.

The digital media universe thus presents a dual challenge: (1) the overload of information, entertainment, and other offerings that constantly need organizing and (2) the lack of assurance of any uniformity in content quality, which necessitates a continual monitoring of credibility on the part of users. With regard to the first point, we know from social cognition research that cues are the primary solution for dealing with information overload of any kind. Even when there is no desperate overload situation, people are known to be "cognitive misers" and will not expend more cognitive energy than necessary to arrive at a particular inference, and so will rely on cognitive heuristics.[25] With regard to the second point, cues can also convey information or stimulate heuristics that assist youth in making credibility assessments automatically.

Cues Transmitted by Technological Affordances

There are at least two ways by which affordances of digital technologies can convey cues pertinent to judgments of credibility. One is the sheer presence of a given affordance because its value-added functionality will be rife with judgment-related cues. For example, the presence of interactivity (a common affordance in modern digital technologies) can transmit cues that imply a greater sense of dialogue in the system, or a higher sense of determination (or contingency) on the part of the user in dictating the nature of information exchange, or simply a more robust flow of communication.[26] Depending upon which of these is salient during a given informational context in which interactivity appears, the heuristic used to guide the receiver's experience and evaluation of message content will be different. The "dialogue" cue might give users the sense that the content is mutually shaped, serving as a trigger for a variety of heuristics relating to participation, democracy, consensus, and so on. The "contingency" cue might trigger the notion of individualization of messages, leading to heuristics pertaining to customization (tailoring, own-ness, etc.). The "flow" dimension of interactivity might evoke heuristics relating to system responsiveness, such as speed, telepresence, and so on. These heuristics may have either a positive or a negative connotation in users' minds in a given situation, thereby shaping their judgment of the content under evaluation accordingly.

A slightly different method by which affordances convey cues involves an active effort by the technology to assemble information that is relevant for making credibility and quality judgments about the underlying content. We see plenty of examples of autogenerated indicators of information or product quality in e-commerce Web sites, often based on prior user traffic or other forms of unobtrusively gathered input from site visitors. A simple example is the presence of counters on home pages, indicating the number of visitors to the site. Social networking sites such as Facebook automatically indicate the number of contacts in any given person's network. These indicators can serve as cues that trigger heuristics pertaining to popularity, insecurity, and so on. More complex examples of autogenerated cues appear in the form of navigational aids offered by algorithms used in search-engine and aggregator sites such as Google News, which transmits cues about the relative recency of the information, among other attributes. These appear as part of—or surrounding—the central content of the site, and emit "information scent" helpful in making quick decisions about the quality of the information available for consumption.[27] These cues tend to be purely informational and quite routinized in their operation and appearance. However, the heuristics triggered by them could hold rich meanings for users, with recency for example translating to timeliness, thereby implying greater newsworthiness and credibility. Likewise, the original source of a given news lead published in Google News can serve to trigger heuristics pertaining to source credibility, expertise, and so on.

In sum, technological affordances in digital media trigger cognitive heuristics that aid credibility judgments by offering both new functions and new metrics that are rich in cues. Given that the overload situation presented by most digital media creates a reliance on cues, today's youth are likely to make quick decisions about the credibility of the information they consume on the basis of these cues. While aspects of the content itself (e.g., headlines) convey cues that trigger heuristics, the central thesis of this chapter is that technological features transmit their own cues that are influential in shaping users' perceptions and processing of content. We are yet to specify exactly which cues are triggered by which technological feature. New models that explicate the specific heuristics stimulated by these cues are sorely needed to help us better understand how youth make snap decisions about credibility in the midst of using digital media. These models can in turn help practitioners develop programs and interfaces to better help users assess credibility in a realistic and effective manner.

The MAIN Model

Ten years of research at The Media Effects Research Laboratory at Penn State University with a variety of digital media have identified four broad affordances that have shown significant psychological effects—Modality (M), Agency (A), Interactivity (I), and Navigability (N). These affordances are present to a greater or lesser degree in most digital media and seem promising in their ability to cue cognitive heuristics pertaining to credibility assessments because they are all structural features that underlie the design aspects or surface-level characteristics

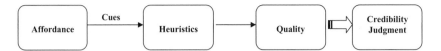

Figure 1
Overview of the MAIN Model.

associated with powerful first impressions of Web site credibility.[28] Clearly, each affordance is richly meaningful from a psychological point of view, but it is unclear what particular meanings they hold for young users of digital media. Research suggests that, depending on how a particular affordance manifests itself to users, it can lead to positive or negative outcomes. For example, if the design of interactive features on an interface successfully cues the convenience aspect of interactivity, users are likely to react positively; but if it cues the need for constant navigation, then it is likely to be viewed as burdensome. In general, calls for interaction with the system have proven to be a double-edged sword, with users preferring them in market surveys but showing a generally negative tendency toward them in experimental studies.[29] Bucy calls this phenomenon the "interactivity paradox."[30] The dominant engineering conviction favors more and more affordances, and users, especially young users, are quite enthusiastic about new structural features in technology, but when they actually use it, the impact on their thoughts, attitudes, and behaviors is often unpredictable even under conditions of good usability.[31]

One reason for such counterintuitive, if not contradictory, findings may lie in the nature of cues transmitted by these technological affordances. It is very likely that a given affordance can convey a variety of different cues leading to a number of different heuristic-based judgments, with some being positive and others negative, resulting in a rather complex equation between the presence of an affordance and the nature of credibility assessments that it can trigger. By identifying the universe of cues transmitted by each of these affordances, we will be able to understand the heuristics that they trigger and the consequent credibility judgments that potentially ensue. This requires an intensive explication of the nature and functioning of these four affordances, which will provide a crucial foundation for understanding youth's information and credibility assessment processes.

What follows is an attempt to uncover as many definitions of each affordance as possible, with a view to identifying the credibility cues that it might trigger. We begin by outlining a simple model whereby a given affordance (such as interactivity in an e-commerce site) conveys a certain cue (e.g., invitation to have a live chat with a customer-service agent) that triggers a heuristic (e.g., service) leading to an automatic deduction that good service means good quality of information and information supply, thus imbuing a high level of credibility to the site (see Figure 1).

Although source and content of digital media are very important in shaping ascribed credibility, the MAIN model is primarily concerned with the technological aspects of digital media that can influence credibility judgments. As such, the starting point is an *affordance* offered by the technology, which means a particular capability possessed by the medium to facilitate a certain action. It is suggestive and perceived by the user.[32] For example, a keyboard affords the possibility of typing in text, whereas the mouse suggests pointing and clicking. The user is an integral part of interpreting the affordance.[33] A music composer might see the mouse as a tool for editing a score online with ease, whereas an avid pianist might see it as a foot pedal and proceed to operate it with her feet. A *cue* is anything in the context of digital media use that might serve as a trigger for the operation of a heuristic. A *heuristic* is simply a judgment rule (e.g., "responsiveness is good customer service") that can result in estimations of content quality. The concept of content *quality* is variously defined but encompasses such considerations as utility, importance, relevance, completeness, level of detail, clarity, variety, accessibility, trustworthiness, uniqueness, timeliness, and objectivity, among many others. Many of these considerations play a critical role in users' perceptions of the credibility of information. For example, trustworthiness and reliability of information have been shown by researchers to be directly linked to credibility.[34]

Next, each of the four affordances is discussed, with a focus on the ways in which the cues embedded in each of the four affordances can trigger heuristics that may play a role in credibility assessments made by youth as they use digital media.

Modality Cues

Modality is perhaps the most structural (i.e., tied to the structure rather than content of the medium) of the four affordances and also the most apparent on an interface. The concept of modality is closely allied with the concept of medium because, historically, media differed according to their modality, with print being predominantly textual, radio being aural, and television being audiovisual. However, the arrival of computer-based media has complicated this modality-based distinction between media by offering content in a number of different modalities. Hence the label "multimedia" that we see applied to digital devices, even though they do not represent many media, but in fact many modalities rolled into one medium.

There are three possible origins of cognitive heuristics within this affordance: (1) each individual modality (e.g., text, aural, audiovisual) may, by its sheer presence, cue a particular heuristic; (2) new modalities unique to digital media could also cue their own heuristics; and (3) combinations of modalities may cue heuristics as well.

The output modality on many digital devices is text-only or predominantly so. Much of what youth consume via e-mail, social networking sites, and digital devices is in the form of text. On Web sites, the most common modalities are text and pictures. On cell phones, it is text and audio. On iPods, especially newer ones, it is text, audio, and video. One could assess psychological differences between these specific modalities by invoking the traditional mass-communication literature on intermedia differences, including differences on perceived credibility.[35] The more interesting question, however, is: what heuristics are triggered in the minds of young users by these particular modalities in the current digital media context, especially given that they can exist in a variety of new configurations on various devices and sites? And, are these heuristics likely to influence assessments of the credibility of the medium and its content?

At first glance, textual modality might appear to be the least credible compared to say the audiovisual modality because textual communication has more intermediaries (the sender has to write what they have seen and the receiver has to decode that writing with all its nuances) and, therefore, leaves more room for noise and deception. Text as a symbol system requires controlled processing whereas audiovisual modality is probably processed more easily because the depiction is more life-like and needs little, if any, decoding or translation. Indeed, many researchers have pointed out that audio is a singularly important characteristic for promoting realism, defined as the transparency between human-human and human-computer interaction, when it comes to the application of social rules.[36] Therefore, the *realism heuristic* would predict that people are more likely to trust audiovisual modality because its content has a higher resemblance to the real world. That is, we trust those things that we can see over those that we merely read about. This heuristic also underlies people's general belief that pictures cannot lie (even in this day and age of digital manipulation) and the consequent trust in pictures over textual descriptions. And, trust, as we know, is a key component of credibility.

However, several recent studies with college-age participants have shown that text-only and text-plus-picture modalities have elicited more positive evaluations from receivers than audio and audiovisual modalities.[37] A common factor across these studies is that they used educational or informational (e.g., news) content. This may have predisposed receivers to apply schemas developed on the basis of their experience with traditional media. Historically, newspapers, the dominant textual medium, are thought to have more stringent gatekeeping standards than broadcast media, and are often associated with policy-shaping news features and editorials. This well-established bias may have governed their assessment of content in these studies. We shall call this the *old-media heuristic*: if a Web site resembles a newspaper in its layout, then this heuristic would be invoked to produce positive credibility evaluations, but if it resembles broadcast media, then its perceived credibility would likely be lower.

This heuristic probably applies only to informational sites and probably only to the Web medium. The vast majority of digital media and content is unlikely to suffer from comparison standards established by traditional media. Advanced digital interfaces, especially those that entertain multimodal input in addition to multimodal output, are usually higher in representational accuracy. In virtual reality systems, for example, the various modalities come together to convey detailed information without ambiguity; in addition, they afford the opportunity to experience motion and being "telepresent" in the represented space. The rendering of the illusory experience is painstakingly carried out with the express purpose of transporting the user to a virtual space. Multiple modalities are believed to extend the speed, range, and mapping of information with greater sensory involvement, thus enlarging the perceptual bandwidth[38] for interaction. So-called perceptual interfaces are likely to provide such sensory immersion that they may cue the *being-there heuristic*. When this heuristic is triggered, i.e., when receivers feel like they are a part of the universe portrayed by the digital media, they are likely to factor the authenticity as well as the intensity of their experience into their credibility evaluations.

On the other hand, the sensory overstimulation experienced during multimodal interactions could just as well cue the *distraction* heuristic.[39] This will be particularly likely when the experience is so all-consuming that the receiver is left cognitively drained. From its earliest conceptualization, multimedia has implied the involvement of multiple senses in processing a stimulus,[40] so it is conceivable that newer digital media push the frontiers of modality usage to the point of sensory overload, although it may be argued that today's youth have a higher threshold than adults given that they have grown up on a regular diet of complex media interfaces. The distraction heuristic is likely to detract users from effortfully evaluating the content of the communication. While such distraction may be desirable under some conditions, the evaluation of credibility of the underlying content is likely to be performed under suboptimal cognitive conditions. Conscious application of the distraction heuristic may amplify the user's systematic processing of content by sensitizing users to credibility issues, whereas automatic application of the heuristic may lead to a directly negative evaluation of credibility.

Somewhat similar is the *bells-and-whistles heuristic* that is quite likely to be associated with multimodal interfaces. Voice-recognition software has increasingly made it possible for us to talk to our devices while operating them with other input modes such as typing, clicking, tapping, and touching. But, as Oviatt points out, the number one myth about multimodal interaction is, "if you build a multimodal system, users will interact multimodally."[41] This is probably because most users approach the introduction of a new modality with some cynicism. Unlike other affordances, modality innovations are very apparent to the user and tend to be flashy, promoting the impression that it is all flash and no substance. The bells-and-whistles heuristic might lead users to conclude that the underlying content is probably insufficiently credible.

But if bells and whistles are the draw, as they might be for younger digital media users, then modality enhancements are likely to cue the *coolness heuristic*, which is a conscious acknowledgment of the "hipness" of the digital device suggested by its newer modalities. Invoking this heuristic might, on the one hand, lead to a directly positive evaluation of credibility (i.e., if it's cool, it's credible), but on the other, raise expectations for underlying content. The bells and whistles of the technology may lead users to expect a commensurately high quality of content and therefore set up a rather high bar for content, with the eventual evaluations dependent on the content itself.

The flipside of this is the *novelty heuristic*, which, if invoked, may prompt a loose association between the innovation signified by the introduction of new modalities and the quality and credibility of the underlying content. Here, the prediction is similar to that made by the elaboration likelihood model for low-involved receivers who are bowled over by the novelty cue. That is, young people who are not particularly involved in the subject matter transmitted by a digital device (say a podcast of a political issue on a blog) may be so enamored by the novelty of the technology (i.e., using podcasts in blogs) that they ascribe higher credibility to the content in that podcast than if they had received the same content through a non-novel delivery mechanism such as a radio broadcast.

Not all new modalities end up triggering the novelty heuristic however. Some modalities that are unique to digital media—animation and pop-ups for example—tend to trigger negative heuristics right off the bat. Given that these modalities often command user attention and arrive unsolicited, they are usually unwelcome and serve to trigger the *intrusiveness heuristic*. When cued, this heuristic is likely to have a negative influence on content evaluations. In fact, based on recent research demonstrating the negative effects of intrusive advertisements, several major Web sites have stopped accepting pop-up ads because they may reflect negatively on the host site.[42]

In sum, by triggering the realism and being-there heuristics, new modalities serve to heighten users' perceptual experience with digital media, with generally positive consequences on credibility evaluations. Newer modalities or combinations of modalities may also cue coolness and novelty heuristics that have the potential to transfer positive assessments of the technology to positive assessments of the content conveyed by the technology. Alternatively, they may trigger the bells-and-whistles heuristic, wherein users are sensitive to their cosmetic value and consciously avoid letting it influence their content evaluations. Finally, some of the newer modalities that are designed to catch the attention of digital media users can cue the intrusiveness and/or the distraction heuristic, leading to negative credibility assessments.

In the absence of strong commitments to content or viewpoints on issues, young users may be particularly likely to rely on these modality-based heuristics, especially given the high visibility of cues that trigger them. They are also less likely than adults to have strong allegiances to particular modalities, implying that they may be quite impressionable when it comes to experiencing new modalities.

Agency Cues

As mentioned earlier, credibility considerations usually center around the source of information. While the source is obvious in most traditional media, the identity of sources in computer-based media is often murky.[43] Is the source of online news a Web site? Or is it the computer itself? Is it the author of the story? Or could it be the news organization that was responsible for putting together a given piece of news? In some ways, all these can be construed as sources.

The agency affordance of digital media capitalizes on this confusion and makes possible the assignment of sourcing to particular entities in the chain of communication, from the front-end box (e.g., computer or television) to an online location (e.g., nytimes.com), from a collection of other users (e.g., polled opinion of one's friends on Facebook) to oneself (e.g., one's space in myyahoo.com or playlist on iPod), among many others. That is, the device (e.g., computer), sometimes in the form of an interface agent, communicates the identity of the source to the receiver. Often, the agent itself is the source, at least psychologically, particularly when there is no other attributed source for a given piece of information. It is not uncommon, for example, for today's youth to attribute sourceness to an online bot-based news aggregator such as Google News. Depending on who or what is identified or perceived by the receiver as the source, particular cognitive heuristics are likely to be triggered about their presumptive abilities to serve as the source, which, in turn, affect the perceived credibility of the information provided by that source.

It is commonplace for us to say that we got something "off the computer." In this case, the psychologically relevant agent is the computer itself. In an experiment where identical online news stories were attributed to either news editors, other users, self, or the computer, study participants rated the stories as being higher in quality when they thought the computer terminal chose them than when they thought news editors chose them.[44] This is probably because of the operation of the *machine heuristic*, implying that if a machine chose the story, then it must be objective in its selection and free from ideological bias. If an interface appears machine-like, then it may cue the machine heuristic, resulting in attributions of randomness, objectivity, and other mechanical characteristics to its performance. This may indeed result in positive credibility judgments. Alternatively, if the interface sports an anthropomorphic look, following recent industry trends, then it is likely to detract from this heuristic and result in credibility judgments that presume a lesser degree of objectivity and other machine-like attributes.

Results from Sundar and Nass showed also that the psychological favorite among all sources was "other users."[45] When other users were attributed as the source of online news, study participants liked the stories more and perceived them to be of higher quality than when news editors or receivers themselves were identified as sources. Furthermore, the stories were rated as more newsworthy compared to when the users themselves selected the stories. These results are probably due to the operation of the *bandwagon heuristic* (if others think that this is a good story, then I should think so too), which has received recent support both in Rieh and Hilligoss's study of youth information seeking (this volume), and in the context of an online recommendation agent whose operation was based on collaborative filtering: Knobloch-Westerwick et al. found that study participants picked more articles from a portal if it featured explicit recommendations, and that strength of the recommendation positively predicted duration of exposure to the article.[46] When the *New York Times* site features a listing of the most e-mailed stories of the day or when Amazon.com indicates to us what others with similar interests have bought, these autogenerated features are assigning agency to the collective other in cyberspace with the purpose of cueing the bandwagon heuristic.

The bandwagon heuristic can be quite powerful in influencing credibility given that it implies collective endorsement and popularity of the underlying content. Collaborative filtering and related technological advancements have dramatically simplified the ability of digital media to dynamically collect and display information about what others are doing, listening, watching, reading, and thinking. The buzz about a given talented musician is instantaneous on social networking sites such as MySpace. It is very simple to obtain an idea of the most downloaded songs on iTunes.com and the most popular chick-lit novels on amazon.com. Furthermore, such cues to bandwagon effects may be particularly powerful for many youth given their motivation to be in on the latest trends, and to constantly orient to their peers and to generally fit in socially. Given the enormous popularity of social networking sites and other such collaborative technologies among our youth, the prominence of others as sources and the bandwagon heuristic they cue with their implicit endorsement of various cultural products, we may be witnessing a shift from independent to social assessment of credibility.[47]

Another heuristic that relies on endorsement is the *authority heuristic*. A common finding across the credibility literature is that one of the major criteria for assigning credibility to a site is whether the source is an official authority or not.[48] The autogenerated source cue in Google News is likely to perform similarly. By revealing the source of the news lead, the site invites readers to apply the authority heuristic to determine the level of credibility of the embedded news item.[49] Another way in which this heuristic is likely to be cued is through interface agents, ideally embodied conversational ones, that specialize in specific topic areas, like Rea, the real-estate agent developed at MIT.[50] The authority heuristic is likely to be operational whenever a topic expert or official authority is identified as the source of content. To the extent the interface agent or even simply a Web site identifies itself as an authority of some sort, it is likely to directly confer importance, believability, and pedigree to the content provided by that source and thereby positively impact its credibility. This heuristic is particularly relevant to younger youth who are relatively reverential about authority because they have been socialized since childhood to listen to authority figures such as parents, teachers, and coaches. And, as Rieh and Hilligoss (this volume) discovered, even college students appear to employ the authority heuristic as a basis for their credibility judgments.

Interface agents do not have to necessarily convey authority to influence credibility perceptions. They can do so simply with "social presence," or the idea that the user is communicating with a social entity rather than an inanimate object. Research has shown that computer users psychologically assume a social presence while interacting with a computer[51] to the point of applying social rules in their interaction,[52] including longer-term affiliations such as loyalty.[53] This is demonstrated even in the absence of any visibly anthropomorphic features of the technology, although if there are cues in the interface that represent human characteristics such as voice, language, and personality,[54] the *social presence heuristic* appears to be more strongly invoked. What this means is that the social presence heuristic may toggle with the machine heuristic and, depending on the nature of the content, one is likely to lead to more positive credibility evaluations than the other. While the machine heuristic is advantageous for objective news selection as detailed above, the social presence heuristic might aid credibility of socioemotional information content. For example, the online chat-bot Ramona (http://www.kurzweilai.net/ramona/ramona.html) is extraordinarily successful in eliciting trust and self-disclosure from users who have little or no prior experience with it.[55] A related heuristic in this context is that of the helper. While users may be cued to Ramona's social presence because of her anthropomorphic presence on the site, they may also see her simply as a helper. Affect-support agents residing in a computer have been generally positively received by users even though the negative affect that needs repairing was caused by the computer (hosting the agent) in the first place.[56] The *helper heuristic* may take an affective path toward influencing credibility evaluations, manifested by such online behaviors as trusting and self-disclosure.[57] It might also have something to do with privileging the user in an otherwise technology-centered medium.

The notion of celebrating the "self" is becoming an increasingly prevalent and popular part of digital media. From blogs to podcasting, and from iPods to myyahoo and YouTube, digital technologies have evolved toward providing users with a strong sense of agency within the medium. They not only allow users to experiment with their identities,[58] but also communicate their identity to others. The agency model of customization[59] argues that imbuing the user with a sense of personal agency will have a powerful effect on attitudes because of its inherent egocentrism. The *identity heuristic* is likely to be triggered whenever an affordance allows the user to assert his or her identity through the technology. Its effect on credibility evaluations is obvious.

In sum, the agency affordance can locate the source of the interaction in the user himself or herself and thus trigger the identity heuristic, or make source attributions to the larger user base and trigger the bandwagon heuristic. Given that a good deal of the usage of digital media by youth is for purposes of self-presentation (i.e., asserting one's identity) and social networking, these heuristics are highly likely to be triggered in their minds and thereby influence their credibility judgments. In addition to locating the source within the user and the larger user base, the agency affordance may simply situate the source within the technology and invoke the machine heuristic or, if the technology possesses cues that invite anthropomorphism, the social-presence heuristic. The agent may under other circumstances channel other sources or feature certain functions that serve to cue the authority heuristic and the helper heuristic, respectively. All these heuristics will have strong effects on credibility evaluations, but their valence is likely to depend on the context of the content being evaluated.

Interactivity Cues

Interactivity is probably the most distinctive affordance of digital media, with most traditional analog media having little of it and some digital media possessing more of it than others. Yet, there is no universally accepted definition for the concept, and each researcher emphasizes a slightly different aspect of interactivity as its definitional core.[60] The term *interactivity* implies both interaction and activity. Particular digital media devices could possess particular attributes that make explicit these two qualities of an interactive device or medium. As heuristics, interaction and activity carry rich connotations. For starters, the *activity heuristic* indicates a departure from the passivity that characterizes usage of traditional media, especially television.[61] At minimum, the use of the mouse while surfing the Web is likely to be much more frequent than the use of a remote-control while watching TV. The level of activity can be even higher with more interactive devices, especially games. In fact, the sheer presence of a joystick (versus a mouse) in an interactive device could cue the user to apply the activity heuristic.

Like many heuristics, the valence of the activity heuristic could be positive or negative depending on a variety of user and situational factors. After a tiring day's work, when one is in the mood to be passively entertained, the activity heuristic would have a negative connotation. Alternatively, as per mood management theory,[62] if the user is bored and is seeking out the digital medium for excitement, the activity heuristic might indeed be a positive force. Greater activity engenders greater dynamism in the medium's offerings, a key criterion for judging relevance of content.[63] Dynamism has also been related to higher perceptions of credibility in traditional source-credibility research, and could operate similarly online.[64] Therefore, dynamism triggered by the activity heuristic may influence users' credibility judgments.

The *interaction heuristic* means that users have the option of specifying their needs and preferences on an ongoing basis, as in the case of tuning one's iPod. Cues on the interface, especially dialog boxes, that solicit user input may trigger the interaction heuristic, leading to greater specificity of the resulting content. Specificity is another relevance criterion[65] that could eventually impact credibility perceptions by showcasing the degree to which the content is specifically referring to user input. Today's youth may be particularly likely to use the interaction heuristic given their early habituation to interactive media. Most everything they consume online is a product of their interaction with the medium. They have enormous interaction opportunities in interpersonal communication venues such as social networking sites and instant messengers. In addition, traditional media products catering to youth increasingly involve the interaction element, from *Dora the Explorer* calling for viewer participation to the *American Idol* host inviting viewers to call in and vote for their favorite contestant.

Interactivity further suggests that the medium is responsive to user needs, and that it is capable of taking into account variations in user input during the course of the interaction.[66] For example, while traveling in a new city guided by a GPS receiver (as opposed to a physical map), the user's constantly changing geographical location serves as the system's input in an ongoing fashion. There are no cues to interaction or activity because the user does not have to actively interact with the device, yet the information output is high in specificity and dynamism. And, assuming that the device is of good quality, the resulting information is accurate as well, thereby enhancing the credibility of the system. Here, the interactivity affordance in the GPS receiver simply cues the *responsiveness heuristic* without confounding it with interaction or activity.

That said, most other interactive devices do involve a fairly high level of interaction and activity in order for the user to realize their full potential. But they differentially cue a host of other heuristics that may influence credibility assessments. The average menu bar in any interactive device, especially if displayed in the form of a series of tabs or as a pull-down list, is likely to cue the *choice heuristic*. Choice is often a desirable feature, but not always.[67] This heuristic conveys not only the greater accessibility of information[68] and level of detail[69] featured in the system, but also potentially the lack of conciseness in representation[70] and the consequent difficulty in information locatability.[71] These are all indicators of information quality (some positive, some negative) with direct implications for judgments of credibility, so the best way to capitalize on the choice heuristic is to trigger it only when the positives outweigh the negatives. If indeed the system has a known problem with locatability of information, or if we know for a fact that the underlying content is not represented in a concise manner, then it would be in the designer's interest to avoid cueing the choice heuristic through the device's interactivity affordance. In learning systems especially, today's youth are quite sensitive to choice (as evident from their behavior in online education portals) and are often attracted to digital venues for education precisely because of the choices and flexibility they offer.

An interesting theoretical possibility is the toggle effect between heuristics. Under certain conditions, the choice heuristic could unwittingly cue the *control heuristic*. Some researchers have found that too much choice can create dissonance and undermine the sense of personal control by overwhelming, rather than empowering, users.[72] User control is considered a key concomitant of interactivity,[73] and several devices explicitly cue the control heuristic by offering users various interface options for controlling the nature of their interaction, from setting the pace of information acquisition[74] to filtering out unwanted content (e.g., pop-up blockers on Web browsers). If a device highlights its ability to afford user control, then it is likely to score high on representational information quality, which is an indicator of the degree to which the user is able to understand and interpret the underlying information,[75] and also the perceived value of the information,[76] thereby enhancing its credibility.

Real-time modifiability of form and content is another defining feature of interactivity[77] especially in the context of creating feelings of telepresence[78] or being transported to a physically different location or a dynamic virtual environment. Virtual reality systems, with their head-mounted displays, strive to cue the *telepresence heuristic* all the time. They deploy the interactivity affordance for the purpose of creating an authentic experience while being geographically stationary. The effect here is clearly psychological, with users perceiving greater responsiveness in the system as well as realism in the content of their interaction, and thereby possibly attributing higher credibility to it.

A related conceptualization of interactivity involves the concept of speed. The speed with which the system responds to the user can be psychologically, even physiologically, significant.[79] A good match between a user's expectations and the system's response can result in an optimal sense of flow, defined as the level of immersion achieved by the user when experiencing a system.[80] The *flow heuristic* may be triggered during the course of experiencing the interactive system and can be tricky to identify and operationalize. But, it is likely to be a significant factor in the minds of young people when they engage with a system. Brought up on a steady diet of videogames that have adjustable and scalable levels, today's youngsters are likely to be extremely reactive to system speed and quite motivated to seek out an optimal level while interacting with digital media. Any system that explicitly features options for adjusting speed (mp3 players, text messaging software on cell phones) is likely to cue the flow heuristic. More often, the heuristic is likely to be triggered in the negative when there is a break in flow, as in the case of most voice-recognition software. Ultimately, the flow heuristic will impact our perceptions of the consistency, compatibility, and reliability dimensions of information quality,[81] with obvious consequences for our evaluations of the system as well as its content. Flow is likely to be an automatically applied heuristic, with good flow creating such a sense of seamlessness in the interaction that users mindlessly apply rules of human-human interaction to human-system interaction.[82] Thus, users may be likely to evaluate the system's credibility positively, just as they would evaluate a person with whom they hit it off.

Interactivity can also be realized in systems that are designed for human-human interactions, the so-called computer-mediated communication applications such as e-mail, instant messaging, chatrooms, bulletin-boards, and social networking sites. Here, the key heuristic is that of "contingency." Message exchange in computer-mediated communication is said to be interactive if and only if the messages are threaded to reflect a sequence of interactions. That is, for a message to be considered interactive, it has to be contingent on not only the immediately preceding message from the interaction partner but also those messages that came before it.[83] This forms the foundation of interactivity definitions that focus on the dialogue and mutual discourse aspects of communication technology.[84] A clear perception of contingency can leave the user with a good feeling about the uniqueness, timeliness, reliability, and relevance of the information exchanged, all of which are likely to positively impact credibility perceptions. The *contingency heuristic* may be triggered by numerous aspects of computer-mediated communication, from the interface features that invite users to get involved in a live interaction to the way the software displays the resulting message threads.

Ultimately, the real value of interactivity is that it gives the user the ability to serve as a source, and not just a receiver, of communication.[85] The affordance enabling the self to act as the source underlies the notion of customization,[86] a key feature of most digital media. When young people go to a portal site and decide which particular features and content domains to consume on a regular basis, they are serving as their own gatekeeper. When they change the desktop to reflect their personal aesthetic preferences, they are customizing. One can even customize digital devices by way of cell phone faceplates and ring tones. All of these customization-related affordances of interactivity serve to cue the *own-ness heuristic*, which can be very powerful psychologically.[87] On the one hand, this heuristic communicates the cognitive, social, and emotional feelings of attachment to one's device or site because the content is largely a reflection of oneself.[88] On the other hand, cueing this heuristic may lead to concerns about one's privacy,[89] because the system necessarily requires the user to divulge personal information as it interactively tailors the content for the user. Therefore, the credibility attributed to the system and the information in it depends to a large extent on how well a given system negotiates these two conflicting cognitions (e.g., trust-building features and the user's prior experience or familiarity with it).

In sum, the interactivity affordance in digital media is capable of cueing a wide variety of cognitive heuristics, ranging from interaction and activity to responsiveness, choice, control, telepresence, flow, contingency, and own-ness. In the past, researchers have attempted to additively combine two or more definitional elements (e.g., synchronicity + two-way communication + user control) to achieve a comprehensive approximation of the notion of interactivity.[90] This has likely led to a mixture of cues in the devices or operationalizations under consideration, with each cue triggering its own cognitive heuristic or multiple cues interacting in unknown ways to stimulate new and unique heuristics. If we are serious about understanding the interaction of our youth with digital media, it is critical to parse the various embedded cues in the interactivity affordance and identify the specific heuristics triggered by them. It is already abundantly clear that interactivity is the hallmark of all digital devices that are successful with young people. At the time of this writing, all of the recent digital media and gadgets that are popular among youth, from Tivo to Nintendo's Wii, have unprecedented levels and ever-richer forms of interactivity.

Navigability Cues

The navigability affordance (i.e., interface features that suggest transportation from one location to another, in keeping with the space metaphors such as "site" and "cyberspace" applied to digital media), more than others, has the dual ability to directly trigger heuristics with different navigational aids on the interface as well as to transmit cues through the content that it generates. To illustrate, the sheer presence of hierarchically organized hyperlinks on a Web site may trigger its own heuristic (e.g., well-organized, easily navigable sites are more credible[91]); in addition, the words on the hyperlinks themselves may trigger a different heuristic, one pertaining more to the nature of content on the site.

The structure of the Web and other digital media allows the interface designer to mimic the nature of the human memory system, particularly the processing of information through associative links.[92] Unlike traditional print media, there is no longer a need to follow a linear narrative style. Instead, the layout could allow users to navigate to different places and process information in a nonlinear fashion. This creates both an opportunity and a challenge for the site architect. Therefore, the hallmark of a good site lies in the ingenuity of its navigational design.

On the one hand, a site that is full of links could cue the *browsing heuristic* and encourage users to skim the site and "check out" the various links. In particular, global and local navigation menus significantly aid the browsing task compared with a simple-selection menu or a pull-down menu.[93] Displaying links in list format as opposed to embedding them within paragraphs[94] is likely to cue the browsing heuristic. On the other hand, a site with a rich layer of hyperlinks, especially if they are interwoven into the main content in a visually integrated way, could give users pause and make them wonder about the relationship between a given link's content and the site's main content,[95] leading to elaborative processing and higher knowledge-structure density.[96] We shall call this the *elaboration heuristic*.

There is evidence for the operation of both browsing and elaboration heuristics during Web use, perhaps simultaneously. Byrne et al. found that users simply read information the vast majority of the time, followed by browsing in search of "something interesting."[97] So, there is clearly a tradeoff between triggering the browsing and the elaboration heuristic, and navigational tools on the site can go a long way in aiding and nurturing these two competing heuristics, probably conditioned by the user's own style of thinking. Regardless of which one of the two heuristics is invoked, their impact on the site's credibility is likely to be positive. While elaboration will likely foster an impression of completeness,[98] the browsing heuristic is likely to give users a positive sense of the lack of bias, verifiability, and variety of offerings on the site.

Good navigability in digital media goes beyond simply providing hyperlinks in various forms. Many, if not most, devices and sites feature navigational aids designed to orient users to the mediated environment and sometimes lead them through particular prescribed paths for maximizing the efficiency of their experience. A clearly organized hierarchical layout of links that lends itself to an effortless visual search is shown to be quite effective in aiding navigation, even when there are a large number of items to display.[99] A map is a common example of a navigational aid, with proven benefits in assisting navigation,[100] and "landmarks" have been known to vastly aid the navigability of virtual environments.[101] Greater visualization in general has a beneficial effect on performance, with users giving positive ratings to orienting features such as the ability to mark user-defined locations in a virtual environment and to quickly undo actions.[102] Typically, most individuals are willing users of such navigational aids and express markedly higher satisfaction when the technology saves them effort.[103]

To users, these aids may cue the *scaffolding heuristic*, whereby they understand the role of navigational aids as helping them. In addition to encouraging a sincere use of the aids offered, this heuristic should also engender an appreciation for the benevolence of the designer. Scaffolding is particularly useful when using new tools[104] and in redesign efforts,[105] and is likely to go a long way in alleviating disorientation, perhaps the single biggest problem with—and complaint about—new media. By improving the clarity, understandability, and appearance of the environment, scaffolding serves to improve representational information quality[106] and thereby credibility perceptions.

Scaffolding can take many forms, including inducing particular affective states in users with specific skill levels. Akin to the flow heuristic triggered by the interactivity affordance, the navigability affordance may cue the *play heuristic* whereby users, especially young people, experience both enjoyment and escapism while using a digital device or site—what Shneiderman[107] calls "fun-in-doing." Interface elements that adjust to the user's skill level and offer highly involving content are likely to trigger a sense of leisure as well as psychological immersion. For anyone who has observed youth during the course of their interaction with a digital system, especially while they are engaged in navigational activities, the play element should be obvious. Perceived play during online search has been shown to be positively associated with attitudes toward the Web site,[108] which may carry over to credibility perceptions.

Getting back to cognitive functions, the critical service rendered by the navigability affordance is in providing cues related to the relative importance of content that one encounters during navigation. Traditional media have well-established ways of communicating prominence of content, by way of bold headlines on the front page, the amount of time devoted to a story on the evening news, and so on. By eschewing gatekeeping for the most part, digital media are left with a tremendous amount of searchable content that has not been formally vetted by professional information brokers. As a result, users are often left with uncertainties regarding the quality of information obtained while navigating.

But, they have adapted. And they use rules that are sometimes problematic, but nevertheless useful. For example, when one encounters the output of a search engine, the first few hits are likely to be the most prominent in terms of initiating further exploration. This is how the search engine cues the *prominence heuristic*—by simply listing the various hits. Some search engines rank the list based on popularity, which clearly privileges established pages and hurts new pages,[109] but researchers are constantly coming up with numerous other criteria for their search algorithms. Ultimately, the credibility of a navigational tool (and by extension the site) will be judged on the basis of the degree to which its output lives up to content expectations created by the prominence heuristic. This is an example of a heuristic that was probably not envisioned by the designers, but one that users decided to follow on their own, based perhaps on habituation with primacy cues in traditional media (e.g., the most important comes first, as in the inverted pyramid newspaper paradigm). As a result, technology design may want to respond to this established heuristic by devising algorithms that would display search results in an order that conforms to psychological expectations.

Perhaps to counter this problem, search engines and other navigational tools have started providing autogenerated cues that seem designed to trigger the *similarity heuristic*. The relevance ranking on some search engines is an example, whereby each hit is accompanied by a rank or score that indicates the degree to which its content matches the search query. This is essentially an automated way of communicating the value of the "information scent"[110] provided by the "proximal cues" in the search engine output. In the literature on information foraging theory,[111] the proximal cues refer to a preview of the actual content; for example, the title and one-sentence snapshot of the hit on the search results page. This is said to emit a scent about the information at the other end of the link. Depending on the user's goals, this scent may be strong or weak, which would then determine the likelihood of clicking on a particular hit. Decisions about the strength of the scent are made by applying the similarity heuristic, which is basically a judgment rule pertaining to the degree of perceived similarity between one's objectives and the promised information.

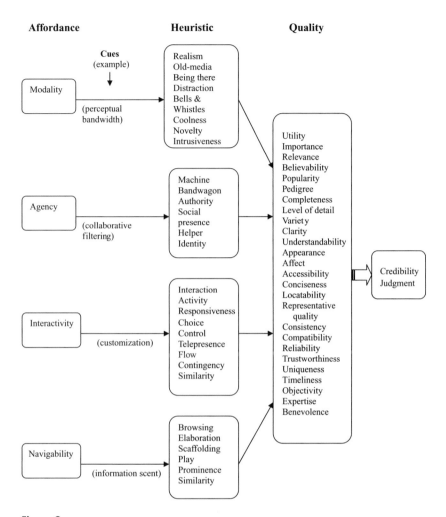

Figure 2
The MAIN Model.

News aggregators also feature automated means of conveying the value of information scent. Google News, for example, offers three distinct "news cues," one each pertaining to source identity, recency, and number of related articles. Each of these is known to cue its own heuristic pertaining to believability, timeliness, and expertise, respectively,[112] but overall, they serve to trigger the similarity heuristic in that they aid the user in making a decision regarding the potential similarity between their interest (to gather news with some particular specifications) and the available stories through the aggregator. Similarity is likely to influence the perception of relevance and thereby contribute to perceived credibility of the cue-providing mechanism, the aggregator in this case.

In sum, the navigability affordance of digital media serves to cue a variety of heuristics that operate at different levels. While the browsing and the play heuristics predispose users to view the navigational structure in terms of variety-seeking and pleasurable psychological immersion, which are particularly salient and prevalent among today's youth, the elaboration and scaffolding heuristics promote a more cognitively intense stance toward the digital medium. Autogenerated navigational aids trigger prominence and similarity heuristics by way of information scent embedded in the content of the output produced by these aids. All these heuristics contribute to credibility assessments by highlighting the relevance, completeness, clarity, and utility of the underlying information.

A simplified, visual representation of the complete MAIN model is shown in Figure 2. The list of cues and heuristics is not exhaustive. Not all cues trigger all the listed heuristics and not all heuristics result in quality evaluations along all the listed criteria. The particular quality evaluations motivated by certain heuristics and the specific heuristics triggered by certain cues were discussed in turn in the preceding sections.

Discussion

Which of the various cues embedded in the four classes of affordances discussed thus far is/are likely to be triggered during a given interaction with the digital medium may depend on the device, user, and context of use, but to the extent that an interface contains features, functions, or simply messages that may cue these heuristics, they are likely to be psychologically significant in shaping user assessments of credibility of the interface, system, and the content within. In general, the broad argument forwarded by the MAIN model is that technological affordances relating to modality, agency, interactivity, and navigability help to explain the perceived credibility of digital media and their offerings, beyond what is explained by content characteristics. Furthermore, it makes the case that these affordances have the power to amplify or diminish content effects on credibility because they indeed deliver the user to the content, and could play this role of a moderator in a variety of psychologically distinct ways.

With their sheer presence, these affordances can trigger heuristics that are likely to predispose users to experience content in a certain way. There can be several layers of heuristics in any digital medium. For example, the very operation of a news aggregator is likely to trigger the machine heuristic given that an algorithm (and not a person) is advertised on the site as performing the gatekeeping function. Moreover, the autogenerated cues relating to recency and source identity in each news lead (produced by the aggregator) are likely to cue the similarity heuristic. Under this condition, the similarity heuristic is operating in the context of a machine heuristic, but a hierarchy prevails such that the machine heuristic is the overarching one and the similarity heuristic is invoked within its realm. Chances are that the effects of the similarity heuristic on credibility may be different, at least in degree if not in kind, when it is triggered in the context of some other overarching heuristic.

While the reality of digital media use is likely to be characterized by the joint operation of several heuristics, it is probably more manageable for researchers to study the cueing of individual heuristics and document their respective contributions to credibility perceptions first. Once our knowledge of their operation is advanced, scholars may be able to propose and test complex interactions between cues and between heuristics. The beauty is that it is relatively simple to ascertain the nature of a heuristic's operation. Unlike some intervening variables in psychological mediation models, heuristics are judgment rules that users employ, which means they carry in their heads a theoretical connection between the presence of a cue and the relevant credibility judgment. So, the users construct and apply the theory, and the researcher simply has to elicit it from them, instead of having to come up with the theoretical connection. Although the elicitation of automatically generated heuristics may prove complicated, self-reports can reliably ascertain the conscious rules of thumb that form the basis of many day-to-day heuristics.

In addition to aiding researchers, the MAIN model offers certain design advantages. These days, the technology community has embraced the idea of involving lay users in the design and development of interfaces. A case in point is the participatory design movement within the human-computer interaction community known as Interaction Design and Children (IDC), which involves working with children as technology design partners.[113] Heuristics used by young people could serve as powerful sources of input for design decisions pertaining to new digital devices and venues because they are likely to result in decisions that are psychologically meaningful to this specific user population, and not simply those driven by engineering considerations. In general, the heuristics-based approach to ascertaining young users' responses to affordances (current and future, hypothetical as well as real) can be used to build effective learning systems in the digital media universe. It will hopefully motivate design innovations that equip interfaces with meaningful features that capitalize on the cues identified in such an analysis for effectively and accurately conveying, as well as assessing, the credibility of accessed information.

In conclusion, the heuristics-based approach advocated here is far more realistic than the checklist approach to credibility evaluations[114] (which, as Metzger points out, is ineffective) because it taps into the natural, automatic ways in which youth make implicit credibility judgments during their interactions with digital media. The list of heuristics in this chapter is by no means exhaustive. At the current time, judging by the success of recent digital media devices, we can say that youth are prone to associate credibility with such surface aspects as trendiness, bandwagon, choice, and play (to name just a few of the heuristics reviewed here). Given many youth's preoccupation with procuring, enjoying, and showing off new gadgets and new features on those gadgets, the four classes of technological affordances identified by the MAIN model are clearly implicated in contributing cues to these surface aspects or heuristics.

As we learn more about the various heuristics that are applied to affordances by young people and how they might influence credibility judgments, we will not only enhance our understanding of the seemingly conflicting findings in the literature about the psychological effects of various affordances, but also gain some insights for promoting critical consumption of digital media in the future. These pointers can in turn constitute training material for media literacy campaigns targeted at young people and new users of the Internet. An understanding of the processes by which technological affordances influence perceived credibility can inform policy concerning adoption of design and technology standards for recognizing, rating, and otherwise distinguishing credible information from the mass of noncredible information in the digital universe.

Notes

1. See, e.g., *Teenage Life Online: The Rise of the Instant-Message Generation and the Internet's Impact on Friendships and Family Relationships* (Pew Internet & American Life Project, June 20, 2001), http://www.pewinternet.org (retrieved November 15, 2006).

2. S. Shyam Sundar, *Self as Source: Agency and Customization in Interactive Media* (paper presented at the 56th annual conference of the International Communication Association, Dresden, Germany).

3. See Andrew J. Flanagin and Miriam J. Metzger, Digital Media and Youth: Unparalleled Opportunity and Unprecedented Responsibility, this volume, for a fuller discussion of these issues.

4. S. Shyam Sundar and Clifford Nass, Source Orientation in Human-Computer Interaction: Programmer, Networker, or Independent Social Actor? *Communication Research* 27, no. 6 (2000): 683–703.

5. Miriam J. Metzger, Andrew J. Flanagin, D. R. Lemus, and R. M. McCann, Credibility in the 21st Century: Integrating Perspectives on Source, Message, and Media Credibility in the Contemporary Media Environment, in *Communication Yearbook* 27, ed. Pamela Kalbfleisch (Newbury Park, CA: Sage, 2003), 293–335.

6. B. J. Fogg, Motivating, Influencing, and Persuading Users, in *The Human-Computer Interaction Handbook: Fundamentals, Evolving Technologies and Emerging Applications*, ed. Julie A. Jacko and Andrew Sears (Mahwah, NJ: Erlbaum, 2003), 358–70; Ben Shneiderman, Designing Trust Into Online Experiences, *Communications of the ACM* 43, no. 12 (2000): 57–59.

7. Richard E. Petty and John T. Cacioppo, *Communication and Persuasion: Central and Peripheral Routes to Attitude Change* (New York: Springer-Verlag, 1986).

8. Shelly Chaiken, Heuristic and Systematic Information Processing and the Use of Source Versus Message Cues in Persuasion, *Journal of Personality and Social Psychology* 39 (1980): 752–66; Shelly Chaiken, The Heuristic Model of Persuasion, in *Social Influence: The Ontario Symposium* 5, ed. Mark P. Zanna, James M. Olson, and C. Peter Herman (Hillsdale, NJ: Erlbaum 1987), 3–39.

9. Serena Chen and Shelly Chaiken, The Heuristic-Systematic Model in Its Broader Context, in *Dual Process Theories in Social Psychology*, ed. Shelly Chaiken and Yaacov Trope (New York: Guilford, 1999), 73–96.

10. Richard M. Shiffrin and Walter Schneider, Controlled and Automatic Human Information Processing: II. Perceptual Learning, Automatic Attending and a General Theory, *Psychological Review* 84 (1997): 127–89.

11. John A. Bargh and Tanya Chartrand, The Unbearable Automaticity of Being, *American Psychologist* 54, no. 7 (1999): 462–79.

12. Chen and Chaiken, The Heuristic-Systematic Model.

13. James Gibson, The Theory of Affordances, in *Perceiving, Acting, and Knowing: Toward an Ecological Psychology*, ed. Robert Shaw and John Bransford (Hillsdale, NJ: Erlbaum, 1977).

14. Marshall McLuhan, *Understanding Media* (New York: Signet, 1964).

15. Mihalyi Csikszentmihalyi and Robert Kubey, Television and the Rest of Life: A Systematic Comparison of Subjective Experience, *Public Opinion Quarterly* 45, no. 3 (1981): 317–28.

16. Donald A. Norman, Affordances, Conventions and Design, *Interactions* 6, no. 3 (1999): 38–43.

17. S. Shyam Sundar, Kenneth Hesser, Sriram Kalyanaraman, and Justin Brown, *The Effect of Website Interactivity on Political Persuasion* (paper presented at the 21st General Assembly & Scientific Conference of the International Association for Media and Communication Research, Glasgow, UK, June 1998).

18. B. J. Fogg, Cathy Soohoo, David R. Danielson, Leslie Marable, Julianne Stanford, and Ellen R.Tauber, *How Do Users Evaluate the Credibility of Web Sites? A Study with Over 2,500 Participants* (paper presented at the ACM conference on Designing for User Experiences, San Francisco, CA, 2003).

19. Shawn Tseng and B. J. Fogg, Credibility and Computing Technology, *Communication of the ACM* 42, no. 5 (1999): 39–44.

20. C. Nadine Wathen and Jacquelyn Burkell, Believe It or Not: Factors Influencing Credibility on the Web, *Journal of the American Society for Information Science and Technology* 53, no. 2 (2002): 134–44.

21. Pamela Briggs, Bryan Burford, Antonella De Angeli, and Paula Lynch, Trust in Online Advice, *Social Science Computer Review* 20, no. 3 (2002): 321–32.

22. Miriam Metzger, Making Sense of Credibility on the Web: Models for Evaluating Online Information and Recommendations for Future Research, *Journal of the American Society for Information Science and Technology* 58, no. 10 (2007).

23. Wendy R. Bolletin, Can Information Technology Improve Education, *Educom Review* 33, no. 1 (1998), http://www.educause.edu/pub/er/review/reviewarticles/33150.html (retrieved January 10, 2007); Sharon Kopyc, Enhancing Teaching with Technology: Are We There Yet? *Innovate* 3, no. 2 (2006), http://www.innovateonline.info/index.php?view=article&id=74 (retrieved January 3, 2007); Jeffrey R. Young, When Good Technology Means Bad Teaching, *The Chronicle of Higher Education* (June 2004): A31.

24. Gunther Eysenbach, John Powell, Oliver Kuss, and Eun-Ryoung Sa, Empirical Studies Assessing the Quality of Health Information for Consumers on the World Wide Web: A Systematic Review, *Journal of the American Medical Association* 287, no. 20 (2002): 2691–700.

25. Susan Fiske and Shelley Taylor, *Social Cognition* (Reading, MA: Addison-Wesley, 1984).

26. S. Shyam Sundar, Sriram Kalyanaraman, and Justin Brown, Explicating Website Interactivity: Impression-Formation Effects in Political Campaign Sites, *Communication Research* 30, no. 1 (2003): 30–59.

27. S. Shyam Sundar, Silvia Knobloch-Westerwick, and Matthias R. Hastall, News Cues: Information Scent and Cognitive Heuristics, *Journal of the American Society for Information Science and Technology* 58, no. 3 (2007): 366–78.

28. See especially Fogg et al., *How Do Users Evaluate the Credibility of Web Sites?*; and Elizabeth Sillence, Pam Briggs, Lesley Fishwick, and Peter Harris, Trust and Mistrust of Online Health Sites, *Proceedings of the Conference on Human Factors in Computing Systems (ACM SIGCHI)* 6, no. 1 (2004): 663–70.

29. S. Shyam Sundar, Social Psychology of Interactivity in Human–Website Interaction, in *Oxford Handbook of Internet Psychology*, ed. Adam Joinson, Katelyn McKenna, Ulf-Dietrich Reips and Tom Postmes (Oxford, UK: Oxford University Press, 2007), 89–102.

30. Erik P. Bucy, The Interactivity Paradox: Closer to the News but Confused, in *Media Access: Social and Psychological Dimensions of New Technology Use*, ed. Erik P. Bucy and John E. Newhagen (Mahwah, NJ: Erlbaum, 2003), 47–72.

31. See, for example, Martijn Hoogeveen, Towards a Theory of the Effectiveness of Multimedia Systems, *International Journal of Human-Computer Interaction* 9 (1997): 151–68.

32. Gibson, The Theory of Affordances.

33. Norman, Affordances, Conventions and Design.

34. Elliot McGinnies and Charles Ward, Better Liked Than Right: Trustworthiness and Expertise as Factors in Credibility, *Personality and Social Psychology Bulletin* 6, no. 2 (1980): 467–72.

35. Richard F. Carter and Bradley S. Greenberg, Newspapers or Television: Which Do You Believe? *Journalism Quarterly* 42 (1965): 35–42.

36. Byron Reeves and Clifford Nass, *The Media Equation: How People Treat Computers, Television, and New Media Like Real People and Places* (New York: Cambridge University Press/CSLI, 1996); John A. Short, Ederyn Williams, and Bruce Christie, *The Social Psychology of Telecommunications* (New York: Wiley, 1976).

37. S. Shyam Sundar, Multimedia Effects on Processing and Perception of Online News: A Study of Picture, Audio, and Video Downloads, *Journalism & Mass Communication Quarterly* 77, no. 3 (2000): 480–99.

38. Jonathan Steuer, Defining Virtual Reality: Dimensions Determining Telepresence, *Journal of Communication* 42 (1992): 73–93; Byron Reeves and Clifford Nass, Perceptual Bandwidth, *Communications of the ACM* 43, no. 3 (2000): 65–70.

39. Sundar, Multimedia Effects on Processing and Perception of Online News.

40. Hans Marmolin, Multimedia from the Perspectives of Psychology, in *Multimedia: Systems, Interactions and Applications, 1st Eurographics Workshop, Stockholm, Sweden April 18–19, 1991*, ed. Lars Kjelldahl (Berlin, Germany: Springer-Verlag, 1991).

41. Sharon Oviatt, Multimodal Interfaces, in *The Human-Computer Interaction Handbook: Fundamentals, Evolving Technologies and Emerging Applications*, ed. Julie A. Jacko and Andrew Sears (Mahwah, NJ: Erlbaum, 2003): 286–304.

42. Jo Best, Pop-ups "Commercial Suicide" for Firms, *silicom.com*, February 2004, http://www.com/hardware/storage/0,39024649,39118629,00.htm (retrieved July 2, 2004); Stefanie Olsen, Google Distances Itself from Pop-ups, *CNet* [Online] (January 29, 2002), http://news.com.com/2100-1023-825507.html (retrieved July 2, 2004).

43. Flanagin and Metzger, Digital Media and Youth.

44. S. Shyam Sundar and Clifford Nass, Conceptualizing Sources in Online News, *Journal of Communication* 51, no. 1 (2001): 52–72.

45. Ibid.

46. Silvia Knobloch-Westerwick, Nikhil Sharma, Derek L. Hansen, and Scott Alter, Impact of Popularity Indications on Readers' Selective Exposure to Online News, *Journal of Broadcasting and Electronic Media* 49, no. 3 (2005): 296–313.

47. See Flanagin and Metzger, Digital Media and Youth.

48. Gunther Eysenbach and Christian Köhler, How Do Consumers Search for and Appraise Health Information on the World Wide Web? Qualitative Study Using Focus Groups, Usability Tests, and In-depth Interviews, *British Medical Journal* 324 (2002): 573–77.

49. Sundar, Knobloch-Westerwick, and Hastall, News Cues.

50. Justine Cassell, Embodied Conversational Interface Agents, *Communications of the ACM* 43, no. 4 (2000): 70–78.

51. Sundar and Nass, Source Orientation in Human-Computer Interaction.

52. Reeves and Nass, *The Media Equation*.

53. S. Shyam Sundar, Loyalty to Computer Terminals: Is It Anthropomorphism or Consistency? *Behaviour & Information Technology* 23, no. 2 (2004): 107–18.

54. Katherine Isbister and Clifford Nass, Consistency of Personality in Interactive Characters: Verbal Cues, Non-verbal Cues, and User Characteristics, *International Journal of Human-Computer Studies* 53 (2000): 251–67; Kwan M. Lee and Clifford Nass, Designing Social Presence of Social Actors in Human Computer Interaction, *Proceedings of the Conference on Human Factors in Computing Systems (ACM SIGCHI)* 5, no. 1 (2003): 289–96.

55. Carey E. Heckman and Jacob O. Wobbrock, Put Your Best Face Forward: Anthropomorphic Agents, E-Commerce Consumers, and the Law, in *Proceedings of the ACM Conference on Autonomous Agents (Agents*

2000), Barcelona, Spain, June 2000, 435–43; Youngme Moon, Intimate Exchanges: Using Computers to Elicit Self-disclosure from Consumers, *Journal of Consumer Research* 26, no. 4 (2000): 323–39.

56. Jonathan Klein, Youngme Moon, and Rosalind W. Picard, This Computer Responds to User Frustration: Theory, Design, and Results, *Interacting with Computers* 14 (2002): 119–40; Timo Partala and Veikko Surakka, The Effects of Affective Interventions in Human-Computer Interaction, *Interacting with Computers* 16 (2004): 295–309.

57. Moon, Intimate Exchanges.

58. Sherry Turkle, *Life on the Screen: Identity in the Age of the Internet* (New York: Simon & Schuster, 1995).

59. Sundar, *Self as Source*.

60. Sundar, Kalyanaraman, and Brown, Explicating Website Interactivity.

61. Csikszentmihalyi and Kubey, Television and the Rest of Life; William Paisley, Computerizing Information: Lessons of a Videotext Trial, *Journal of Communication* 33 (1983): 153–61.

62. Dolf Zillmann, Mood Management: Using Entertainment to Full Advantage, in *Communication, Social Cognition, and Affect*, ed. Lewis Donohew, Howard E. Sypher, and Edward T. Higgins (Hillsdale, NJ: Erlbaum, 1988): 147–71.

63. Linda Schamber, Users' Criteria for Evaluation in a Multimedia Environment, in *Proceedings of the 54th Annual Meeting of the American Society for Information Science 28*, ed. José-Marie Griffiths (Medford, NJ: Learned Information, 1991): 126–33.

64. See Metzger et al., Credibility in the 21st Century.

65. Schamber, Users' Criteria for Evaluation in a Multimedia Environment.

66. Carrie Heeter, Implications of New Interactive Technologies for Conceptualizing Communication, in *Media in the Information Age: Emerging Patterns of Adoption and Consumer Use*, ed. Jerry Salvaggio and Jennings Bryant (Hillsdale, NJ: Erlbaum, 1989): 217–35.

67. Sheena S. Iyengar and Mark R. Lepper, When Choice Is Demotivating: Can One Desire Too Much of a Good Thing? *Journal of Personality and Social Psychology* 79, no. 6 (2000): 995–1006.

68. Richard Y. Wang, A Product Perspective on Total Data Quality Management, *Commmunications of the ACM* 41, no. 2 (1998): 58–65.

69. Richard Y. Wang and Diane M. Strong, Beyond Accuracy: What Data Quality Means to Data Consumers, *Journal of Management Information Systems* 12, no. 4 (1996): 5–34.

70. Ibid.

71. Dale L. Goodhue, Understanding User Evaluation of Information Systems, *Management Science* 41, no. 12 (1995): 1827–44.

72. Barry Schwartz, Self-Determination: The Tyranny of Freedom, *American Psychologist* 55 (2000): 79–88.

73. Frederick Williams, Ronald E. Rice, and Everett M. Rogers, *Research Methods and the New Media* (New York: Free Press, 1988).

74. William P. Eveland Jr. and Sharon Dunwoody, An Investigation of Elaboration and Selective Scanning as Mediators of Learning from the Web Versus Print, *Journal of Broadcasting & Electronic Media* 46, no. 1 (2002): 34–53; Katelyn Y. A. McKenna and John A. Bargh, Plan 9 from Cyberspace: The Implications of the Internet for Personality and Social Psychology, *Personality and Social Psychology Review* 4, no. 1 (2000): 57–75.

75. Yang W. Lee, Diane M. Strong, Beverly K. Kahn, and Richard Y. Wang, AIMQ: A Methodology for Information Quality Assessment, *Information & Management* 40 (2002): 133–46.

76. Dan Ariely, Controlling the Information Flow: Effects on Consumers' Decision Making and Preferences, *Journal of Consumer Research* 27, no. 2 (2000): 233–48.

77. Steuer, Defining Virtual Reality.

78. James R. Coyle and Esther Thorson, The Effects of Progressive Levels of Interactivity and Vividness in Web Marketing Sites, *Journal of Advertising* 30, no. 3 (2001): 65–77.

79. S. Shyam Sundar and Sriram Kalyanaraman, Arousal, Memory, and Impression-Formation Effects of Animation Speed in Web Advertising, *Journal of Advertising* 33, no. 1 (2004): 7–17; S. Shyam Sundar and Carson B Wagner, The World Wide Wait: Exploring Physiological and Behavioral Effects of Download Speed, *Media Psychology* 4 (2002): 173–206.

80. Mihalyi Csikszentmihalyi, *Flow: The Psychology of Optimal Experience* (New York: Harper & Row, 1990).

81. Lee et al., AIMQ: A Methodology for Information Quality Assessment.

82. Clifford Nass and Youngme Moon, Machines and Mindlessness: Social Responses to Computers, *Journal of Social Issues* 56, no. 1 (2000): 81–103.

83. Sheizaf Rafaeli, Interactivity: From New Media to Communication, in *Advancing Communication Science: Merging Mass and Interpersonal Processes*, ed. Robert Hawkins, John Weimann, and Suzanne Pingree (Newbury Park, CA: Sage, 1988): 124–81.

84. John Pavlik, *New Media Technology: Cultural and Commercial Perspectives* (Boston: Allyn and Bacon, 1996); Harper A. Roehm and Curt P. Haugtvedt, Understanding Interactivity of Cyberspace Advertising, in *Advertising and the World Wide Web*, ed. David W. Schumann and Esther Thorson (Mahwah, NJ: Erlbaum, 1991): 27–39; Williams, Rice, and Rogers, *Research Methods and the New Media*.

85. John December, Units of Analysis for Internet Communication, *Journal of Communication* 46 (1996): 14–38; Sundar and Nass, Conceptualizing Sources in Online News.

86. Sundar, *Self as Source*.

87. S. Shyam Sundar and Sampada Marathe, *Is It Tailoring or Is It Agency? Unpacking the Psychological Appeal of Customized News* (paper presented at the 89th annual convention of the Association for Education in Journalism and Mass Communication, San Francisco, CA, August 2006).

88. Jan O. Blom and Andrew F. Monk, Theory of Personalization of Appearance: Why Users Personalize Their PCs and Mobile Phones, *Human-Computer Interaction* 18 (2003): 193–228.

89. Ramnath K. Chellappa and Raymond G. Sin, Personalization versus Privacy: An Empirical Examination of the Online Consumer's Dilemma, *Information Technology and Management* 6 (2005): 181–202.

90. Yuping Liu and L. J. Shrum, What Is Interactivity and Is It Always Such a Good Thing? Implications of Definition, Person, and Situation for the Influence of Interactivity on Advertising Effectiveness, *Journal of Advertising* 31, no. 4 (2002): 53–64.

91. As found by Fogg et al., *How Do Users Evaluate the Credibility of Web Sites?*

92. William P. Eveland Jr., Juliann Cortese, Heesun Park, and Sharon Dunwoody, How Web Site Organization Influences Free Recall, Factual Knowledge, and Knowledge Structure, *Human Communication Research* 30 (2004): 208–33.

93. Byeong-Min Yu and Seak-Zoon Roh, The Effects of Menu Design on Information-Seeking Performance and User's Attitude on the World Wide Web, *Journal of the American Society for Information Science and Technology* 53, no. 11 (2002): 923–33.

94. Kushal Khan and Craig Locatis, Searching through Cyberspace: The Effects of Link Display and Link Density on Information Retrieval from Hypertext on the World Wide Web, *Journal of the American Society for Information Science and Technology* 49, no. 2 (1998): 176–82.

95. Eveland and Dunwoody, An Investigation of Elaboration and Selective Scanning.

96. Eveland et al., How Web Site Organization Influences Free Recall.

97. Michael D. Byrne, Bonnie E. John, Neil S. Wehrle, and David C. Crow, The Tangled Web We Wove: A Taskonomy of WWW Use, in *Proceedings of the Conference on Human Factors in Computing Systems (ACM SIGCHI)* (1999): 544–51.

98. Wang and Strong, Beyond Accuracy.

99. Anthony J. Hornof, Cognitive Strategies for the Visual Search of Hierarchical Computer Displays, *Human-Computer Interaction* 19 (2004): 183–223.

100. Eyal Haik, Trevor Barker, John Sapsford, and Simon Trainis, *Investigation into Effective Navigation in Desktop Virtual Interfaces* (paper presented at the ACM conference on Web 3D, Tempe, AZ, February 2002).

101. Norman G. Vinson, Design Guidelines for Landmarks to Support Navigation in Virtual Environments, in *Proceedings of the Conference on Human Factors in Computing Systems (ACM SIGCHI)* (1999): 278–85.

102. H. Sayers, Desktop Virtual Environments: A Study of Navigation and Age, *Interacting with Computers* 16 (2004): 939–56.

103. Nada N. Bechwati and Lan Xia, Do Computers Sweat? The Impact of Perceived Effort of Online Decision Aids on Consumers' Satisfaction with the Decision Process, *Journal of Consumer Psychology* 13, no. 1–2 (2003): 139–48.

104. Kathleen Luchini, Chris Quintana, and Elliot Soloway, Design Guidelines for Learner-Centered Handheld Tools, *Proceedings of the Conference on Human Factors in Computing Systems (ACM SIGCHI)* 6, no. 1 (2004): 135–42.

105. Keith S. Jones, J. Shawn Farris, and Brian R. Johnson, Why Does the Negative Impact of Inconsistent Knowledge on Web Navigation Persist? *International Journal of Human-Computer Interaction* 19, no. 2 (2005): 201–21.

106. William H. Delone and Ephraim R. McLean, Information Systems Success: The Quest for the Dependent Variable, *Information Systems Research* 3, no. 1 (1992): 60–95.

107. Ben Shneiderman, Designing for Fun: How Can We Design User Interfaces to Be More Fun? *Interactions* (2004): 48–50.

108. Charla Mathwick and Edward Rigdon, Play, Flow, and the Online Search Experience, *Journal of Consumer Research* 31, no. 2 (2004): 324–32.

109. Junghoo Cho and Sourashis Roy, *Impact of Search Engines on Page Popularity* (paper presented at the ACM conference on WWW, New York, NY, 2004).

110. Peter Pirolli, Computational Models of Information-Scent Following in a Very Large Browsable Text Collection, in *Proceedings of the Conference on Human Factors in Computing Systems (CHI'97), Atlanta, GA* (New York, ACM Press, 1997): 3–10.

111. Pirolli and Card, Information Foraging.

112. Sundar, Knobloch-Westerwick, and Hastall, News Cues.

113. Allison Druin, The Role of Children in the Design of New Technology, *Behaviour & Information Technology* 21, no. 1 (2002): 1–25; Guha et al., Working with Young Children as Technology Design Partners; Gene Chipman, Jerry A. Fails, Sante Simms, and Allison Farber, Working with Young Children as Technology Design Partners, *Communications of the ACM* 48, no. 1 (2005): 39–42.

114. Metzger, Making Sense of Credibility on the Web.

Trusting the Internet: New Approaches to Credibility Tools

R. David Lankes

Syracuse University, School of Information Studies

It has been said that the Stone Age did not end because humans ran out of stones. Instead, Stone Age technology was superseded by new tools and capabilities. At some point in history, it simply became more advantageous to adopt new methods and tools rather than trying to solve problems inherent in older methods. Society may soon be at this inflection point in terms of how people, and particularly youth, identify credible information, abandoning traditional methods of determining credibility that are based on authority and hierarchy for digital tools and new network approaches. Far from being a negative development, new methods and tools for determining credibility may reflect a more distributed and open approach than in the past. Such an approach has important implications for how youth are educated, how policy is determined, and how future information systems are built.

This chapter first highlights some reasons why youth, the institutions that serve them, and society as a whole are moving online, as well as some of the consequences of this move—namely, the paradox of "information self-sufficiency." A reformulated vision of credibility is offered in this context, which highlights features of digital information and networks. Then, a shift among credibility tools and techniques from traditional authority models to more of a "reliability approach" is discussed. Based on this, a framework for understanding the implications of information self-sufficiency for learning in a networked digital world is presented. This framework is used to highlight the often invisible effects that technology has upon credibility. Finally, implications of this are explored and current and anticipated developments on the Internet are considered. The chapter concludes by discussing implications of the information self-sufficiency paradox in the context of the education of youth in the current digital media environment.

The Shift Toward Increased Information Self-Sufficiency

There is little doubt that in the United States and other developed countries, citizens are increasingly relying on the Internet to gather information. Seventy-three percent of U.S. adults are Internet users, and 42 percent of Americans (about 84 million) now have broadband connections at home, up from 29 percent in January 2005.[1] The numbers are even more striking for youth. Lenhart, Madden, and Hitlin recently reported that 87 percent of youth in the United States ages 12 to 17 are Internet users, 51 percent of whom say that they use the Internet on a daily basis.[2] Other estimates indicate that half of children in grades 1–5 are online, as are 80 percent of high school students.[3]

Increasing Internet reliance is also evidenced by the dramatic increase of self-service options available to Internet users. Today, individuals are expected to book their own airline tickets, determine their own retirement plans, and even decide between life-and-death medical treatments using Internet tools and information available on the Web, without the assistance of traditional information intermediaries.[4] However, the quality of these services varies. Examples of bad self-service options abound and nearly everyone has a horror story of getting tangled in a phone tree or diving deep into a company Web site desperately looking for a phone number to call or person to e-mail. Yet, there are also plenty of examples where online self-support systems and customer service have been designed and implemented well. Examples include Lands' End live chat support service[5] and package tracking through UPS, FedEx, and other overnight carriers, to name a few.

The trend toward online self-support services and "disintermediation" more generally[6] is also apparent in nonprofit and governmental sectors. For example, the National Science Foundation has supported extensive research into "digital government" that seeks to provide support of digital integration over a wide variety of government tasks such as electronic voting, public comments, security, and more.[7] In the K–12 arena, Rice discusses several national policy initiatives involving the use of digital media to expand educational opportunities for U.S. students.[8]

Youth in particular are increasingly dependant upon online systems and support. From homework help services such as Tutor.com to completely virtual high schools,[9] school-based learning is increasingly complimented by online services. As early as 2001, for example, Lenhart, Simon, and Graziano noted "71% of online teens say that they used the Internet as the major source for their most recent major school project or report."[10] This increasing use and reliance on the Internet means that for a growing percentage of students the quality of online services and self-support options can directly affect their learning.[11]

Presumably, the chief advantage to customers of online information self-sufficiency is greater control and satisfaction. However, this may not be the reality. ServiceXRG found that of the 60 percent of customers who used Web self-service, only 23 percent reported that they found what they were looking for online,[12] suggesting that only a small minority who choose to use online self-service features are able to find content that satisfies their needs. Thus, and ironically, many customers turned online actually require *additional* customer support. Unfortunately, such outcomes are not atypical.[13]

This shift to digital over physical media, however, is only partly a response to citizen demand for increased self-service. Another important factor is economic pressure felt by organizations to minimize cost by eliminating expenses such as printing and customer service personnel. According to the Web consulting firm Adaptive Path, in the last few years companies have "pushed labor-intensive tasks out to the customer, and they did so in a way that provided the customers with direct access to and control over information that they care about."[14] The advantage to organizations is substantial cost savings. For example, ServiceXRG, a market research firm, found that whereas first contact closure cost of phone transactions is $49.10, it is $36.70 when done via e-mail, and only $11.60 via Web self-service.[15]

The awkwardness with which some organizations have shifted the responsibility of support from employees to users is understandable given that the transition to digital methods of information creation, storage, analysis, and distribution has happened in an astoundingly short period of time. In less than fourteen years, the U.S. federal government, for example, has gone from mandating executive agency Web sites (initially little more than simple online brochures), to requiring electronic voting,[16] Web-based submittals of grant applications,[17] and electronic banking transactions. There simply has been too little time and too much change in the Internet environment to formalize and codify "good online service." To put it bluntly, what users need in order to take charge of their own online decision making is at best an art and, more often than not, a series of trial-and-error solutions.

Moreover, what may be called "information self-sufficiency" or "disintermediation" is far from an Internet-only phenomenon. Anyone who has checked into a flight at the airport knows that the number of touch screens is steeply on the rise, while ticket agents are in steep decline. Libraries now have self-checkout kiosks as do grocery and other retail stores. Information self-sufficiency is obvious in a world where so many aspects of life are either online (e.g., online banking, music downloads, shopping, medical information, government documents access) or are facilitated by online transactions (e.g., electronic fund transfers, traffic management systems, automated payroll systems). In the end, information self-sufficiency has dramatic impact: it affects how products are marketed, how organizations manage information, how courts assess liability, and even how the current and future workforce is trained.

Information Self-Sufficiency and the Heightened Importance of Credibility

Although information self-sufficiency could (and should) be examined in a number of ways—including economic, political, and even in terms of social and class roles—this chapter concentrates on the effects of information self-sufficiency on credibility, or the believability (i.e., the trustworthiness and expertise) of some source of information. Indeed, credibility, particularly in the context of youth and the Internet, is fundamental to the long-term success of information self-sufficiency and, by implication, the success of digital media themselves. An emphasis on credibility is crucial in the success of society's digital migration because information is increasingly disconnected from its physical origin and, as a consequence, the credibility of information has taken on new complexities, with new implications.

Consider the simple act of buying a book over the Internet. When people buy a book online, they are not basing their buying decision on a single, physical item. They are instead basing the buying decision on information *about* a book (e.g., its price, author, shipping terms, reviews). Even if they had previously checked the book out of a library, or paged through it at the local bookstore (where they could have bought the book based on the information it contained *and* the physical attributes of the book such as whether it is in good shape, etc.), in the online environment they are simply putting in an order for a book based on some proxy, such as a digital image of a physical item.

This seemingly mundane and obvious fact actually has sweeping implications for credibility on the Internet. In particular, for any online transaction that involves delivery of some physical item, a central means of determining credibility—physical examination and testing—is gone, or is at least greatly diminished (since one can usually return the book after a physical inspection at the end of the process). No more is it possible to review a signature to make sure it is original. No more is examination of the quality of paper used in a publication practical. No more can one audit a physical inventory prior to purchase.

Another example that serves to illustrate the point is a digital fingerprinting system for use by law enforcement personnel in New York State. When suspects are arrested, instead of inking fingers and making cards with copies of fingerprints, in many jurisdictions prisoners now place their fingers on glass and have them digitized. The system was intended to speed up processing of fingerprints, and to make them more accessible for searches (P. Lorenzo, personal communication). However, removing the physical collection of fingerprints had an unintended consequence. At one arrest a processing officer took a suspect's name and date of birth, and simply copied a fingerprint already stored under that name and date of birth into the new case file (which was against policy). It turns out the date of birth and name given by the suspect were false, and the prints copied belonged to a prisoner already incarcerated. More striking, when the mistake was revealed, and the suspect's prints were actually scanned, it was discovered that he was wanted for another crime—murder. This mistake was possible, and undetectable, in a digital networked environment because every transaction is an information-only event: that is, transactions exist only as digital information with no physical record or artifact. As such, some transactions work better in the digital environment than others.

For example, while buying books online has become popular, buying homes online is still a rarity. This is due both to the size of the transaction, and also to how much of an object's information is intrinsic and how much is extrinsic to its physical form.[18] The more mass produced and standardized an item is, the more information can be "separated out" from that item. In the case of the book, nearly all of the information within the book—including the author, the price, the title, and even the visual images of the pages themselves—can be recreated accurately in digital form. Thus, the information is extrinsic to the physical item. With a house, however, the condition of the roof, the true color of the paint, the "feel" of the neighborhood, and the creakiness of the floors are all intrinsic qualities that need physical inspection to assess accurately. This also explains why buying a new car online is not only possible, but is a growing industry. Although it is a large transaction, new cars are fairly standard, so a test drive of a car in New York is assumed to be identical to test driving the same make and model in California. Therefore, buying that new car in California does not require a second test drive. The same cannot be said of a house. Houses are unique, and so the information relevant to a buying decision is intrinsic to the house.

Since information is the only evidence available to people when making an online transaction (e.g., buying something, talking to someone, learning about something), the credibility of that information is essential. Moreover, methods of building trust, and methods to test assertions have changed. For example, if one goes to buy a book online, that person can no longer test the book to see if it is complete and in good condition prior to delivery. They must now trust the online vendor of that book. This is the great paradox in information self-sufficiency on the Internet: *end users are becoming more responsible for making information determinations, but because they have fewer physical cues to work with, they are becoming more dependent on the information provided to them by others.*

This paradox is complicated further by the fact that people are simply unable to, or fail to, recognize many of the more technical influences on the information with which they are provided in the first place. In fact, there is a great deal of information manipulation that occurs that is *never* perceptible to the user. Built into the tools themselves are filters, assumptions, biases, and outright distortions that can never be factored into a user's credibility decision.[19] Indeed, there has been much discussion and research of how the media used to access information can affect perceptions of the credibility of that information.[20] There have also been a number of studies into how the online environment itself affects credibility.[21] Together, this work highlights how credibility can be both determined and manipulated by technical elements, such as load time of Web pages or site design.[22] Research also points out that while technology influences credibility decisions, it is often invisible to the end user.[23]

Perhaps because these things are so invisible to most people, this point is completely missed in many examinations of how users make credibility decisions online.

Youth in particular are increasingly dependent on software and hardware tools while accessing information and services on their own within the digital environment. Put simply, there is no way to be on the Internet without some intermediating piece of technology. Be it a Web browser, a cell phone, or some other tool, information flowing to and from the Internet, as well as information crucial for determining credibility, all flow through seemingly invisible agents of code and silicon. The Lankes/Eisenberg Architecture[24] can be used to highlight the kind of information manipulation that occurs solely in the province of the tools of the digital environment. This architecture divides the Internet and, by extension, digital networks into four distinct layers: infrastructure, application, information service, and user. Each of these layers can manipulate information in a way that is completely transparent to the recipient. Consequently, there are implications of each layer in terms of youth learning.

Infrastructure is composed of hardware (e.g., routers, protocols) used to move information from one place to another on the Internet, and the organizations, such as Internet Service Providers (ISPs), that provide and maintain these mechanisms. This layer is often the most invisible to end users, yet can have a profound impact on the information available to users to enable them to make credibility assessments. For instance, many people do not realize that infrastructure providers can easily block traffic to and from certain destinations, and can make such blocked traffic invisible. When a school blocks access to certain Web sites, they may post a message to a student's browser stating that the site is blocked, or they can more simply provide a "site not found" indication to a user's browser, the same error it would send if the user misspelled a URL. One component of people's credibility assessments in the online environment is the comprehensiveness of the information they obtain.[25] As such, filtering programs used in schools may negatively influence students' perceptions of the comprehensiveness, and perhaps even the impartiality, of Internet-based information. In addition, ISPs can block access to any application, disabling software such as instant messaging or social networking at the network layer. The user, not aware of such a block, would only know that their IM (instant messaging) program did not connect to a server and may assume that the error lies in the remote server, thus erroneously affecting their credibility assessment of the remote server, rather than the infrastructure provider.

Applications on the Internet consist of software that allows information to be exchanged between different actors on the network. Applications include Web browsers and instant messaging clients, as well as high-level protocols such as HTTP that transfer Web pages. This broad category covers everything from e-mail applications that automatically mark incoming messages as "junk mail" to the Simple Mail Transfer Protocol (SMTP) that enables e-mail over the Internet, including spam. Spam filters are excellent examples of technology affecting credibility in a nearly invisible way. Many schools have implemented spam filters based on opaque and often propriety algorithms at the organization level, discarding numerous e-mail messages before any human eyes ever see them. While this type of protection from inappropriate or harmful content can be good, it can also have the unintended consequence of inadequately preparing youth for the digital world they may encounter outside the school environment. Indeed, as both Harris[26] and Weingarten[27] argue, blocking young people's exposure to information that may not be credible is probably not the best strategy for teaching students to identify and defend themselves against such information, which they will almost certainly encounter at some point in their lives.

Information services are organizations that use applications and infrastructure to meet users' informational needs on the Internet, such as Google and MySpace. From a credibility standpoint, there are ample studies that look at how information services such as Google skew results in their search engines.[28] In fact, most search engines, including Google, determine the "quality" and "relevance" of sites using a "link-popularity" metric. This metric selects which Web sites to display and the order in which to display them on the search results page based on how many other sites link to a site. Consequently, more popular pages are selected and are displayed higher in the search results. Because few people go beyond the first few pages of the search output, however, "even if a page is of high quality, the page may be completely ignored by Web users simply because its current popularity is very low."[29] This kind of a system sets up a sort of "popularity equals credibility" heuristic[30] that could be dangerous or at least disadvantageous to students' learning. As another example of the bias inherent at the level of information services, and the resulting credibility implications, top results tend toward shopping and technology services in Google.[31] Without knowing this, youth may assume that top results are the "best" regardless of context.

Finally, the *user layer* is composed of individuals and groups, such as teachers and students, who primarily seek and consume information on the Internet to meet their own information needs. Of course, users bring their own biases to both information consumption and production that may affect their credibility perceptions as well as learning. Perhaps the best example is the online encyclopedia Wikipedia. While the collaborative editing afforded by Wikipedia may in fact produce credible information, users must be cognizant that contributors and their contributions may be biased, uninformed, or outdated and should evaluate the information accordingly. A young person using Wikipedia for class assignments who is unaware of the process and accompanying pitfalls of collective editing is thus vulnerable to relying on misinformation.

Decisions at each of these layers can affect credibility judgments by all Internet users, but perhaps particularly by youth, given their heavy reliance on digital media, coupled with meaningful developmental and experiential differences between youth and adults.[32] In the end, having tools as intermediaries deepens the information self-sufficiency paradox by making youth more independent in their information seeking, while simultaneously making them more dependent not only on the information they receive but on the tools they use to access this information.

Shifting Credibility from Authority to Reliability

One outcome of this paradox is a shift from an authority-based approach to credibility to a "reliability approach." This shift represents a sea change from the way in which credibility has traditionally been conceived. Whereas credibility has historically been tied to concepts of authority and hierarchy, in the reliability approach, users determine credibility by synthesizing multiple sources of credibility judgments.[33] Both the need for synthesis and the richer set of resources to be synthesized are products of the pressure for participation enabled and imposed by networked digital media.

Traditional approaches to credibility strongly emphasize authority, where a trusted source is used to inform an individual's credibility determinations. In essence, trusted sources are used to "vouch" for the credibility of a given piece of information. People may have many such authority sources, and may themselves serve as an authority in various settings. The process of becoming or choosing an authority is a process of developing trust and seeking coherence and consistency in the authority.

Some claim that authority is dead on the Internet, for example, some have said Wikipedia (http://en.wikipedia.org/wiki/Main_Page) and group editing have become at least as authoritative as traditional methods for producing encyclopedias, if not more so.[34] Others feel that blogging will supersede or at least parallel the authority of traditional news outlets.[35] There are indeed a number of ways in which traditional means of authority have been supplanted by open, flat structures for information creation and credentialing. However, to call this tantamount to the death of authority is, at best, an imprecise use of terminology. This new paradigm is not without authority, but more sophisticated methodologies may be required for evaluating it.[36] Moreover, while they may not have been as celebrated or accessible as they are currently, history is replete with examples of waves of centralization and decentralization of authority. The dramatic increase in information self-sufficiency has merely led to celebrating the large-scale nature of this decentralization today.

Beyond this historical view, most people use the term *authority* to refer to a single entity, or small set of entities. That is, authority has traditionally been conceived of as hierarchical and centralized. For example, libraries have come together to invest the power of authority in a given institution. For example, the Library of Congress keeps a file of book authors' names, birth, and death information. When citing an author (or including them in a library record) someone can consult these authority files for proper spelling, aliases, and confirmation of an author's identity. This can be thought of as "authority by consent," where all parties in a situation or context agree on who is the authority—that is, who provides the accurate information.

Nonetheless, it might be more precise to use the terms *authoritarian* and *authoritative* to clarify traditional notions of authority. *Authoritarian* is defined as the enforcement of an authority: in essence, the removal of choice by force of law, policy, structure, or some other means. *Authoritative*, on the other hand, is authority granted on the basis of perceptions of trust and expertise. The former is active and enforced, the latter is earned. Wikipedia is more likely to be the death of an authoritarian view that encyclopedias come from only Britannica, Groliers, or other large publishing houses, than it is to be the death of authority per se.[37] Thus, the problem of determining the credibility of Internet-based information is not a crisis of authority, but rather a crisis of choice. There are simply currently more choices about whom to trust. Although this is true for virtually all media venues to some degree, the scale of choice makes the Internet particularly affected by shifts in authority.

Libraries have been wrestling with this issue of shifting modes of authority since at least the early 1990s. Many in the library community—though not all, of course—have reacted to the overwhelming number and variety of information choices available to their clients via the Internet by adopting an authoritarian view that the library is where to get good, accurate, and credible information, while the open Internet is filled with bad and wrong information. One famed tag line of the time was, "Information on the Internet is free, but you get what you pay for." Many want the library to become a preferred provider of information, yet the concept of "preferred" only works in an authoritarian view when there is someone who can make others prefer or select something over something else.

This resistance to the democratization of authority among librarians is ironic because there are few professionals better suited to the authoritative world of the Internet than are librarians. They have a culture of open and free expression and access to ideas. They are generalists who move agilely across different topical domains. They are skilled at searching out information, and locating potential biases in information. Their enterprise (i.e., the library) has little invested in the production of information, and much invested in the consumption of information products from a wide variety of sources. Furthermore, librarians already have a reputation as authoritative, not authoritarian.

The resistance to the democratization of authority is not limited to librarians. Teachers, college professors, doctors,[38] and indeed just about any information intermediary has had to wrestle with the new environment of plurality in authority. For some areas of the economy, the effects have been drastic. For example, the travel industry has been rocked by the growth in online bookings.[39] And, although people may not be buying houses online, they are using Internet real estate listing services to even the marketplace.[40] Perhaps one of the most striking examples of the role of authority can be seen in the insurance industry. As Levitt and Dubner note, the simple act of allowing consumers to directly compare term life insurance rates from different organizations over the Internet, rather than depending on the authority of a life insurance salesperson, led to the cost of term life insurance in the United States to drop by $1 billion.[41] Interestingly, in this case the concept of an authority in a field (an insurance agent) was actually used to mask truly credible information (in the form of lower prices).

The decentralization of authority has turned out to be particularly attractive for teenagers. This shift against stated authority and hierarchy on the Internet is perfectly matched to teenagers' own internal shift against authority of all types.[42] Note, for example, that the most common tools used by teens include IM, MySpace, and Google, all of which allow for a sort of level playing field, where the "right" or authoritarian answers are virtually indistinguishable. IM, a peer-to-peer technology that allows for instant access to friends and social peers, may constitute a wide network of potential experts in this environment built by the teen, not imposed by some adult "expert." In other words, the technology allows greater opportunity for young people to themselves become authoritative experts in many areas, potentially even shifting the power balance between children and adults in some cases. Eysenbach makes a parallel argument for how digital media have impacted the relationship between doctors and patients.[43]

Not surprisingly, many adults feel it is a problem that teens may not look to vetted and traditional sources of "valid" information. Their answer to the problem is often phrased in educational terms: "If only we show them the good stuff, they'll use it." This approach has several guises, normally in terms of literacy: digital literacy, information literacy, information problem solving, and those approaches that rely upon checklists to determine "right" and "wrong" information. However, while these approaches can have a positive effect in certain populations, such as undergraduates and elementary school children, under certain conditions they do not always "fix" the problem.[44]

Of course, the concept of multiple authorities existed prior to the Internet. But, the cost in terms of time, money, and even reputation to seek out a multitude of authorities was very high. With the Internet and other digital media, the range of possible authorities has expanded greatly. Before the Internet, for example, a young person might have to rely on his or her local television news or newspaper to predict the weather. Now he or she can go to the Weather Channel, AccuWeather, or even the National Oceanic & Atmospheric Administration for weather information. The task then becomes determining from a number of sources which among them is most credible.

Moreover, a consequence of the culture of information self-sufficiency is that people, even youth, can more easily become authorities themselves. Not only do users have more sources to choose from, but now they can also access data and information directly, thereby avoiding traditional authority sources altogether.[45] For example, now young people can gather weather data directly from a variety of satellites and radar installations (including home-based weather stations), and train themselves, until they feel they have sufficient expertise and trustworthiness to credibly interpret information. As users take it upon themselves to become authorities by directly evaluating, synthesizing, and even producing information themselves, the notion of a singular authority ends, and "reliability" becomes the predominant form of credibility assessment.

Reliability commonly refers to something or someone perceived as dependable and consistent in quality. If you have a reliable car, it is one that runs well over time. Reliability to the scientist is simply the consistency of data, such that the same treatment (e.g., questions, experiments, or applications) yields the same result over time. If an authority approach is exemplified by believing that a given news anchor will give a credible answer, then switching from news station to news station looking for commonalities in the same story exemplifies a reliability approach. Reliability approaches to credibility can be seen in the physical world. The fact that a person's signature is seen as a marker of credibility in legal settings is the belief that a person signs his or her name in a reliable fashion. Reliability is also seen in the cornerstone of good journalism: to confirm information with a second source.

Authority and reliability approaches are often used in conjunction in both the physical and digital world. In the aftermath of Hurricane Katrina in New Orleans in 2005, many residents turned to chat rooms and community-run Web sites to resolve contradictory and often false information coming from traditional channels and sources (including the federal government and the mass media). Local Web sites, such as NOLA.com, allowed communities to come together and share information. Users were able to hear from multiple sources, including eyewitnesses and residents, and to get a more accurate, complete, and thus credible picture of the situation in the neighborhoods. Users who provided the most consistently accurate information became trusted authorities, and traditional authorities (the government and the mass media) were deemed less credible than the users. This is but one example of how digital media have turned credibility on its head.

Perhaps the most common way to become an authority, however, is through reliability. If someone consistently gives out testable and *accurate* information, they are often seen as an authority.[46] Experts are not simply people with the most experience, but people who have the longest track record in using their experience successfully. The true power of reliability, however, is not only in its capacity to create authority but in its power to destroy it as well. While the necessary degree of reliable performance for authority status varies across contexts (e.g., a baseball player who bats .350 is considered outstanding even though he hits the ball less than half of the time, but a mathematician would not be considered an expert if she got math answers right only half of the time), it is clear that agents giving out unreliable information over time will lose their authority status and, by extension, their credibility.

Authority and reliability also have "halo effects," meaning that a person who is seen as an authority in one area may be presumed to be an authority in other domains as well, even without proven performance. This can be seen, for example, in celebrity product endorsements. Likewise, unreliable performance in one area can cast doubt on performance in other areas. Like an accountant who cheats at Monopoly, or a minister who cheats on his wife, loss of credibility in one area can cast suspicion on one's other domains of authority. These halo effects become even more pronounced in the digital environment when the information about and from an agent (person, organization process) can be more voluminous, diverse, and mobile than in offline environments.

Ultimately, reliability and authority anchor the endpoints of a continuum of approaches to credibility. With authority, preexisting agreements are in place and assumed: the conversation is over. With reliability, by contrast, the conversation is open and ongoing. Networked digital media enhance this conversation and thus are more likely to encourage users to seek out more information and other people to come to a credibility judgment compared to traditional media. Since digital networks bring to youth an overwhelming amount of information and people to engage with in arriving at a credibility judgment, there is pressure for the tools they use to incorporate some ability to participate, or engage in a conversation with people and sources. Builders of digital network tools and information services have begun to respond by being more open and by creating more opportunity for user participation in content creation and dissemination. In so doing, the tools built for users today to find and use credible information facilitate reliability approaches to credibility assessment, and thus learning via constant "conversation."

Digital Media and Credibility by Reliability

Recent trends in digital media facilitate the shift to a reliability approach of credibility assessment. The Internet is by its very design open, providing only minimal control at the network level. The guiding technical protocol of the Internet, Transmission Control Protocol/Internet Protocol (TCP/IP), simply breaks data into packets and makes sure these packets get to the proper destination with fidelity. What these data packets contain, what they do, and how they do it is completely ignored by most users. From this very simple packet-switching technology, Internet users have built e-mail, the Web, instant messaging, and all of the services that users enjoy today. Indeed, the Internet's interoperability, open access, and decentralized control are especially well suited to innovation on the scale of the individual user.[47]

As a result, even higher-level Internet functions are not defined or controlled by the Internet itself. Indeed, there is no central authority that controls the Internet, beyond its basics such as domain name registration and the structure of TCP/IP. Even so-called governing bodies such as the World Wide Web Consortium (W3C) merely suggest standards that are often embellished, altered, or ignored by software developers.[48] The Internet is, in a very real sense, an agreement, and an ongoing conversation where organizations and individuals share information.

This open architecture and decentralized control provide enormous capacity for participation, which contributes to accurate credibility assessment through reliability among multiple shared perspectives and experiences. Yet, there is nothing inherent in digital networks that makes infrastructure participatory. There are many historical examples of large-scale networks that were centrally controlled, where infrastructures were provided to users with little input by those users. Commercial online networks ranging from CompuServe, Prodigy, and America OnLine to not-for-profit Freenets and BitNet networks were "black boxes" that only allowed users to manipulate pre-made tools. These are historical examples, however, because, even in the case of AOL, these proprietary networks have either been superseded by the Internet, or have had to radically change their underlying infrastructures to accommodate the Internet.[49] Thus, although involvement in the infrastructure and at the level of specific software applications is not a certainty, the Internet's evolution appears to favor involvement and participation.

Indeed, involvement and participation have led many Internet software designers to view the very process of software development as a means toward credibility. For instance, so-called open source software at its most basic is when the developer of a piece of software makes the underlying source code of the software application available to the public. Anyone with sufficient programming skills can then take the source code and analyze it, add to it, or incorporate it into another software package. On the Internet, this simple concept has been expanded to a more complex approach to any system development.[50] While anyone with sufficient skill can use open source software, if they improve or expand the original code, they must give the additions back to the open source community.

Open source software and the associated movement propose a new concept of credibility in terms of tools: credible tools are ones that are built in the open, where a conversation on the merits and structure of infrastructure can be debated and tested. This stands in stark contrast to more traditional models of credible software development. In a traditional approach to software development, credibility is defined by the organization that produced the software. This organization would have some standing in the community, good practices, and a proven track record of quality products (i.e., authority). Interestingly, this is often proffered in terms of security. A system is "secure" if few have access to its inner workings, and if the few programmers who put it together used a common quality process. The open source approach takes an opposite stance: To be secure, software must first be transparent and then tested by others (i.e., be reliable). The idea is that, if everyone can see the code, and can test it, flaws will be easier to find and because the process of implementation is tested in public, everyone can trust the product. Open source advocates would argue that by being able to dissect and test all aspects of a piece of software, right down to the very source code, they can better determine both the trustworthiness of a tool as well as the expertise of the tool's creators (i.e., its credibility).

While there is an ongoing debate between the "open" and "closed" software development approaches, there is no question that it has changed the shape of tool building on the Internet. For example, the Internet produced the concept of "open beta" where software products were made available to any Internet user to test while still in production. Over time, these beta test processes run longer, sometimes never leaving beta (i.e., "continuous beta"). Even traditional software developers such as Microsoft and Adobe have moved toward a more open approach "to enlist a large army of bug testers to help iron out any kinks"[51] in their products.

This openness goes a long way toward addressing the information self-sufficiency paradox among youth, but only for those with sufficient technology skills and education. That is, youth with sufficient technical skills now have the ability to choose and shape the tools themselves. Skilled youth who are wary of a given Web browser can use another one, or even write their own, often in concert with others sharing a similar concern. If a school wants to know exactly how its e-mail program is filtering spam, it can now shop multiple filtering packages until it finds the right one, sometimes evaluating the very source code of the filter.

This ability of *skilled* users fluent in the technologies of the Internet has important implications for youth and education. If society wants youth to be truly able to make credibility decisions in digital networks, then youth must understand the technical nature of the network itself—from the use of tools to the creation of tools. Simple use skills, such as browsing the Web, are insufficient to truly understand the role that tools play in the credibility of Internet-based information. Furthermore, if schools and other institutions prevent youth from participating in the underlying infrastructure,[52] they are limiting youths' ability to resolve the information self-sufficiency paradox and, by extension, limiting youths' ability to learn about and act upon credibility.

This limitation, and youths' reaction to limiting access to the underlying infrastructure of digital networks, can be seen in content filtering put in place at many schools and libraries today. When faced with limited access to the Web, many youth have begun to document the limitations of the filters themselves. Privacy organizations and civil liberties groups have joined students in challenging the efficacy of filters, and have called for change.[53] Because the infrastructure that these filters are built upon is open, and because the filter is not part of the network itself, it can be modified or replaced by those who possess the skills to do so. Suddenly the invisible nature of the network itself is visible—and indeed debatable.

The "Credibility Conversation"

To be effective both at constructing reliability-based credibility assessments and in working collaboratively to build innovative technical tools, youth must be able to engage in appropriate conversations with appropriate others via the Internet. Accordingly, Nielsen/NetRatings indicates that teens' usage of digital media is shifting. While the top sites for youth ages 12 to 17 used to be those offering a selection of instant messaging buddy icons, in the last three years the most popular sites have shifted to social networking sites or those providing assistance with social networking content, profiles, and page layouts.[54] While social networking sites such as MySpace, the Facebook, and others are relatively recent, teens' desire for online social interaction is not new. Teens have preferred social uses of the Internet for some time. For example, in 2001 Lenhart, Raine, and Lewis found that extremely popular uses of the Internet among teens included e-mail, instant messaging, and visiting chat rooms.[55] Teens' desire for social Internet experiences also shows up in institutional education settings, where Simon, Graziano, and Lenhart found that a large percentage of teens "say they use e-mail and instant messaging to contact teachers or classmates about schoolwork."[56]

Beyond simply a person's age or cultural fads, the migration to social applications on the Internet is in part due to the very nature of learning. Conversation theory,[57] for example, proposes that learning and knowledge are gained through the interaction of agents around ideas as they go back and forth describing an idea. This interaction can then be used to develop new understandings and new knowledge through a process that contemporary learning theorists call *scaffolding*: one idea building upon another. Learning conversations can take place between two individuals (say a teacher and pupil), two organizations (negotiating a set of academic standards), or even two societies (debating over the best way to educate youth).

Framed by conversation theory, the utility of social interactions in online learning environments (be they formal or informal) for youth is obvious. As youth engage in conversations they learn, and the online environment allows for a greater scale and scope of conversants. Furthermore, as they encounter systems for learning in the digital environment, they may seek out tools to aid in interactions and conversation. The tools they seek out do not simply present credibility information, or third-party credibility assessments, but instead allow youth to participate in the conversation, and therefore the process of credibility verification and knowledge creation. Indeed, recent research suggests that members of open-source online communities are able to effectively build collective knowledge through "virtual re-experience," whereby individuals share their work using online tools to co-construct applicable knowledge.[58] Clearly, among other uses, youth are well poised to take advantage of precisely this type of conversation.

The concepts of openness, and indeed participation, in the development of tools exemplified in the open source movement can also be seen at the level of the Web sites and remote resources that users access on the Internet. Information services are under increasing pressure to open their sites and resources to youth participation. Information services today understand the power of participation. Where once services might count hits to a Web page, or unique visitors, today whole industries are devoted to analyzing a user's path through a Web site to discover what information he or she encountered, where this information led to successful "goal conversion," such as buying a product or, in an educational context, learning a piece of information, and where the information led to confusion or exiting a site. Educational organizations are now beginning to understand that the true power of the Internet for learning is not simply wide-scale and one-way distribution of information, but instead is getting closer to what is happening inside users' (learners', customers') brains. This trend follows larger forces at work in the educational setting that have resulted in the shift from accreditation and evaluative education bodies to outcomes evaluation and performance standards.[59]

Recognition of the increasingly participatory nature of information services can also be seen in the rise of social networking sites, where the information service is little more than an infrastructure for user-contributed conversations and artifacts. Such services are the purest example of a trend finding its way into a large number of Web sites: users contributing to the ongoing conversation about an artifact (such as a book listed on Amazon), fact (such as an entry in Wikipedia), place (such as Flickr communities devoted to a given city), or other entity. In much the same way that traditional tool developers feel an increasing pressure for community input, content providers are also feeling an equal pressure for community input on their content. Part of this pressure comes from users who see participation as a crucial part of assessing the *credibility* of these artifacts, facts, and topics.

The advent of services that allow greater user involvement, such as blogs, social networks, and recommender, rating, or commenting in e-commerce and other sites, has led to increased demand by youth and other users for involvement in Internet services of all types. Key issues here in terms of credibility are, can one trust a person one has encountered online, and does that person know what he or she is talking about? Increasingly youth and others are looking to user-submitted comments, editorial reviews, and open conversations on a given topic, artifact, or idea to determine trust and expertise. And, in many cases where sites do not provide these functions, the youth community can take advantage of the open nature of the Internet to create their own. This has led to the rise of an entire class of network destinations known as "protest sites" devoted to user discontent with a given institution, person, brand, or product. In the physical world, youth might be limited in their protests to complaints to the principal or reliance on third parties such as better business bureaus, but online youth and others can seek out and build communities of discontented users regardless of geographic location.[60] Moreover, users new to the brand or item can now easily find such sites, allowing them to incorporate the dissenting views, as well as the official information, when making credibility decisions. In this way, youth can compensate for their relative lack of life experience[61] by leveraging that of others. Of course, these user communities gain strength in numbers and are assessed in terms of their reliability, rather than their authority, as discussed earlier.

This style of grassroots organization has quickly spread from the consumer to the political arena. With an open network, opposing voices that challenge the credibility of some "official" information have equal access to the network and, at times, equal weight compared to official information outlets and forums. This type of information "leveling" afforded by open digital networks can also be seen in schools. Youth, dissatisfied with either the information available to them from their classes, schools, and teachers, or with the venues for complaint, have turned to the digital environment to disseminate information of protest or information otherwise unavailable within the school. For example, there are now several sites rating teachers, professors, and classes. Blogs, MySpace, and other community sites are filled with "counter information" meant to provide greater context to, or to at least raise concerns about, the credibility of a given piece of information.

Of course, the Web also provides ample opportunity for users to post false information. There are many examples of "astroturfing," whereby marketing firms have set up seemingly grassroots sites that actually promote particular products or approaches.[62] Certainly youth may put up false information on protest sites as well, either intentionally or unintentionally. The result is that credibility may be harder to determine for any piece of information. False information also increases pressure on information services to provide opportunities for community feedback, in essence inviting protestors and commentators into a controlled space where an organization can respond to counterinformation.

This pressure for a voice on the part of youth can be expected to result in more opportunities for discussion and conversation in both existing and emerging forms of digital media. It is not surprising that the distinctions between information seeking, learning, and communicating are breaking down. Where once users would e-mail (or instant message) in one application, and search the Web in another, they are now doing both simultaneously. This is not a simple matter of convenience, but rather is based on users' implicit or explicit preference for knowledge acquisition through conversation. Given what is happening on the Web in terms of social uses and applications, it appears that users are looking to talk with others in order to better evaluate what they find and to synthesize this information into actionable knowledge.

It is also likely that the trend of tracking users' conversations online will continue and will be enhanced. Information retrieval systems may well develop into conversational retrieval tools that link information by how others have used such information in their conversations. Just like libraries used to produce pathfinders and annotated bibliographies, users will soon be able to find a piece of information, such as a Web site, and follow that information to all of the other public information used in a given conversation. Such a holistic context will allow users to make credibility determinations about an item in the full context in which it resides. Digg.com provides an excellent present-day example of such a system.[63] When a Digg.com user finds an interesting news story on the Web, he or she can mark it, allowing other Digg users to not only view the site, but to discuss it in an online forum. What this does, in essence, is elevate the interest of one user to a group's consideration and evaluation.

Youth may understand this type of information seeking better than adults. Through e-mail, instant messaging, and texting, youth already create close-knit "research" teams that share findings and implicit credibility assessments.[64] Credibility in these contexts is not determined by the individual, or even the individual in interaction with a Web resource, but within a community engaged in a larger conversation. For school assignments, students may use sources they determine to be credible from their past experience, their heuristic appeal,[65] the input of experts such as teachers and librarians, and from others, including their peers. This "credibility conversation" may, however, extend past the actual assignment and well into the evaluation of that assignment. A low grade, or follow-up from teachers, may have an impact on how a student evaluates credible sources in the future, and how he or she conveys information about the sources to others (via social networks or otherwise) who may want to use those sources in the future.[66] The grades and feedback that the peer group receives should also influence future credibility decisions. However, unless credibility is made explicit in this large and ongoing conversation, it will be ignored. That is, if teachers, parents, adults, and peers do not make credibility part of the discussion, and if there is no consistent result from either embracing or ignoring credibility, it will become invisible, not cognitively attended to by youth, and therefore not assimilated into knowledge. This situation is made worse by the growing educational environment that emphasizes "high-stakes" testing, which minimizes rich assessments and interactions between student and teacher.[67]

The need to highlight credibility in conversations has implications for educational policy makers as well. If youth are exposed only to vetted and "safe" resources, often pruned of a great deal of context and conversation, how are students to gain the invaluable skills required to determine credibility on their own, outside of guided environments? Harris identifies such "conservative attitudes" as a structural challenge that must be overcome.[68] What policy makers must understand is that, as Weingarten[69] and Harris[70] argue, the unintended consequence of creating "safe" learning environments is an environment that limits learning about credibility.

The fact that technology constrains youth information before youth are able to make credibility decisions has startling implications for education. To begin, a common strategy to prepare youth to make informed credibility decisions is based around educational programs normally under some literacy rubric such as information literacy, digital literacy, or media literacy.[71] These programs typically present young people with various strategies and checklists to determine the quality of information they find via digital media.[72] While this approach makes sense for much of the information a student might access through digital networks, it does not make sense for all Web-based information. For example, how can one judge the credibility of information at a given URL when the true URL is masked by inline frames that show content from some third-party destination as if it were just a part of a normal page? Although this is a specific feature of the Web today, there are sure to be many analogs in future digital technologies. Moreover, there is no amount of literacy instruction that can prepare the average young person for the effects of a network infrastructure that they cannot control directly.

Conclusion and Recommendations

This chapter described the growth of information self-sufficiency and the related paradox where users are simultaneously more responsible for decisions, while also more dependent on information provided by others and the tools used to manipulate information. It discussed how the Internet and digital networks that allow for community participation in the construction of the underlying network and infrastructure have become the predominant model for existing and future digital media, and how this has led to credibility assessment by reliability rather than by authority. It presented a model in which knowledge is gained through conversation and reflection, and argued that digital networks and tools must address this reality. Finally, it showed how this need for participation and involvement has influenced information services, and how users themselves define and assess credible information.

Primary aims of the chapter have been to highlight trends that will most likely endure, continue, or expand as future digital media develop, and to show how youth are both affecting and being affected by these trends. Large-scale digital networks have extended youths' ability to build their own social networks to aid in the assessment of credibility. They have also allowed youth to participate in the networks in meaningful ways, in essence elevating their own personal credibility in certain domains. However, this new reality has serious implications for youth, as well as for society as a whole.

To prepare youth to make fully informed credibility decisions, they must become fluent in the tools that facilitate the conversation and become aware of potential biases in the network technology itself. As noted by Harris, schools may be an ideal place to do this, but they are limited in their ability to do so.[73] Without technical fluency, however, students become dependent on, and often unaware of, the stakeholders who control the network's infrastructure and the policies they create.[74] Yet, as others in this volume have pointed out, the extent to which youth are involved shapes the Internet and the services available. The omnipresent nature of the digital environment is necessitating more technical fluency and greater explicit consideration of credibility and technology at an earlier age.

So, what are the implications for youth and credibility in the digital environment? The first is that youth, with enough training, now have equal opportunity to access the infrastructure they increasingly depend on. Unlike previous media technology widely adopted by youth, such as radio, television, and the phone system, youth can not only adopt technology, they can shape it at its most fundamental levels—at the level of infrastructure. Furthermore, with the global nature and low cost of entry to the Internet, innovations that are started by a teenager in one schoolhouse or bedroom can become an internationally adopted standard. These changes highlight the possibility that, with the emphasis of open source on public function testing as a means to credibility rather than credibility determined by the reputation of the code's corporate origin, youth with sufficient technical skills can enter the infrastructure development arena on an equal footing to established organizations. This implies that any attempt to prepare youth for life in the digital world should incorporate some fluency in the basic technologies of the network, and the ethical guidance in how such technologies should be implemented.

Indeed, youth have now come to expect involvement in all aspects of information in the network. Schools, business, governments, and other institutions and organizations must change to accommodate this expectation. If not, youth will migrate their attention to venues that allow for conversation and debate of information, or create their own. This is perhaps the most important implication for youth from the increasing requirement for participation on the network. Youth can and will increasingly expect to shape their information domain, and define credible information on their own terms. Any system that seeks to either impose an authority view of credibility, or that seeks to change behavior, must now be done with the understanding that youth can simply bypass these attempts and create counter-structures. Furthermore, these alternative credibility structures can have a global reach and build communities of like minds across divisions of geography, race, gender, age, and other demarcations.

Thus, there appears to be a pressing need to educate youth to assess credibility in participatory ways, thereby steering the potentially negative implications of digital networks toward positive outcomes. Because youth in particular are more self-sufficient in decision making, and also more dependent on the information that others are providing to them, digital media increase the importance of credibility, as well as their ability to make credibility judgments effectively. Learning through "conversation," typified by collaboration with others, is one avenue toward reliable credibility assessments. In the end, this is perhaps the most realistic and effective means by which to increase knowledge among youth increasingly reliant on digital media for the information that is central in their lives.

Notes

1. Mary Madden, *Internet Penetration and Impact* (Pew Internet & American Life Project, 2006), http://www.pewinternet.org/PPF/r/182/report_display.asp (retrieved November 15, 2006).

2. Amanda Lenhart, Mary Madden, and Paul Hitlin, *Teens and Technology: Youth Are Leading the Transition to a Fully Wired and Mobile Nation* (Pew Internet & American Life Project, 2005), http://www.pewinternet.org/pdfs/PIP_Teens_Tech_July2005web.pdf (retrieved December 15, 2006).

3. National Center for Education, Rates of Computer and Internet Use by Children in Nursery School and Students in Kindergarten through Twelfth Grade: 2003 (2005), http://nces.ed.gov/pubsearch/pubsinfo.asp?pubid=2005111 (retrieved February 26, 2007).

4. See Gunther Eysenbach, Credibility of Health Information and Digital Media: New Perspectives and Implications for Youth, this volume, for a similar argument.

5. Jules Abend, Lands' End Uses Internet to Expand Sales, Personalize Customer Service; Bobbin, 1999, FindArticles.com, http://www.findarticles.com/p/articles/mi_m3638/is_10_40/ai_55609089 (retrieved December 15, 2006).

6. See Gunther Eysenbach, Credibility of Health Information and Digital Media, this volume.

7. Dg.o, The National Science Foundation's Digital Government Research Program, 2006, http://www.digitalgovernment.org/ (retrieved December 15, 2006).

8. Kerry Lynn Rice, A Comprehensive Look at Distance Education in the K–12 Context, *Journal of Research on Technology in Education* 38, no. 4 (2006): 425–48.

9. Florida Virtual School, http://www.flvs.net/educators/fact_sheet.php (retrieved December 28, 2006).

10. Amanda Lenhart, Maya Simon, and Mike Graziano, The Internet and Education: Findings of the Pew Internet & American Life Project, 2001, 2, http://www.pewinternet.org/PPF/r/39/report_display.asp (retrieved December 28, 2006).

11. Miriam J. Metzger, Andrew J. Flanagin, and Lara Zwarun, College Student Web Use, Perceptions of Information Credibility, and Verification Behavior, *Computers & Education* 41 (2003): 271–90; Rice, A Comprehensive Look at Distance Education in the K–12 Context.

12. Tina Miteko, Driving Value from Every Online Customer Interaction: The Power of Intent-Driven Personalization, *Customer Inter@ction Solutions* 24, no. 8 (2006): 38.

13. Matthew L. Meuter, Amy L. Ostrom, Robert I. Roundtree, and Mary Jo Bitner, Self-Service Technologies: Understanding Customer Satisfaction with Technology-Based Service Encounters, *Journal of Marketing* 64 (2000): 50–64; Allard van Riel, Veronica Liljander, and Petra Jurriens, Exploring Consumer Evaluations of E-Services: A Portal Site, *International Journal of Service Industry Management* 12, no. 4 (2001): 359–77.

14. Lane Becker, Self-Service Web Applications: Less Cost, More Value, 2002, http://www.adaptivepath.com/publications/essays/archives/000063.php (retrieved November 15, 2006).

15. Tina Miteko, Driving Value From Every Online Customer Interaction, 38–41.

16. Federal Election Commission, Help America Vote Act of 2002: Public Law 107-252, http://www.fec.gov/hava/hava.htm (retrieved November 15, 2006).

17. Grants.gov, http://www.grants.gov/ (retrieved November 25, 2006).

18. Joanne Silverstein, *Information Technology and Commerce: Attributes of Emerging Online Business* (doctoral dissertation, Syracuse University, 1997).

19. Batya Friedman, Peter H. Kahn Jr., and Alan Borning, Value Sensitive Design and Information Systems, in *Human-Computer Interaction in Management Information Systems: Foundations*, eds. Ping Zhang and Dennis Galletta (Armonk, NY, and London: Sharpe, 2006): 348–72.

20. B. J. Fogg, *Persuasive Technology: Using Computers to Change What We Think and Do* (New York: Morgan Kaufman, 2002); B. J. Fogg, Cathy Soohoo, David R. Danielson, Leslie Marable, Julianne Stanford, and Ellen R. Tauber, How Do Users Evaluate the Credibility of Web Sites?: A Study with Over 2,500 Participants, in *Proceedings of the 2003 Conference on Designing for User Experiences*, San Francisco, CA, 2003, 1–15; Miriam J. Metzger, Andrew J. Flanagin, Keren Eyal, Daisy Lemus, and Robert M. McCann, Bringing the Concept of Credibility for the 21st Century: Integrating Perspectives on Source, Message, and Media Credibility in the Contemporary Media Environment, in *Communication Yearbook 27*, ed. Pamela J. Kalbfleish (2003), 293–335; Miriam J. Metzger, Andrew J. Flanagin, and Lara Zwarun, College Student Web Use, 271–90; C. Nadine Wathen and Jacquelyn Burkell, Believe It or Not: Factors Influencing Credibility on the Web, *Journal of the American Society for Information Science and Technology* 53, no. 2 (2002): 134–44; Joseph B. Walther, Zuoming Wang, and Tracy Loh, The Effect of Top-Level Domains and Advertisements on Health Web Site Credibility, *Journal of Medical Internet Research* 6, no. 3 (2004): e24, http://www.jmir.org/2004/3/e24/ (retrieved January 3, 2006).

21. Andrew J. Flanagin and Miriam J. Metzger, Digital Media and Youth: Unparalleled Opportunity and Unprecedented Responsibility, this volume; B. J. Fogg, Jonathan Marshall, Othman Laraki, Alex Osipovich, Chris Varma, Nicholas Fang, Jyoti Paul, Akshay Rangnekar, John Shon, Preeti Swani, and Marissa Treinen, What Makes Web Sites Credible? A Report on a Large Quantitative Study, *Proceedings of the SIGCHI Conference on Human Factors in Computing Systems*, Seattle, WA, March 31–April 4, 2001, 61–68.

22. Andrew J. Flanagin and Miriam J. Metzger, The Role of Site Features, User Attributes, and Information Verification Behaviors on the Perceived Credibility of Web-based Information, *New Media and Society 9*, no. 2 (2007): 319–42.; B. J. Fogg, Jonathan Marshall, Alex Osipovich, Chris Varma, Othman Laraki, Nicholas Fang, Jyoti Paul, Akshay Rangnekar, John Shon, Preeti Swani, and Marissa Treinen, Elements That Affect Web Credibility: Early Results from a Self-Report Study, *CHI '00 Extended Abstracts on Human Factors in Computing Systems*, The Hague, Netherlands, 2000, 287–88; Fogg et al., What Makes Web Sites Credible?

23. Melody Y. Ivory and Rodrick Megraw, Evolution of Website Design Patterns, *ACM Transactions on Information Systems* 23, no. 4 (2005): 463–97.

24. R. David Lankes, *Building and Maintaining Internet Information Services: K–12 Digital Reference Services* (Syracuse, NY: ERIC Clearinghouse on Information & Technology, 1999).

25. Metzger et al., Bringing the Concept of Credibility for the 21st Century.

26. Frances Jacobson Harris, Challenges to Teaching Credibility Assessment in Contemporary Schooling, this volume.

27. Fred W. Weingarten, Credibility, Politics, and Public Policy, this volume.

28. See, e.g., Junghoo Choo and Sourashis Roy, Impact of Search Engines on Page Popularity, in *International World Wide Web Conference: Proceedings of the 13th International Conference on World Wide Web* (New York: ACM Press, 2004), 20–29.

29. Choo and Roy, Impact of Search Engines on Page Popularity, p. 1.

30. See S. Shyam Sundar, The MAIN Model: A Heuristic Approach to Understanding Technology Effects on Credibility, this volume.

31. Abbe Mowshowitz and Akira Kawaguchi, The Consumer Side of Search: Bias on the Web, *Communications of the ACM* 45, no. 9 (2002): 56–60.

32. Matthew S. Eastin, Toward a Cognitive Developmental Approach to Youth Perceptions of Credibility, this volume; Flanagin and Metzger, The Role of Site Features.

33. Flanagin & Metzger, The Role of Site Features.

34. Thomas Chesney, An Empirical Examination of Wikipedia's Credibility, *First Monday* 11, no. 11 (2006), http://www.firstmonday.org/issues/issue11_11/chesney/index.html (retrieved January 4, 2006); Jim Giles, Internet Encyclopedias Go Head to Head, *Nature* 438 (2005): 900–1; Felix Stadler and Jesse Hirsh, Open Source Intelligence, *First Monday* 7, no. 6 (2002), http://firstmonday.org/issues/issue7_6/stalder/index.html (retrieved January 4, 2007); Aaron Weiss, The Power of Collective Intelligence, *netWorker* 9, no. 3 (2005): 16–23.

35. Tanni Haas, From "Public Journalism" to the "Public's Journalism"? Rhetoric and the Reality in the Discourse on Weblogs, *Journalism Studies* 6, no. 3 (2005): 387–96; Thomas J. Johnson and Barbara K. Kaye, Wag the Blog: How Reliance on Traditional Media and the Internet Influence Credibility Perceptions of Weblogs among Blog Users, *Journalism and Mass Communication Quarterly* 81, no. 3 (2004): 622–42.

36. Deborah L. McGunines, Honglei Zeng, Paulo P. da Silva, Li Ding, Dhyanesh Narayanan, and Mayukh Bhaowal, Investigations into Trust for Collaborative Information Repositories: A Wikipedia Case Study, *Proceedings of the Workshop on Models of Trust for the Web*, WWW2006, May 22–26, Edinburgh, UK, 2006, http://ebiquity.umbc.edu/_file_directory_/papers/274.pdf (retrieved January 4, 2007); Nikolaos Th. Korfiatis, Marios M. Poulos, and George Bokos, Evaluating Authoritative Sources Using Social Networks: An Insight from Wikipedia, *Online Information Review* 30, no. 3 (2006): 252–62.

37. Susan L. Bryant, Andrea Forte, and Amy Bruckman, Becoming Wikipedian: Transformation of Participation in a Collaborative Online Encyclopedia, in *Proceedings of the 2005 International ACM SIGGROUP Conference on Supporting Group Work*, Sanibel Island, FL, 2005, 1–10.

38. See Eysenbach, Credibility of Health Information and Digital Media.

39. Rob Law, Kenith Leung, and R. James Wong, The Impact of the Internet on Travel Agencies, *International Journal of Contemporary Hospitality Management* 16, no. 2 (2004): 100–7; Clive Wynne, Pierre Berthon, Layland Pitt, Michael Ewing, and Julie Napoli, The Impact of the Internet on the Distribution Value Chain: The Case of the South African Tourism Industry, *International Marketing Review* 18, no. 4 (2001): 420–31.

40. James E. Littlefield, Yeqing Bao, and Don L. Cook, Internet Real Estate Information: Are Home Purchasers Paying Attention to It? *Journal of Consumer Marketing* 17, no. 7 (2000): 575–90; Risa Palm and Michelle Danis, The Internet and Home Purchase, *Tijdschrift voor Economische en Sociale Geografie* 93, no. 5 (2002): 537–47.

41. Steven D. Levitt, and Stephen J. Dubner, *Freakonomics: A Rogue Economist Explores the Hidden Side of Everything* (New York: William Morrow, 2005).

42. Eysenbach, Credibility of Health Information and Digital Media.

43. Ibid.

44. Carrie Lowe, Yale University's PACE Research Center and the Big6™, 2005, http://big6.com/showarticle.php?id=459 (retrieved November 15, 2006).

45. See Eysenbach, this volume, for a similar argument.

46. For a greatly expanded discussion of attributes of authority and countervailing factors, see Richard Thomas De George, *The Nature and Limits of Authority* (Lawrence: University Press of Kansas, 1985).

47. Andrew J. Flanagin, Craig Flanagin, and Jon Flanagin, Technical Code and the Social Construction of the Internet, unpublished manuscript.

48. Jeffrey Zeldman, *Designing With Web Standards* (Berkeley, CA: New Riders Press, 2003).

49. Richard Wray and Dan Milmo, AOL Tries to Survive by Going Free, 2006, http://business.guardian.co.uk/story/0,1835908,00.html (retrieved January 2, 2007).

50. Eric S. Raymond, *Cathedral and the Bazaar: Musings on Linux and Open Source by an Accidental Revolutionary* (Sebastopol, CA: O'Reilly Media, 2001).

51. Galen Fott, Adobe Photoshop CS3 Beta, 2006, http://www.pcmag.com/article2/0,1895,2074376,00.asp (retrieved January 6, 2007).

52. See Harris, Challenges to Teaching Credibility Assessment.

53. For an example, see PEACEFIRE, 2006, http://www.peacefire.org/ (retrieved December 29, 2006).

54. Market Wire, U.S. Teens Graduate from Choosing IM Buddy Icons to Creating Elaborate Social Networking Profiles, According to Nielsen//NetRatings, 2006, http://www.marketwire.com/mw/release_html_b1?release_id=171656 (retrieved December 28, 2006).

55. Amanda Lenhart, Lee Rainie, and Oliver Lewis, Teenage Life Online: The Rise of the Instant-Message Generation and the Internet's Impact on Friendships and Family Relationships, 2001, http://www.pewinternet.org/PPF/r/36/report_display.asp (retrieved December 15, 2006).

56. Maya Simon, Mike Graziano, and Amanda Lenhart, The Internet and Education: Findings of the Pew Internet and American Life Project. 2001, p. 6. http://www.pewinternet.org/PPF/r/39/report_display.asp.

57. Gordon Pask, *Conversation Theory: Applications in Education and Epistemology* (New York: Elsevier, 1976).

58. Andrea Hemetsberger and Christian Reinhardt, Learning and Knowledge-Building in Open-source Communities: A Social-Experiential Approach, *Management Learning* 37, no. 2 (2006): 187–214.

59. See Harris, Challenges to Teaching Credibility Assessment.

60. Peter S. Jenkins, Leafleting and Picketing on the "Cydewalk" – Four Models of the Role of the Internet in Labour Disputes, *UCLA Journal of Law and Technology* 7, no. 1 (2003).

61. See Eastin, Toward a Cognitive Developmental Approach to Youth Perceptions of Credibility.

62. Wikipedia, Astroturfing, 2006, http://en.wikipedia.org/wiki/Astroturfing (retrieved December 29, 2006).

63. http://digg.com/.

64. Chris Davies, Geoff Hayward, and Linariah Lukman, *Digital Technologies: A Review of Research and Projects* (2006): 14–19, http://www.futurelab.org.uk/download/pdfs/research/lit_reviews/futurelab_review_13.pdf (retrieved December 29, 2006).

65. Sundar, The MAIN Model.

66. Soo Young Rieh and Brian Hilligoss, College Students' Credibility Judgments in the Information-Seeking Process, this volume.

67. Brett D. Jones and Robert J. Egley, Looking through Different Lenses: Teachers' and Administrators' Views of Accountability, *Phi Delta Kappan* 87, no. 10 (2006): 767–71; Harris, Challenges to Teaching Credibility Assessment.

68. Harris, Challenges to Teaching Credibility Assessment.

69. Weingarten, Credibility, Politics, and Public Policy.

70. Harris, Challenges to Teaching Credibility Assessment.

71. Ibid.

72. Miriam Metzger, Making Sense of Credibility on the Web: Models for Evaluating Online Information and Recommendations for Future Research, *Journal of the American Society for Information Science and Technology* 58, no. 10 (2007).

73. Harris, Challenges to Teaching Credibility Assessment.

74. See Weingarten, Credibility, Politics, and Public Policy.

Credibility of Health Information and Digital Media:
New Perspectives and Implications for Youth

Gunther Eysenbach

University of Toronto, Department of Health Policy, Management, and Evaluation;

Centre for Global eHealth Innovation, University Health Network, Toronto

The Special Role of Health Information

Searching for health information online is often said to be one of the most common activities on the Internet.[1] Such sweeping (and only partially accurate) claims are mostly based on survey data, such as the Pew Internet & American Life Report,[2] which found that "80% of adult Internet users, or about 93 million Americans, have searched for at least one of 16 major health topics online." The report concluded that "this makes the act of looking for health or medical information one of the most popular activities online." Other surveys from industrialized countries have arrived at similar conclusions. For example, Statistics Canada concluded that between 1999 and 2003 health information was the most prevalent Internet activity each year aside from e-mail and "general browsing," well ahead of such things as searching for travel information, government information, or electronic banking.[3] Surveys further show that these trends also apply to young people.[4] For example, a recent survey of 1,100 U.S. teens ages 12–17 found that 31 percent reported seeking health information online (representing 6 million people), and that teens' use of the Internet for this purpose was up 47 percent since 2000.[5] Another survey found that three quarters of youth between the ages of 15 and 24 have used the Internet to get health information.[6]

However, the impression these survey data are generating that most people are using the Web mainly for health information is misleading. For example, other uses may be underrepresented. Social desirability biases can lead people to answer questions about how they use the Web in a manner they deem socially acceptable. As a result, searching for pornography, for example, is a prevalent activity on the Web[7] that may be underreported in a survey.

Another issue with survey research in this domain is that the definition of "health" is sometimes problematic. For example, fitness, sports, wellness, diet, and food information may or may not be regarded as health information, with no clear-cut boundaries.[8] For example, Lenhart et al. observed that "when we ask adult Internet users if they ever go online to simply look for 'health or medical information'. . . 66% report doing so. However, when we ask about a wide range of health topics (e.g., 'Have you ever looked online for information about exercise or fitness?' or 'For information about immunizations or vaccinations?') 80% of adult Internet users say they have researched at least one of those specific health topics at some point."[9] Similar results were found for youth in the same study.

Finally, surveys often do not accurately assess the prevalence of day-to-day health information-seeking activities. To gauge these, one has to directly observe Web traffic or monitor what information people are searching for on a daily basis. Indeed, several independent studies using these more "direct" methods to gauge online activities by tapping into the data sets from various search engines have concluded that the actual volume of health-related searches on the Internet as a proportion of all searches conducted each day is around 5 percent. By comparison, searches for issues related to entertainment, shopping, pornography, research, places (e.g., searching for cities, landmarks) or business (e.g., stocks, personal finance) are much more popular.[10] Thus, survey and search data combined suggest that searching for health information is a popular, but not necessarily *frequent*, activity for most people (chronically ill people being a notable exception).

This usage pattern of health information has several implications: although people may know where to go for news, weather, movie reviews, shopping, and business information, health and medical questions arise infrequently enough such that people do not necessarily have a trusted brand name or portal in their mind as they begin a search. Thus, whereas people may be savvy and experienced enough to evaluate the credibility of a general news Web site or an e-commerce site, they may have insufficient experience and expertise with health Web sites, which are generally not used on a day-to-day basis. This may be particularly true for many young health information seekers, who may not have experienced a lot of prior health problems in their lives.

While trusted commercial health portals (e.g., WebMD) and noncommercial, government-sponsored health portals (e.g., Healthfinder, MedlinePlus, Canadian Health Network) exist, people with specific health problems or questions mostly enter a health-related search term directly into a search engine, not necessarily going through a portal site.[11] For example, in one study among youth, only 16 percent said they go directly to a particular site to research a health issue, while the majority said they used a general search engine (60 percent). Another 23 percent reported that they "just came across" health information while browsing the Web.[12] Yet, surprisingly few cases of harm due to online health information have been reported, with the majority due to self-medication[13] and/or self-diagnosis. One systematic review concluded that only a few cases of harm have been reported in the medical literature.[14] Indeed, as part of the European MedCERTAIN project, researchers set up a special database of adverse events related to the Internet to systematically collect cases where consumers have been harmed by health-related Internet information, but very few cases have actually been submitted.[15]

Nonetheless, and in spite of its low prevalence to date, the potential for physical and mental harm caused by people applying dubious, low-quality, or untrustworthy information illustrates the importance of considering the credibility of online health information in particular. While generally most encounters with dubious information may result in negative financial, social, or personal consequences, health information can literally be a matter of life and death. Therefore, educating consumers and providers of health information and services about how to avoid "low quality" information becomes paramount. Because top-down quality assurance mechanisms provided by the government and other entities are not realistic or—at least in Western countries—not ethically acceptable solutions,[16] consumer education on how to identify quality information is crucial.

In addition to the potential harm caused by online health information (which in this chapter includes information on Web sites, but also information delivered through other Internet channels, such as e-mail or in newsgroups, and, by extension, also information delivered through other digital media such as mobile devices), the enormous potential benefits of the Internet and digital media for public health must also be considered. The fact is that there is a great deal of high-quality information on the Web that is published by trusted organizations. It is important for these organizations to appear credible enough to initiate a behavior change in consumers. Thus, to understand how people assess the credibility of a site, source, or piece of information is a key task in the development of any health education or health promotion undertaking and, thus, an important area of research. This latter "positive" aspect of the importance of credibility research in the health arena is often overlooked in the literature, and has been overshadowed by discussions and research focusing on the harmful potential of low-quality information on the Internet.[17]

How Do Consumers Access and Assess Health Information?

Many adults say that they (still) trust their doctors more than the Internet, yet in many cases the Internet is the first channel of information consulted. Hesse et al. suggest that physicians remain the most highly trusted information source to patients, with 62 percent of adults expressing "a lot" of trust in their physicians.[18] When asked where they preferred going for specific health information, 50 percent reported wanting to go to their physicians first. However, when asked where they *actually* went, only 11 percent reported going to their physicians first, while 48 percent said they went online first. It is obvious that either the degree of mistrust in health information does not run as deeply as surveys suggest, or that the convenience and accessibility of Internet information outweighs quality concerns at least for some health problems, and/or that consumers have found ways to cope with less trustworthy information, or—most likely—a combination of those factors.

In reality, consumers likely triage their conditions with the easiest or most appropriate information source first, and may end up using both Internet information and doctors in a complementary manner. Indeed, the convenience of accessing online self-care information rather than visiting a health professional is often cited as a motivation for using the Internet before seeing a doctor. For example, in one focus-group study, a teenager said, "I wanted to know how to get rid of a wart on my toe without the doctor—so I looked on the Internet and it told me stuff like how to get rid of plantar warts."[19] At the same time, many consumers recognize the limitations of self-care and will be more wary to bypass health professionals if they have a more serious disease. For example, in the same study, another teenager said, "You're not going to go on the Internet if you have cancer . . . if you've got a big tumor or something."[20] Still, even for serious diseases such as cancer, consumers are known to consult the Internet before and/or after a physician visit. This is especially true for patients who are younger,[21] more highly educated, and those with more severe diseases.[22] Overall, patients generally describe the health information they find from the Internet as trustworthy, and the majority of patients use that information as a basis for discussions with their doctor.[23]

Although "the Internet" typically receives a lower average trustworthiness rating than a concrete person ("my doctor") in surveys, this does not necessarily mean that people do not perceive *some* Internet resources as *more* trustworthy than their doctors. However, while some people may have completely lost trust in their own doctor and, consequently, turn to Internet-based Web doctors or medical webmasters for advice instead, for most people consulting the Internet has more to do with a desire to obtain as much information and as many perspectives as possible, to make sure nothing important has been missed, and as a coping strategy.[24]

Once on the Internet, most adults[25] and youth[26] are very aware that credibility evaluation of health information is paramount. A Pew Internet Survey stated that "compared to other Internet users, health seekers show greater vigilance in checking the source of online information" and that 86 percent of people seeking health information "are concerned about getting health information from an unreliable source online."[27] However, while people often claim that the source of the information is their primary yardstick when evaluating credibility,[28] direct observational research in a lab setting shows that health consumers rarely look at the credibility of the source.[29] Consistent with other research on credibility,[30] these studies further conclude that, in reality, consumers are more impressed by surface credibility markers, such as Web site design (e.g., whether it appears "professional"). Some consumers even use markers such as the picture of the site owner to determine credibility of the site and its information.[31]

Role of Digital Health Information for Youth

Adolescence is a period where individuals face multiple health-related challenges and questions. For example, questions arise as teens discover their sexuality or experiment with drugs and alcohol, and concerns arise owing to common medical conditions that tend to manifest themselves during adolescence including, for example, acne, mental health disorders such as schizophrenia and depression, smoking, or eating disorders such as obesity or anorexia.[32] This coincides with a phase of life where cognitive abilities develop rapidly,[33] and when most adolescents have easy access to the Internet at home and/or at school.[34]

Young people may be especially vulnerable to problems with regard to online health information seeking. For example, Rideout argues that the Internet is likely an especially important source of health information for young people in particular, given that they are often concerned with issues that may be sensitive and hard to talk about, and because many young people have not yet established a relationship with a doctor other than their family doctor.[35] The implications of this, she says, are unclear: "Increased access to health information could create a more informed and healthful youth. On the other hand, if the quality of online information is not high or the source unknown, increased reliance on the Internet could lead to greater misinformation and skepticism."[36] Of course, "young people" constitute a heterogeneous group, and whether online health information seeking leads to an informed or a misinformed youth is likely to be a function of an individual's age, maturity, cognitive development, and information literacy.[37]

Health information-seeking behavior varies depending on the age of youth. For instance, two representative surveys focusing on youth conducted in 2000 and 2001 by different research groups (Pew and the Kaiser Family Foundation, respectively) arrived at very different conclusions regarding the relative importance of health information compared to other types of information that young people sought online. The Pew report surveyed people between the ages of 12 and 17, while the Kaiser report surveyed "youth" between the ages of 15 and 24. The Pew Internet survey found that looking for health-related information ranked *lowest* compared to other topics among teenagers who are online. Looking for health information was reported by only 26 percent of teenagers.[38] In contrast, the Kaiser Family Foundation survey found that as many as 75 percent have used the Internet at least once to find health information.[39] These discrepant findings are most likely a result of the two surveys dealing with different age populations, with younger teenagers seeking health information to a lesser extent than older youth.

The Pew report also noted that health information seeking seemed to increase by age. Older girls and boys were the most likely to look for health, fitness, or dieting information (40 percent of girls and 26 percent of boys ages 15–17 reported that they had done so). In contrast, only 18 percent of the younger (ages 12–14) teens said they had looked for health information online.[40] Moreover, a good proportion of these health-related searches are related to topics pertaining to sexual health or drugs.[41] With awakening sexuality and increasing autonomy, certain health-related issues become important, while traditional sources of information (parents, teachers) are often challenged and begin to lose authority in the eyes of teens.

Nonetheless, the Kaiser Family Foundation survey found that among young people ages 15–24, the most significant (and most credible) sources of health information continued to be traditional sources such as health classes at school, parents, and doctors.[42] Furthermore, information from parents, school, TV, and friends is trusted much more than Internet information. Only 17 percent said they trusted Internet-based information "a lot," whereas 85 percent said they trusted doctors, 68 percent said they trusted parents, 30 percent said they trusted TV, and 18 percent said they trusted friends "a lot" when it came to health information.[43] That said, the Internet is a much more abstract and variable entity than "parents" and, when thinking of the Internet, most respondents primarily think of the variable quality of information on the Web, rather than thinking of specific Web sites they use. Also, when assessing the trustworthiness of Internet information, many respondents may not consider other Internet tools such as e-mail, chat, instant messenger, or social networking sites, which may actually help them to identify credible information on the Web.[44]

Gray and colleagues speculate that youth do not use the Internet as their "first port of call" when looking for health information, but rather as a last resort,[45] but little or no direct observational data exist to support or refute this hypothesis. Furthermore, as the foregoing review suggests, age or maturity of the youth in question and the perceived severity of the young person's medical condition should also be considered. For sensitive or embarrassing health topics that are not perceived as "severe diseases" including, for example, pregnancy and birth control, sexuality, drug and alcohol abuse, violence, smoking, depression, and weight loss, information is often sought from the Internet, sometimes as the primary source.[46] In summary, while adults and youth both often say they trust other sources more than sources on the Internet, only preadolescent youth seem to consult primarily other sources (parents) first, whereas adolescents and adults often use the Internet before consulting other sources, including health professionals.[47] One explanation for this difference may lie in the fact that during adolescence, teenagers become more autonomous and increasingly learn to rely less on traditional authority figures and intermediaries, which in turn is a result of increased cognitive abilities and skills[48] combined with a tendency and desire to challenge authority or societal rules as a means to establish individuality. The theory that *autonomy* (desired or actual) is a critical variable explaining differences in information seeking and information-appraisal behavior is explored in greater detail later.[49]

What Is Special about Credibility in Digital Media?

Flanagin and Metzger note several factors about digital media that raise credibility concerns,[50] but specific considerations in the context of health information warrant special attention. For example, the lack of quality control (e.g., editorial boards, peer review) on the Internet, coupled with the extremely cheap publishing process online, result in less need to adhere to the highest publishing standards.[51] Although there is of course a large amount of information online that has gone through some sort of peer review,[52] many people, and perhaps youth in particular, have difficulties discriminating between peer-reviewed (or editor-controlled) and non–peer-reviewed material.[53] For example, in a study with college students, nearly half of the respondents had trouble discriminating between primary and secondary sources of information, as well as between references to journal articles and other published documents, and when presented with questionable Web sites on nonexistent nutritional supplements, only 50 percent of respondents were able to correctly identify the Web site with the most trustworthy features.[54]

Part of the trouble in discerning trustworthy sites from dubious ones is the result of a *deficit of context*, which can be particularly deleterious for health information.[55] For example, a Web site created by an individual can look equally professional and credible as the home page of, say, a professional organization, making it more difficult for consumers to distinguish who sponsored the Web site.[56] Also, search engines often send consumers directly to a particular Web page on a site, bypassing the home page, thereby making it difficult to discern who is behind a certain Web site and what the authors' motives and qualifications are.[57] Together, these issues, coupled with ambiguity about why, how, and for whom Web information is produced, have been referred to as "context deficit."[58] Context is particularly important in medicine, as information does not necessarily have to be inaccurate in order to have the potential to harm—accurate information that is taken out of context can also be harmful.[59]

Another aspect of the context deficit presented by digital media is the blurring of lines between different genres of information, in particular between advertising and informational content.[60] In the medical domain, such blurring reached headlines in September 1999, when one of the once-leading health portals, http://DrKoop.com, was criticized for lack of "Web ethics." In an article published in the *New York Times*, the site (partly owned by former U.S. Surgeon General C. Everett Koop) was accused of inadequately distinguishing between editorial content and promotion. For example, DrKoop.com published a list of hospitals designated as "the most innovative across the country," not revealing the fact that these hospitals actually paid for the listing. Moreover, the site was criticized for calling advertisers "partners." In addition, DrKoop.com violated the medical ethics guidelines of the American Medical Association by making money through referring patients to other physicians without revealing this fact. The incident sparked the development of codes of ethics for health Web sites.[61]

Additional concerns are particularly relevant for the health field. For example, digital information by its very nature is cheap and easy to multiply or copy online. Multiple copies of a piece of information can lead to a lack of editorial ownership and control, with no one person responsible for taking it down or updating all copies. The original custodian or creator of the information, who is the one most familiar with the information, is unable to exert control over the multiple copies disseminated in a digital universe. Compounding this problem, health information has a particularly short half-life and needs to be continuously updated in order not to lose its value and validity.

Other features of digital health information make credibility and quality considerations important as well. The ability to mass-customize interactive applications can lead to higher involvement by users and, thus, perhaps greater impact on individuals.[62] According to a recent review, interactive health care applications developed by domain experts appear to have largely positive effects on users, in that users tend to become more knowledgeable, feel better supported socially, and may have improved behavioral and clinical outcomes compared to nonusers.[63] A meta-analysis comparing Web-based interventions versus non–Web-based interventions found improvements in outcomes such as increased exercise time, increased knowledge of nutritional status, increased knowledge of asthma treatment, increased participation in health care, slower health decline, improved body shape perception, and eighteen-month weight loss maintenance.[64] Interactive digital media clearly have a significant potential and perhaps even an advantage over traditional media to engage people, to establish credibility, and to lead to changes in behavior.[65] However, interactivity also poses dangers if the wrong message is delivered in a credible and engaging way. In the end, the enormous reach of digital media brings a potential to affect the health of large populations, both positively and negatively.

Another aspect that makes quality and credibility considerations particularly important in health communication is that people use digital media to retrieve information "on demand" and "just-in-time," for example, by typing in a respective query into a search engine when and where they need it ("My child has fever, so let's see what I can find on the Internet"). As a result, they are more likely to apply this information and act on it immediately. Of course, mobile devices and future "ambient/ubiquitous" computing applications further increase the just-in-time accessibility of information. By contrast, health information in traditional "push" media (e.g., newspaper, TV, radio) is usually only relevant to and applicable for a small proportion of users who encounter it more or less by chance.

A related problem is the larger effect of what has been called "self as source,"[66] which is the influence of people's prior attitudes and knowledge, biases, and misconceptions on the kind of information they encounter. This influence is enhanced in "information pull"-based digital media, because people have greater control over what information they retrieve compared to "push" media. For example, entering "rapid cure for lung cancer" in a search engine leads to qualitatively different articles on cancer than entering "small cell carcinoma treatment," and a search query including the phrase "evidence that X is caused by Y" will return preferably documents confirming that indeed X is caused by Y (even if it is not true), thereby presenting a biased search result that confirms the bias in the recipient.

A final reason why digital media are different with regard to health information is that content and cues helping to assess the credibility of that content can be delivered separately, and both can be dynamically and intelligently tailored to the individual. The Internet is not a static medium such as a newspaper, book, or patient leaflet, where once a person has obtained misinformation there is little health professionals can do to correct the information. On a decentralized, electronic medium, peers and intelligent systems can give consumers additional information about a topic from other sources and perspectives, which can mediate (reduce or enhance) their trust in a message in a personalized, tailored way. This process shall be called "apomediation" henceforth,[67] and is explicated in the following sections. Apomediation will be used to illustrate that the networked environment not only provides new challenges for credibility, but also provides new solutions.

From Intermediation to Disintermediation and Apomediation

Much of the debate on quality and credibility in the digital age is a result of a social process of "disintermediation" through digital technologies, and the health industry is no exception. Just as in many other areas of life (e.g., the travel industry), information and communication technologies empower consumers to access pertinent information or services directly, cutting out the middleman or gatekeeper (or *intermediary*), such as the travel agent, real estate agent, librarian, pharmacist, health professional, or journalist.[68] With direct and convenient access to abundant health information on the Internet, consumers may now bypass the expert intermediary and gain direct access to unfiltered information.[69] Apart from "general" health information found on the Internet, consumers may also be able to access their own personal health information from their electronic health record.[70] Similarly, youth can bypass traditional gatekeepers and authorities such as parents or teachers. In this situation, consumers must assume new responsibilities.[71]

As the role of "human" intermediaries diminishes or changes, consumers and patients are finding new ways to locate relevant and credible information. The agents that replace intermediaries in the digital media context may be called "apomediaries," because rather than mediating by standing "in between" (inter-) consumers and the services or information they seek, they "stand by" (apo-) and provide added value from the outside, steering consumers to relevant and high-quality information without being a requirement to obtain the information or service.[72] While the traditional intermediary is the "expert," apomediaries consist of a broader community including experts, parents, teachers, peers, and the like, who are networked in a digital environment.

While intermediaries typically engage in "upstream filtering," apomediaries enable and facilitate "downstream filtering." Upstream filtering is characterized by a limited number of gatekeepers (usually experts, authorities, professionals) setting quality criteria, performing evaluations, and giving access only to selected information that has been vetted by them. In contrast, "downstream filtering" is characterized by third parties (experts, authorities, professionals, peers) mainly communicating selection criteria to users, with evaluations and eventual filtering taking place further "downstream" by end users or apomediaries. In so doing, these evaluations incorporate the values and preferences of individual end users.[73] An extreme example to illustrate upstream versus downstream filtering can be seen in the following: some countries such as Saudi Arabia direct all international Internet traffic through a central proxy farm with content filters to block access to pornographic and other "inappropriate" material, which can be referred to as an "upstream" filtering approach.[74] By contrast, labelling of pornographic material using metadata (i.e., electronic labels) provided by the author or a community of users empowers end users to set their own thresholds on what is acceptable for them, which can be referred to as downstream filtering.[75] Upstream filtering, however, need not be synonymous with censorship. "Weaker" forms of upstream filtering include Internet portals that include only links selected by experts, the traditional peer-review process for publishing academic papers, and the traditional editorial process for news articles. Downstream filtering, by contrast, is exemplified by editorial control based on user rankings and social bookmarking, by Web sites such as Digg, where news stories and Web sites are submitted by users, and then promoted to the front page through a user-based ranking system.[76] Apomediaries—such as users and friends in the case of Digg—can help users navigate through the onslaught of information afforded by networked digital media, giving additional credibility cues and supplying further metainformation. Other examples of apomediaries and apomediation tools include consumer ratings on amazon.com or epinions.com; technologies like PICS or MedPICS labels that enable machine-processable dissemination and interpretation of user ratings;[77] collaborative filtering and recommender systems as exemplified by StumbleUpon.com; and other second-generation Internet-based services and tools that let people collaborate on a massive scale and share information online in new ways, including social networking sites, social bookmarking, blogs, wikis, communication tools, and folksonomies.[78]

Parallels between Disintermediation during Adolescence and Digital Disintermediation

Some interesting parallels exist between processes of disintermediation in health care and other industries, and the individual emancipation process that takes place during adolescence. As mentioned earlier, one of the key themes during adolescence is that as children grow into teenagers they become more autonomous and rely less on traditional authority figures. They strive to become more independent and desire to reduce the influence of traditional intermediaries (e.g., parents), with peers (apomediaries) partly taking over the role of these former intermediaries.

Ling describes adolescence as a time when emancipation from one's parents is of central concern.[79] As such, teens have a strong motivation to "establish themselves as independent social actors who are outside the sphere of their parents." Peers become important as teens make the transition to adulthood by helping them "to work out a relationship to the various facets of adult life," which they do in part by providing "the teen with a sphere in which he or she can assert control and participate more fully in decision making." Ling further argues that teens' desire for autonomy in part drives their avid use of digital media because "these modes of communication facilitate emancipation" since they lower the threshold for social interaction by giving teens more freedom, control, and privacy to access peers or others outside of the family.[80]

Thus, for younger users of digital media, the disintermediation/emancipation process takes place at two levels during adolescence. One is the naturally occurring emancipation process from parents, guardians, teachers, and other traditional authorities; the other is an empowerment and emancipation process that is enabled and supported by the digital tools for communication that youth use, which themselves reinforce and enable disintermediation and apomediation. These parallels will be explored further, as part of the dynamic disintermediation/apomediation model, which is explained in greater detail next.

The Dynamic Disintermediation/Apomediation Model

One impact of networked digital media is that people are being pushed to be more informationally self-sufficient.[81] For adolescents and adults alike, autonomy (a person's ability and motivation to think, feel, and make decisions on his or her own) thus becomes the common basis for disintermediation/apomediation. While autonomy is a key theme during adolescence, "the development of autonomy does not end after the teen years. Throughout adulthood, autonomy continues to develop whenever someone is challenged to act with a new level of self-reliance."[82]

In health care, new autonomy challenges include the patient journey after diagnosis of a chronic disease. For example, an elderly patient newly diagnosed with Type II Diabetes might initially rely on health professionals (intermediation), but later may develop sufficient autonomy through increased knowledge and self-efficacy to obtain health information from the Internet (disintermediation). The information she relies on may range from Web sites to using a network of peers in newsgroups as apomediaries, thereby relegating the former intermediary (her doctor) to just one actor among many others in an apomediation network. In other situations, however (e.g, finding a newly spotted tumor), the same individual might fall back to the intermediation model, opting not to bypass a health professional, before she again becomes sufficiently motivated and capable to do independent research on the Web, thereby moving to an apomediated model.

What predicts whether in a given situation an intermediary is preferred over an apomediation model, provided both are options? While personality traits and developmental factors may broadly predispose individuals to generally prefer one approach over the other, the decision to use apomediaries versus intermediaries remains largely *dynamic and situational*.[83]

As will be argued later, this has implications for individuals' credibility assessments. As stated above, *autonomy* (desired or actual) seems an important prerequisite for bypassing traditional authorities. Autonomy is generally associated with variables such as knowledge, ability, and self-efficacy. Thus, it is plausible to argue that the better informed individuals are, and the better they know what information or services they need, the less likely they will require and seek an intermediary. In the health context, compared to a person with an acute illness, a knowledgeable person with a chronic condition, such as diabetes, will have a greater capacity and perhaps inclination to critically appraise information found on the Internet, and may have less need for an intermediary, at least for satisfying information needs (medical treatment being a different matter).

Cognitive abilities and literacy also play a role. A more mature adolescent eager to learn about sexuality is less likely to rely solely on an intermediary such as a parent or teacher than is a younger child with limited cognitive ability and "eHealth literacy," which includes media, computer, health, and functional health literacy skills.[84] Indeed, studies find that with increased media literacy of the recipient (including the ability to distinguish different types of information such as editorial content versus advertising) and prior knowledge about message content, the effects of source expertise on credibility can be attenuated such that the credibility of "experts" and other authorities decreases.[85] Finally, *self-efficacy*, or the belief that one has the capabilities to execute the actions required to manage a situation, is a further prerequisite to bypass the intermediary. Self-efficacy, in turn, is fueled by experience, social modeling ("If they can do it, I can do it as well"), and positive reinforcement.[86]

The dynamic intermediation/disintermediation/apomediation (DIDA) model presented in Figure 1 proposes how disintermediation is initiated, sustained, and can be reversed through a process called "reintermediation." The model proposes that information, which is often initially mediated and filtered by an intermediary, usually increases knowledge and self-efficacy and, hence, autonomy. The dotted arrow indicates that if individuals do not perceive they have enough knowledge, self-efficacy, and autonomy, they will continue to rely on an intermediary. However, once a critical threshold of knowledge, self-efficacy, and autonomy is exceeded, individuals may feel sufficiently empowered to bypass the intermediary and to rely more on apomediaries. Furthermore, in cases of perceived success, for example, when consumers find what they want and are reassured by apomediaries that what they found is credible, a positive feedback loop is created, where self-efficacy and autonomy are further fueled and the consumer is even more encouraged to prefer apomediation over experts or intermediaries in future similar situations. Here again, there are interesting parallels to what is happening during adolescence as youth gradually emancipate themselves from traditional authority figures and become increasingly self- and peer-reliant.

As mentioned above, the decision to use an intermediary or to bypass the intermediary is situational, and the positive-feedback loop can be broken at any time, leading to a process of reintermediation. For example, this is likely to occur if the apomediation approach is perceived to be a failure, or if the individual is confronted with a new situation, where knowledge, self-efficacy, and/or autonomy are perceived as insufficient (e.g., a new, threatening medical condition).

The DIDA model has limitations in that it does not apply to situations where external factors "force" people into apomediation. For example, patients may choose to consult the Internet rather than a health professional because they do not have health insurance, or simply because they do not have time to see a doctor.[87] In both cases, the decision to abandon an intermediary is made for reasons that are unrelated to a desire for more autonomy. On

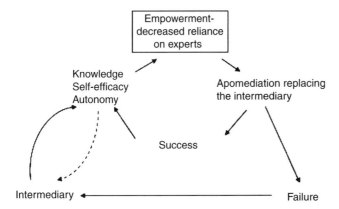

Figure 1
Dynamic intermediation/disintermediation/apomediation (DIDA) model.

the other hand, even in these situations it might be argued that patients have a higher desire for autonomy than other patients in a similar situation who are willing to pay a consultation fee or who go through the inconvenience of scheduling an appointment. The DIDA model is also only applicable in the context of information seeking. However, intermediaries, such as physicians, parents, teachers, also have other roles that go far beyond information filtering. So, users may on one level "bypass" the intermediary when it comes to information seeking and information evaluation, but this does not necessarily mean that the relationship with the intermediary ends.

The power relationship between the recipient and the intermediary does, however, change as a result of disintermediation, which may create conflicts. For instance, a significant minority of health care providers see their authority challenged by the abundance of health information accessible via digital media, perceive a deterioration in the physician-patient relationship as a result, and fear a negative impact on the quality of health care or health outcomes, although most embrace the shift brought about by technology from a paternalistic to a partnership model of health care.[88] Parents may be similarly irritated when their children search for information on birth control on the Internet, for instance, rather than discussing this with them or with a physician. In this way, the DIDA also helps to explain some of the perceptions and frustrations that intermediaries often have with the disintermediation process, as they tend to see predominantly the "failures," for instance, patients finding irrelevant or misleading information on the Internet.

Challenges and Limitations of Apomediation

The power shift that occurs during disintermediation creates new challenges for both the intermediary and the newly empowered user and patient. One of the challenges, particularly in the context of health care and youth, is the question of personal relevance, interpretation, and contextualization. Even information that is accurate can be detrimental when applied in the wrong context. In fact, when physicians express discontent about patients bringing stockpiles of Internet printouts into the doctor's office, the primary complaint is not so much about the quality or credibility of that information in an objective sense, but its irrelevance for the specific patient or potential misinterpretations by the patient. In one survey, 73.8 percent of general practitioners said that Internet information brought in by patients is generally accurate, and 65 percent even said much of the information was new to them, but only 44.7 percent said that the patient had correctly interpreted the information. A different survey found that those health care providers who thought that much of the information patients brought in was irrelevant also had more negative views on how the patient–physician relationship was affected by such information.[89] This is not surprising, because contextualizing and interpreting information is one of the key roles of intermediaries, especially in the health care context. Moreover, contextualizing and interpreting information is likely a bigger challenge for youth than for adults, owing to limited life experience, education (in the case of younger youth), as well as limited functional health literacy and topical knowledge.[90] That said, however, older youth may benefit from higher levels of computer and new media literacy, greater free time, their natural curiosity and persistence, and a strong network of peers, with whom they stay connected through digital technology such as instant messaging, social networking, and other applications,[91] which may help to compensate for young people's knowledge and experiential deficits.

Given this picture, it is a curious omission from the literature that the degree to which apomediaries actually succeed in the same way as intermediaries, such as physicians or parents, in filtering and interpreting health information is largely unexplored. While there have been data on the "self-corrective" nature of digital media, for example, that inaccurate statements on mailing lists are corrected by peers[92] and studies of the relative accuracy of Wikipedia,[93] little is known to what degree apomediation helps to filter *relevant* information and to contextualize that information. There is tremendous opportunity for research on this topic.

In addition, various apomediation tools such as "tabulated" credibility[94] have further significant limitations, in that they may lead to the promotion of opinion rather than fact. As Grohol notes, "Even if a website collates a bunch of people's opinions and gives them numbers, that doesn't elevate the information presented to 'fact.' It is still opinion. And such opinion is no substitute for medical advice, professional advice, or an empirical research study."[95] To illustrate this point, Grohol presents the example of a Web site that allows members to rate medication. If a user sees that 90 percent of members report that a certain medication gives them a headache, they will likely conclude that they should avoid taking that medication. That conclusion may be false, however, since the data presented on the Web site say nothing about how well the sample is representative of the population or whether the medication can plausibly be linked to headaches. He writes, "Headaches are very common in the general population—everyone gets them. Randomized controlled research studies have methods in place to measure whether a symptom is likely caused by a specific medication or not. Generally people's website self-reports, however, do not have such careful data collection methods."

Of course, medication-rating Web sites do actually exist (e.g., askapatient.com). Few adverse effects have been noted, perhaps because, if used correctly, such systems merely complement and do not necessarily replace interactions with an intermediary. As discussed earlier, intermediaries do not necessarily disappear, but can remain an actor in the apomediation network, even if their roles have changed. Indeed, narrative, experiential-based information, if interpreted correctly, should be seen as a valuable complement to information from health care intermediaries or from scientific studies. However, the question of whether and to what degree patients are actually misled by rating or recommender systems is important, as is the question of to what degree the success of apomediation systems is domain-dependent (i.e., should the same apomediation tools that seem to work in entertainment and other areas be used in health care?).

Credibility Implications of Disintermediation/Apomediation

The shift from intermediaries to disintermediation/apomediation has implications for several credibility constructs. Some credibility implications include the hypothesis that there is an association between apomediation/intermediation and the way credibility is evaluated, the hypothesis that credibility of a specific message might be boosted through disintermediation/apomediation, the notion that disintermediation/apomediation may help to reinstate trust in intermediaries, the prominence of experiential information in apomediated environments, and the idea of applying network theory to apomediation networks to develop new tools to direct consumers to credible information. Each will be considered in turn below.

Correlations between Apomediation/Intermediation and Credibility Assessment

How people evaluate credibility is likely to be different in an apomediated environment than in an intermediated environment and is probably related to their preference for one or the other. Specifically, within intermediated environments, information is prefiltered by the gatekeeper or authority and is presented as credible to users. With disintermediation, apomediaries provide users *guidance* in locating and evaluating information. With this in mind, it is hypothesized that people who possess or desire greater autonomy, be they mature teenagers, people with chronic illnesses, or anyone else, will prefer apomediation as an approach to determining credibility. As a consequence of relying less on "authorities" and more on peers, it is further hypothesized that message credibility will be more important than source credibility for these people. Furthermore, people using an apomediary approach to credibility assessment are probably more prone to employ a "spectral evaluation" rather than a "binary evaluation" approach, acknowledging "shades of grey" rather than "black and white" answers.[96]

By contrast, people choosing an intermediary are likely to be those who are less autonomous and as a result need or want authoritative answers from traditional intermediaries. These people could include, for example, younger children, older seniors, incapacitated or illiterate people, or people with acute diseases or in other "new" situations. In this situation, more emphasis is likely placed on source credibility. These hypotheses come with some important limitations that will be discussed below, and it should also be acknowledged that within each environment, considerable interindividual and intersituational variation exists in terms of what credibility evaluation strategies are employed. For example, time constraints, technical abilities, and motivation will affect people's credibility evaluation strategies.

These considerations are grounded in the observation that several variables that predict an individual's preference for disintermediation/apomediation, including *autonomy*, *self-efficacy*, and *knowledge*, are also correlated with an individual's *motivation* and *ability* to process messages and influence credibility judgments. According to the elaboration likelihood model (ELM) of persuasion,[97] higher motivation (which is affected by a person's involvement with an issue, including knowledge and personal relevance of some topic) and ability (a person's cognitive abilities, degree of literacy, or time available) will lead to more effortful processing of a message, while lower motivation and ability will privilege an evaluation of environmental characteristics of the message, such as the attractiveness or qualifications of the source, or message presentation elements, as primary credibility cues. Fogg and Tseng[98] extend this model to hypothesize that people with lower motivation and ability are more likely to adopt a binary evaluation strategy (i.e., something is "credible" or "not credible"), whereas people with higher motivation and ability employ a spectral evaluation strategy. If we accept that in most cases autonomy is positively correlated with general motivation and ability, and if we accept that these variables also predict whether or not somebody prefers a disintermediation/apomediation approach to credibility assessment, then the argument presented here is plausible.

Of course, these very general predictions that may characterize broad trends come with important limitations and exceptions, such as the fact that the model only works if people have a choice between seeking an intermediary or not. For example, if disintermediation occurs as a result of the intermediary not being available, the user is forced into an apomediary model regardless of whether the prerequisite "autonomy" is present. Also, the way in which the credibility of a message is evaluated is primarily determined by the situation, since the environment (intermediation or disintermediation/apomediation) in which individuals find themselves cannot always be controlled. In other words, in practice it may be easier to "switch" between evaluation strategies than between environments.

This gives rise to situations where intermediaries are used, but motivation and ability of the receiver are high, creating an apparent contradiction with the argument that autonomous (motivated and knowledgeable) individuals will prefer apomediation and employ the credibility evaluation strategies outlined above. For example, educated (i.e., able) and motivated cancer patients who seek out a health professional (intermediary) might prove an exception to the rule as they likely screen message credibility carefully, as well as employ a sophisticated spectral evaluation approach despite using an intermediary. Two explanations are possible: First, one could argue that the primary reason for relying on the intermediary in this case is for treatment rather than informational purposes. Second, information needs, information-searching behavior, and credibility-assessment strategies of patients evolve and change during the course of their care,[99] and thus the notion that patients with severe illnesses always have high motivation and ability may be an oversimplification. In particular, motivation and ability are often low immediately after diagnosis (due to fear and denial), but then increase over time.[100]

Boosting Credibility through Disintermediation

"Direct" or unmediated information is often perceived as more credible than mediated information because mediation through a gatekeeper brings "greater opportunity to impute motives and intentions of the communicator."[101] As such, disintermediation has the potential to increase the perceived credibility of information, especially under circumstances where the intermediary is perceived as not completely neutral or where the credibility of the gatekeeper is unclear or questionable. This is particularly relevant in the health care system, where doctors are often paid per service by insurance companies or governments, and where payers are under considerable cost pressures, leading to a perceived rationing of available services.

Against this background, many consumers mistrust intermediaries, which are seen as part of a flawed system and not neutral. For example, many consumers view the traditional health care system as being biased against alternative medicine, as health care professionals are incentivized to offer expensive therapies for which they are reimbursed more generously, as opposed to therapies which are "natural" but for which they cannot charge much.[102]

Such mistrust creates the desire to bypass the intermediary, and boosts trust in information that has been received from other sources. Under this logic, it is possible that a sufficiently autonomous patient who receives information through a health professional may have bigger concerns about its credibility than another patient who finds the identical information independently from an intermediary on the Internet. In addition, the very fact that in digital apomediated environments information usually has to be more actively pursued rather than just being provided by an intermediary, may increase its salience, which in turn may lead people to attribute more importance to that information.[103] While youth are unlikely to rationalize their mistrust of traditional health intermediaries in this way, questioning and mistrusting traditional authorities is a natural part of adolescence, and information mediated through traditional authorities such as parents, teachers, and even health care professionals may be perceived as biased. Information from trusted peers who are experiencing the same health concerns or experiences, on the other hand, may in fact be seen as more credible. This may be particularly true for information on sensitive topics related to sex, alcohol, or drugs, which constitute a good proportion of the health information that teens seek.

Reinstating Trust in the Intermediary

It can also be hypothesized that intermediaries who voluntarily "step aside" to allow and facilitate consumers' direct access to information and participation in services can help to re-instate trust in the intermediary, provided that the consumer possesses the respective desire for autonomy and the abilities to cope with that information. For example, health professionals who actively encourage patients to access their own health records (electronically or otherwise) can help to restore patients' trust in the medical system.[104] However, this works only if information provided through more direct channels is not perceived as contradictory to the information provided by the intermediary. If that is the case, recipients may attribute the discordance to intermediary bias, thus undermining the trust relationship. For example, youth accessing information on issues of sexuality through the Internet may lose trust in parents and teachers if the information found through the apomediaries contradicts the information provided by intermediaries.

The principle of "trust your users to gain trust" can also be exemplified by the success of recent Internet tools such as wikis or blogs, and by online companies and services that have employed a "trust your users" philosophy, such as Amazon, epinions, eBay, YouTube, MySpace, and the like. While the traditional dogma on the Web was creating trust and quality through tightly controlled editorial content management, the new emerging philosophy is to allow and encourage participation and content creation by users with little or no "upstream" barriers.

The Importance of Experiential Information in Apomediated Environments

While traditional wisdom from credibility research suggests that perceived accuracy is a hallmark for message credibility,[105] it would be a mistake to assume that accuracy only refers to evidence-based information based on research, or that this type of information would automatically have more credibility for health consumers than do anecdotes. In a focus group with patients, Glenton and colleagues found that people "often made treatment decisions in a context of great pain and despair," which left them with little energy to perform laborious information searches or to care what the research said.[106] "Instead, they often gathered information about treatments through the personal anecdotes of friends and neighbors, and, in most cases, this experience-based information was considered to be more relevant than the evidence-based information." Not only can experiential information from apomediaries and peers be more *relevant* for patients, it may also be perceived as more or at least equally *credible* as information based on scientific research.

Similarly, the notion that source expertise is communicated primarily through author credentials is not always true in the health care context. Here, "expertise" is not only expressed by such credentials as professional degrees and qualifications, but also by firsthand experience. Thus, experience-based credibility can be seen as an additional dimension of source credibility.[107] Source credibility research finds that similarity in attitudes with a speaker positively influences credibility perceptions.[108] By extension, similarity of experiences (similarity of symptoms, diagnoses, etc., in the health care context) also contributes to credibility perceptions. In the context of youth, this idea is expressed by the term *street credibility*, which is defined as "commanding a high level of respect in a certain environment due to experience in or knowledge of issues affecting that environment."[109]

Applying Network Theory to Apomediaries: Credibility Hubs

Apomediaries can be seen as highly complex networks of individuals and tools guiding consumers to credible information. Networked environments are typically seen as more equitable and democratic in structure compared to hierarchical environments, where a relatively small set of intermediaries holds most of the power. However, network theory[110] teaches us that most networks turn out not to be random networks in which all nodes have roughly the same number of links, but instead are scale-free networks, where a rich-gets-richer phenomenon leads to the emergence of highly connected nodes, called "hubs." Hubs emerge in scale-free networks because of growth (i.e., the continued addition of new nodes or actors) and preferential attachment of links to nodes that already have more links.[111] In the context of this chapter, these hubs can be called *credibility hubs*. Credibility hubs are highly connected and influential nodes (e.g., "opinion leaders"), and are partly a result of what Sundar[112] calls the bandwagon heuristic of credibility assessment ("If others think something is good, then I should think so too"). The implication is that not all apomediaries are equal; there is likely to emerge a small number of highly influential nodes whose recommendations carry more weight in influencing credibility perceptions.

Interestingly, former intermediaries may initially have a good chance of becoming a credibility hub, because they are already well connected. For instance, a professional medical organization has a preexisting social network that leads to other organizations' linking to their Web site, leading their Web site to appear at the top of Google search results, making the Web site appear more credible, which in turn leads to more people to link to it, and so on. An interesting psychological phenomenon that may help to create credibility hubs through a rich-gets-richer mechanism is that people attribute statements they believe to credible sources. For example, participants in an experiment who were exposed to a statement many times not only came to believe the statement, but were also likely to attribute it more often to *Consumer Reports* (a credible source) than to the *National Enquirer* (a not-so-credible source).[113] Such psychological mechanisms may further increase the trustworthiness of often-cited sources.

Despite the fact that former intermediaries may initially have a better chance of becoming credibility hubs in an apomediation network, network theory also shows that entirely new hubs may emerge with relative ease,[114] making the landscape much more fluid than in an intermediation environment, where credibility hubs tend to be relatively static. In any case, there is tremendous opportunity to analyze apomediation networks not only for research purposes, but also to develop tools that can help guide consumers to trustworthy information. Semantic Web tools, which allow machine-processable descriptions of trust relationships, combined with social network analysis, have been proposed as a possible approach to develop "intelligent" applications that enable consumers to find credible health information on the basis of what a network of actors says about other actors,[115] and there is now an emerging area of research looking at the question how trust relations in Web-based social networks can be modeled, calculated, mined, and integrated into applications.[116]

New Perspectives on Source and Message Credibility

As the previous section argued, the shift from intermediaries to apomediaries has implications in terms of how people assess credibility and what is deemed credible. Moreover, this shift from a gatekeeper/singular authority environment to a network environment where people are guided to information through others/multiple authorities, perhaps even constitutes a paradigm change for users and for researchers, whose thinking is still primarily influenced by the old intermediary model. The following section explores some new perspectives on source and message credibility in networked digital environments.

Source Credibility in a Networked World

Source credibility is traditionally seen as a cornerstone of credibility judgments. A piece of health information attributed to a high school freshman can appear less credible than the same piece of information attributed to a medical expert, in particular if the message receiver has limited knowledge of the topic discussed.[117] A number of quality instruments and credibility checklists for content producers refer to the provision of authors' names as an ethical tenet, as well as a predictor for "quality" information.[118] However, there are considerable problems in defining author or "source" in the digital environment.[119] In fact, aspects of the technology may cause users to pay less attention to and assign less weight to source cues than they do to message cues when determining credibility than they do in intermediated environments. Fogg's prominence-interpretation theory supports this view, claiming that credibility is a product of the prominence and interpretation of credibility cues.[120]

In digital environments, source cues may be less prominent than in traditional media or face-to-face interactions, owing to the difficulties in determining who the source is in digital media environments and the relative paucity of source cues on many Web sites. As a result, it may actually be easier for the user to try to corroborate the message, for example by clicking on the first hits in a search engine, to see what multiple people have to say, rather than investigating in-depth each specific site for its source(s) and source credentials. Ironically, some users even praise the relative "source anonymity" on the Internet as an advantage of the medium, as illustrated by the following quote of a teenager, who said on the Internet "people can meet people and share their ideas without their race, religion, or physical attractiveness becoming a factor. This optional facelessness allows true freedom and interaction without bias."[121] What the teenager implies is that, ideally, people should focus on the message rather than the source, especially if there is reason to believe that source attributes may unfairly negatively influence message acceptance by the receiver. By extension, teenagers striving for autonomy may appreciate the fact that the Internet allows them to conceal their age, as it may detract from their credibility in adults' eyes.

Second, in terms of users' interpretation of credibility cues, digitally sophisticated users (and youth in particular) may be well aware that on the Internet, credentials suggesting expert status can be easily misrepresented, as can identities, making interpretation of source cues difficult. Hence, users may intuitively feel that even if they would investigate source expertise cues, the legitimacy of those cues would still remain questionable. Indeed, many young people have multiple online identities themselves: A Pew survey in 2000 found that 56 percent of teens reported having more than one screen name or e-mail address, 24 percent have pretended to be someone else online, and 33 percent have lied about themselves for various purposes, some to gain access to age-restricted Web sites.[122] Most users are also aware that it is relatively easy to misrepresent expert status online. The fact that anyone with sufficient technological access and skill can create a Web site and claim to be an expert on a topic is well known. Thus, sophisticated users will cross-check facts rather than rely on asserted claims of expert status. This observation is grounded in empirical work[123] that shows that consumers collect bits and pieces of information from different Web sites without necessarily paying a lot of attention to who authored each information bit.

In summary, young people may not spend a lot of energy looking at authors' names and verifying source expertise. Although additional research is required to resolve the various dimensions of source credibility today, the influence of visible source credibility cues that can be easily interpreted such as brand name recognition,[124] surface credibility,[125] site design,[126] concordance of the message when obtained from different sources,[127] and perhaps apomediary credibility (as discussed next) are all important to consider today.

Apomediary Credibility

Apomediaries are human or technological agents that guide users to trustworthy sources and messages by, for example, recommending certain sources or messages. Apomediaries themselves are not necessary to obtain that information, in contrast to the more traditional intermediary model. Intermediaries are often conceptualized as the "source" (although in many cases they just mediate between the true source and the recipient, as, for example, do journalists), and as such, most of the source credibility literature deals with the credibility of the intermediary.[128] Apomediaries, on the other hand, should not be conceptualized as sources because they are recommenders or referrers to other sources. That said, however, the credibility of the apomediary certainly has an influence on perceptions of the credibility of the recommended source.

Consumers may evaluate the trustworthiness of various apomediaries differently, depending on whether they are humans or electronic tools. For some types of apomediaries, people may rely largely on community mechanisms to sort out less trustworthy members, such as friends, peers, or users of electronic rating and recommender systems where the reputation of the user is measured (e.g., Slashdot's "karma" mechanism). In this situation, access to or standing within the community are the primary conveyors of trust. This type of credibility assessment may be particularly appealing to younger Internet users, given their popularity and apparent comfort with social networking via digital media. However, whether or not these mechanisms are effective is unclear.

Message Credibility

Message credibility is commonly seen as being associated with attributes such as perceived message accuracy and completeness. However, the relationship between message "quality" attributes such as accuracy and completeness and perceived message credibility is not simple or linear.[129] Consequently, developers of health information designed for public dissemination should not assume that all they have to do is make their information "accurate" and complete in order for users to find it credible.

Relationship between Accuracy and Perceived Message Credibility

According to Fogg, credibility is an inherently subjective concept that is created from an individual's interpretation of various source, media, and information elements.[130] The subjectivity of credibility interpretations implies that different audiences may perceive the same information from the same source to be differently credible, supporting the notion that accuracy and completeness are not necessarily predictors of message credibility. Indeed, evidence-based health information provided by sources with the best credentials can be perceived as not credible as when, for instance, an otherwise high-quality Web site delivering evidence-based information is negatively affected by bad design and navigational issues (broken links, etc.). In addition, research has shown that evidence-based health information may not be trusted by some because of negative attitudes and mistrust toward research and researchers as the source of information.[131]

While it is sometimes easy to spot blatantly inaccurate information, in medicine there are often "grey" areas with no "correct" answer. This reality is not always understood by laypersons, who may expect that there is a clear-cut answer to most medical questions. In fact, there may even be an inverse relationship between accuracy (in a sense of truthfulness to the facts as found in clinical research) and perceived credibility: For many medical problems, a vast body of conflicting evidence exists, and if all the contradictions and scientific uncertainty were "accurately" represented by a physician or on a Web site, many patients would be more skeptical than trusting, since uncertainty negatively affects credibility.[132] By contrast, sources that give simple, unconditional, nonconflicting information, even to the point of oversimplifying things to the extent that they really cannot be called "accurate," may appear more credible, at least for people who adopt a "binary" evaluation strategy as described earlier.[133]

Although it would be nice to be able to measure the relationship between actual and perceived message accuracy, research on the quality of health information on the Internet has revealed significant methodological difficulties in measuring the "actual" accuracy and comprehensiveness of online health information in an objective and reliable manner.[134] One common methodology used to assess accuracy and comprehensiveness is to extract facts from evidence-based clinical guidelines and to check whether these facts are present or absent on a health Web site. While the gold standard of accuracy is "evidence-based medicine," in many cases the evidence is poor or conflicting, and it may be difficult or impossible to determine the "truth." Even in the presence of clinical guidelines, standards for medical practice often vary regionally, signalling yet another problem for a global medium.

A related problem is that no clear standards exist on how, or how much, medical information should be conveyed to consumers. Questions such as the degree to which and how information should be simplified, and how to best communicate risks are hotly debated. In reality, then, quality of content can only be determined if there is a clear answer to a medical question and if there is an evidence base that says how to best convey this information to consumers. Unfortunately, both of these elements are often absent in the medical literature. It is not surprising, then, that patients sometimes seek, and have more trust in, experiential information from peers, rather than information based on research. On the Internet, experiential information is by far more prevalent than research information. It is important for consumers to realize, however, that while anecdotes are "accurate" representations of a single person's experience, they may not be generalizable, reliable, or applicable, which is why anecdotes are generally dismissed by physicians as a basis for medical decision making. However, they remain "accurate" information at some level, and it is still an open question to what degree the body of "opinions" and "experiences" on the Internet conflicts with the research evidence, and to what extent it may be misleading or helpful for patients.

Completeness in a Hyperlinked World

"Comprehensiveness" or "completeness" of content is an important quality criterion used by information scientists[135] and evaluators of health information on the Internet.[136] It is also important from the point of view of a commercial health information provider, who generally aims to keep consumers on their Web site, avoiding links to other Web sites and often striving to provide a broad scope of information to enhance "stickiness" and credibility of the Web site. Some empirical work shows that the more information provided, the more a Web site is trusted by consumers.[137] This is perhaps a result of promoting "comprehensiveness" as a quality or credibility criterion in the literature, or more likely is a result of people being easily impressed by an information-filled page or site, and inferring authority from the pure volume of information.

However, from the point of view of a user, public health researcher, or policy maker, completeness of a given single Web site in a networked world may not be of primary importance, as long as further information can be easily found on other Web sites. This is because people typically gather information from various sites and complementary information is often only a mouse-click away.[138] From the user's perspective, there may be nothing wrong with a Web site that deals with one narrow topic in depth (e.g., treatment options for a particular health condition) but that provides links to other sites with additional information rather than providing "comprehensive" information about a disease (e.g., epidemiology, diagnosis, prognosis, and treatment). In fact, it has been shown that some people trust specialists more than generalists[139] owing to their presumed deep knowledge, highlighting that "comprehensiveness" or "completeness" should not be misunderstood as coverage of a broad scope of topics.

In sum, while information completeness may be a valid concern in the offline world, consumers in the networked, hyperlinked world are not necessarily looking for the "one-stop shopping" Web site. Part of the attractiveness of the Internet is in fact its diversity. While consumers do look for convenience, and some have difficulty searching and finding information on the Internet, much of the younger generation will likely not perceive clicking from site to site as a major inconvenience. As a consequence, content developers should not necessarily always strive for completeness, particularly when information that is outside their particular content expertise is covered on other sites, and educators should not necessarily promote completeness as a definitive quality criterion in this context.

Language and Message Credibility

High-quality and credible health Web sites targeted to youth may also have some special requirements concerning language. While "professional" language has been mentioned by adults as a marker for credibility,[140] age-appropriate nonpatronizing language is important to engage kids and will likely enhance the "street credibility" of the content producer. Young people may not be persuaded by material that "preaches" in an adult voice, especially in sensitive health areas involving sexual or drug-related information. Again, there are parallels to what "autonomous" adults prefer, who also have a dislike for patronizing, "doctors know it best" language.[141] The implication is that language should be tailored to the autonomy level of the audience to positively influence users' credibility judgments.

Next-Generation Education Assessment Tools

A recent review of 273 instruments designed for patients and consumers to assess the credibility of health information concluded that "few are likely to be practically usable by the intended audience."[142] Most of these tools are simple checklists, reflecting the observation made earlier that many tools and perspectives on credibility do not adequately take into account the unique features of a digital networked environment. A prime example is the DISCERN instrument, which was developed for printed patient education brochures[143] but is advocated as a tool to be used in the Internet context.[144] While aspects of these tools may well be useful in the networked world,[145] as also shown for DISCERN,[146] there is a shortage of tools that specifically exploit the strengths of the Internet.

A second generation of educational tools that takes the networked digital environment into account is required. Educational and technological tools should capitalize on the advantages of networked environments, which include the ability for users to rely on multiple sources of information, to cross-check information on other Web sites, and to verify the credibility and reputation of the source using the Web itself. As Meola notes, rather than promoting a mechanistic way of evaluating Internet resources, a contextual approach is needed, which includes reminding users that they can and should corroborate information on the Web.[147] It is exactly those techniques and processes that should be taught and reinforced through process-oriented applications and tools.

An example of such a second-generation educational tool—though certainly still in need of improvement—is the FA4CT (or FACCCCT) algorithm, developed in the context of an Internet "school" for cancer patients.[148] FA4CT is intended for use by consumers to find and check medical facts on the Internet in three steps: (1) Find Answers and Compare from different sources, (2) Check Credibility, and (3) Check Trustworthiness (reputation). To use FA4CT, consumers who seek information on the Web are instructed to first formulate their medical question as clearly as possible, preferably in a way that allows a yes/no answer. They are then instructed to translate this question into search terms and to conduct an initial Google search query to locate three Web sites that contain an answer to their question. If there is no consensus in the three answers provided, each Web site is evaluated for credibility by checking the currency of the information, its use of references, determining the site's explicit purpose, disclosure of sponsors, interests disclosed and conflicts found, how balanced the information appears to be, and the level of evidence provided for claims. These criteria are based on empirical studies and reflect markers that have been shown to predict information accuracy.[149] If after elimination of less reliable Web sites there is still no consensus, users are asked to enter the name of the source into Google to check what others on the Web have to say about that source, in an effort to arrive at a reputation score.

Cross-checking of facts as a strategy does have its limitations and, apart from one small study,[150] there is limited evidence demonstrating that this strategy is indeed suitable to find "accurate" information. There are also potential pitfalls to this strategy including misinformation, rumors, and myths that may spread as fast as credible information on the Internet. Moreover, because information may be mirrored or "syndicated" simultaneously on hundreds of Web sites, it may falsely appear to support a fact from multiple perspectives, while in reality a single source is responsible for the content. Perhaps the biggest threat in applying the cross-checking strategy is that if consumers do not formulate their queries in a neutral way, they will find mainly information that supports their own preconceived view (as discussed earlier). Thus, a certain degree of Internet literacy is required to implement this strategy effectively and, ideally, promoting the strategy of corroboration should be combined with educating users how to perform unbiased searches as well as how to avoid other potential pitfalls. Finally, more general limitations of process-oriented approaches include that such processes and techniques are time-intensive and cognitively demanding.

Conclusion

This chapter argues that digital media technologies have caused a paradigm shift in the ways in which people, both young and old, seek and find health information that they consider credible. As a result of disintermediation, traditional intermediaries are being both complemented and replaced by "apomediaries," who stand by consumers to guide them to trustworthy information, and/or provide credibility cues for information or sources. Table 1 summarizes the differences between intermediary and apomediary environments.

It is further argued that different degrees of desire, ability, and actual autonomy are related to the preference for an apomediated versus intermediated information environment. In particular, the chapter draws analogies between the technological disintermediation process afforded by digital media, and the naturally-occurring disintermediation process that takes place during adolescence. Both processes reflect the desire of e-consumers and adolescents to, under certain circumstances, emancipate themselves from traditional authorities, and to gain and maintain autonomy. While the disintermediation and emancipation processes are enabled, supported, and reinforced by digital media, in both cases information recipients have to reach a certain degree of cognitive ability, prior knowledge, self-efficacy, and autonomy to use them effectively.

Of course, none of these correlations are absolute and, in many cases, information consumers will dynamically switch back and forth between intermediated and apomediated environments, as well as use them simultaneously. However, the journey through adolescence and the journey of a chronic disease patient are two situations where profound shifts in autonomy typically occur, with consequences for how credibility is assessed throughout this continuum.

Indeed, another premise of this chapter is that these environments affect how credibility is assessed. It is hypothesized that with disintermediation, tools, influential peers, and opinion leaders become more important. As such, the recommendations of apomediaries may become equally or more important than source credibility as it has been defined traditionally. This is not to say, however, that visible and easy-to-interpret source cues, including brand names, will not continue to affect credibility perceptions in the online world. Rather, they will likely be one of many credibility cues that information seekers will consider, and may become less important as the cues provided by apomediaries, perhaps especially for younger information seekers who may be more comfortable using the social networking potential afforded by digital media.

On the basis of these ideas, the chapter suggests that the tools of network analysis may be useful in studying the dynamics of apomediary credibility in a networked digital world. The networked environment also supports the evaluation of messages, in addition to sources, through cross-checking of facts from multiple sources. One concern arising from the apomediated environment is that it may promote "mass opinion" more than "fact," making

Table 1
Dichotomies in intermediation versus apomediation environments.

Dimension	Intermediation Environment	Disintermediation/Apomediation Environment
Overarching Issues		
Environment	Managed	Autonomous
Power	Centralized; power held by intermediaries (experts, authorities)	Decentralized; empowerment of information seekers and youth
Dependence	Information seekers dependent on intermediaries (physicians, parents); intermediaries are *necessary*	Information seekers are emancipated from intermediaries as apomediaries (peers, technology) provide *guidance*; apomediaries are *optional*
Nature of Information Consumption	Consumers tend to be passive receivers of information	Consumers are "prosumers" (i.e., coproducers of information)
Nature of Interaction	Traditional 1:1 interaction between intermediary and information seeker	Complex individual- and group-based interactions in a networked environment
Information Filtering	"Upstream" filtering with top-down quality assurance mechanisms	"Downstream filtering" with bottom-up quality assurance mechanisms
Learning	More formal; learning through consumption of information	More informal; learning through participation, application, and information production
Cognitive Elaboration	Lower cognitive elaboration required by information receivers	Higher elaboration required by information seekers; higher cognitive load unless assistance through intelligent tools
User	More suitable for and/or desired by preadolescents, inexperienced or less information-literate consumers, or patients with acute illness	More suitable for and/or desired by older adolescents and adults, experienced or information-literate consumers, or patients with chronic conditions
Credibility Issues		
Expertise	Based on traditional credentials (e.g., seniority, professional degrees)	Based on first-hand experience or that of peers
Bias	May promote facts over opinion, but opportunity for intermediary to introduce biases	May bestow more credibility to opinions rather than facts
Source Credibility	Based on the believability of the source's authority; source credibility is more important than message credibility	Based on believability of apomediaries; message credibility and credibility of apomediaries are more important than source credibility
Message Credibility	Based on professional and precise language, comprehensiveness, use of citations, etc.	Based on understandable language, knowing or having experienced issues personally
Credibility Hubs	Static (experts)	Dynamic (opinion leaders)
Credibility Evaluations	Binary	Spectral

credibility a popularity contest, and that this may be particularly hazardous in the medical context given its special nature and consequentiality.

The ideas raised in the chapter also indicate practical implications of the apomediation model for developers of digital information and media, such as health Web sites geared specifically for children. Governments and other traditional authorities, while certainly having credibility due to brand name recognition, do not typically do a very good job of creating credible health Web sites for youth because they nearly always look and sound like government Web sites, and they lack the "street credibility" to keep many youth engaged with the site or message. Under the rubric developed in this chapter, good Web sites for youth should allow young people to share their voices and connect with others in a safe, positive, supportive, moderated, online community. They should allow youth to be creators of content, rather than conceive of them as merely an audience to "broadcast" to. Engaging and credible Web sites are about building community, and communities are built upon both personal and social needs.

Finally, this chapter points out that some of the core dimensions of message credibility as traditionally conceived, such as message "accuracy" or "completeness," are problematic in a domain such as medicine, where accuracy or completeness are difficult or impossible to measure objectively. Rather, it is suggested that evaluations of the accuracy of a message in this context are primarily a function of user needs and expectations. This opens some new perspectives for enhancing the credibility of online health messages. Unlike traditional media, digital media allow mass-customization to recipients' needs and expectations, as well as individual tailoring of message content.[151] What has been done to a lesser degree is tailoring credibility cues that can be used to increase the persuasiveness of the message. Such message tailoring can be equally useful for adult and youth health information seekers, as it takes into account different developmental levels and different levels of autonomy. More sophisticated educational tools that take into account the advantages afforded by digital media are required to help consumers find the information they need to become healthier individuals.

Notes

1. Susannah Fox and Deborah Fallows, Internet Health Resources, 2003, http://www.pewinternet.org/pdfs/PIP_Health_Report_July_2003.pdf. Archived at: http://www.webcitation.org/5I2STSU61.

2. Ibid., p. ii.

3. Statistics Canada, Household Internet Survey, 2003, http://www40.statcan.ca/l01/cst01/comm09a.htm?sdi=internet. Archived at: http://www.webcitation.org/5I2fNukJs.

4. Susannah Fox and Mary Madden, Pew Data Memo, Generations online, 2005, http://www.pewinternet.org/pdfs/PIP_Generations_Memo.pdf. Archived at: http://www.webcitation.org/5MGIFTboq.

5. Amanda Lenhart, Mary Madden, and Paul Hitlin, Teens and Technology: Youth Are Leading the Transition to a Fully Wired and Mobile Nation, July 27, 2005, http://www.pewinternet.org/pdfs/PIP_Teens_Tech_July2005web.pdf. Archived at: http://www.webcitation.org/5NBw8JH3M.

6. Victoria Rideout, Generation Rx.com: How Young People Use the Internet for Health Information, 2001, http://www.kff.org/entmedia/upload/Toplines.pdf. Archived at: http://www.webcitation.org/5I8qkgufL.

7. Greg Pass, Abdul Chowdhury, and Cayley Torgeson, A Picture of Search, 2006, http://www.ir.iit.edu/~abdur/publications/pos-infoscale.pdf. Archived at: http://www.webcitation.org/5I2Tms4Qk.

8. Donald L. Patrick, J. W. Bush, and Milton M. Chen, Toward an Operational Definition of Health, *Journal of Health Social Behavior* 14 (1973): 6–23.

9. Lenhart, Madden, and Hitlin, *Teens and Technology*, 42.

10. Gunther Eysenbach and Christian Köhler, What Is the Prevalence of Health-Related Searches on the World Wide Web? Qualitative and Quantitative Analysis of Search Engine Queries on the Internet. *Proc AMIA Annual Hall Symposium* (2003): 225–29; Gunther Eysenbach and Christian Köhler, Health-Related Searches on the Internet, *JAMA: The Journal of the American Medical Association,* 291 (2004): 2946; Amanda Spink, Yin Yang, Jim Jansen, Pirrko Nykanen, Daniel P. Lorence, Seda Ozmutlu, and H. Cenk Ozmutlu, A Study of Medical and Health Queries to Web Search Engines, *Health Information and Libraries Journal* 21 (2004): 44–51; Pass, Chowdhury, and Torgeson, A Picture of Search.

11. Gunther Eysenbach and Christian Köhler, How Do Consumers Search for and Appraise Health Information on the World-Wide-Web? Qualitative Study Using Focus Groups, Usability Tests and Indepth Interviews, *British Medical Journal* 324 (2002): 573–77.

12. Rideout, Generation Rx.com.

13. Mark I. Hainer, Naoky Tsai, Steven T. Komura, and Charles L. Chiu, Fatal Hepatorenal Failure Associated with Hydrazine Sulfate, *Annals of Internal Medicine* 133 (2000): 877–80; Steven D. Weisbord, Jeremy B. Soule, and Paul L. Kimmel, Poison On Line—Acute Renal Failure Caused by Oil of Wormwood Purchased through the Internet [published erratum appears in *New England Journal of Medicine* 337(20) (1997): 1483], *New England Journal of Medicine* 337 (1997): 825–27.

14. Anthony G. Crocco, Miguel Villasis-Keever, and Alejandro Jadad, Analysis of Cases of Harm Associated with Use of Health Information on the Internet, *JAMA: The Journal of the American Medical Association* 287 (2002): 2869–71.

15. Gunther Eysenbach and Christian Köhler, Does the Internet Harm Health? Database of Adverse Events Related to the Internet Has Been Set Up, *British Medical Journal* 324 (2002): 239.

16. Gunther Eysenbach, Gabriel Yihune, Kristian Lampe, Phil Cross, and Dan Brickley, Quality Management, Certification and Rating of Health Information on the Net with MedCERTAIN: Using a med-PICS/RDF/XML Metadata Structure for Implementing eHealth Ethics and Creating Trust Globally, *Journal of Medical Internet Research* 2 (2000): (suppl2) e1; Gretchen P. Purcell, Petra Wilson, and Tony Delamothe, The Quality of Health Information on the Internet, *British Medical Journal* 324 (2002): 557–58.

17. Gunther Eysenbach, The Impact of the Internet on Cancer Outcomes, *CA: A Cancer Journal for Clinicians* 53 (2003): 356–71; Thomas Ferguson and Gilles Frydman, The First Generation of E-Patients, *British Medical Journal* 328 (2004): 1148–49.

18. Bradford W. Hesse, David E. Nelson, Gary L. Kreps, Robert T. Croyle, Neeraj K. Arora, and Barbara K. Rimer, Trust and Sources of Health Information: The Impact of the Internet and Its Implications for Health Care Providers: Findings from the First Health Information National Trends Survey, *Archives of Internal Medicine* 165 (2005): 2618–24.

19. Nicola J. Gray, Jonathan D. Klein, Peter R. Noyce, Tracy S. Sesselberg, and Judith A. Cantrill, Health Information-Seeking Behaviour in Adolescence: The Place of the Internet, *Social Science and Medicine* 60 (2005): 1467–78.

20. Ibid., 1472.

21. Michael S. Sabel, Victor J. Strecher, Jennifer L. Schwartz, Timothy S. Wang, Darius L. Karimipour, Jeffrey S. Orringer, Timothy Johnson, and Christopher K. Bichakjian, Patterns of Internet Use and Impact on Patients with Melanoma, *Journal of the American Academy of Dermatology* 52 (2005): 779–85.

22. Kathryn E. Flynn, Maureen A. Smith, and Jeremy Freese, When Do Older Adults Turn to the Internet for Health Information? Findings from the Wisconsin Longitudinal Study, *Journal of General Internal Medicine* 21(2006): 1295–301.

23. Genni M. Newnham, W. Ivon Burns, Raymond D. Snyder, Anthony J. Dowling, Nadia F. Ranieri, Emma L. Gray, and Sue-Ann Lachlan, Information from the Internet: Attitudes of Australian Oncology Patients, *Internal Medicine Journal* 36 (2006): 718–23.

24. Gunther Eysenbach and Thomas L. Diepgen, Patients Looking for Information on the Internet and Seeking Teleadvice: Motivation, Expectations, and Misconceptions as Expressed in E-Mails Sent to Physicians, *Archives of Dermatology* 135:1999: 151–156.

25. Susannah Fox and Lee Rainie, The Online Health Care Revolution: How the Web Helps Americans Take Better Care of Themselves (Washington, DC: The Pew Internet and American Life Project, 2000), http://www.webcitation.org/NVu.

26. Hesse, et al., Trust and Sources of Health Information.

27. Fox and Rainie, *The Online Health Care Revolution*, 6.

28. Eysenbach and Köhler, How Do Consumers Search for and Appraise Health Information on the World-Wide-Web?; Fox and Rainie, *The Online Health Care Revolution*.

29. Eysenbach and Köhler, How Do Consumers Search for and Appraise Health Information on the World-Wide-Web?

30. B. J. Fogg, Cathy Soohoo, David R. Danielson, Leslie Marable, Julianne Stanford, and Ellen R. Trauber, How Do Users Evaluate the Credibility of Web Sites? A Study with Over 2,500 Participants (paper presented at the Proceedings of the 2003 Conference on Designing for User Experiences, San Francisco, CA), http://portal.acm.org/citation.cfm?doid=997078.997097; C. Nadine Wathen and Jacquelyn Burkell, Believe It or Not: Factors Influencing Credibility on the Web, *Journal of the American Society of Information Science & Technology* 53 (2002): 134–44.

31. Eysenbach and Köhler, How Do Consumers Search for and Appraise Health Information on the World-Wide-Web?

32. British Medical Association, Board of Science and Education, Adolescent Health, 2003, http://www.bma.org.uk/ap.nsf/AttachmentsByTitle/PDFAdolescentHealth/$FILE/Adhealth.pdf. Archived at: http://www.webcitation.org/5LmPtPZ8e.

33. Matthew Eastin, Toward a Cognitive Developmental Approach to Youth Perceptions of Credibility, this volume.

34. Harvey Skinner, Sherry Biscope, and Blake Poland, Quality of Internet Access: Barrier Behind Internet Use Statistics, *Social Science & Medicine* 57(2003): 875–80.

35. Rideout, Generation Rx.com.

36. Ibid., p. 1.

37. Eastin, Toward a Cognitive Developmental Approach; F. J. Harris, Challenges to Teaching Credibility Assessment in Contemporary Schooling, this volume.

38. Amanda Lenhart, Lee Rainie, and Oliver Lewis, Teenage Life Online: The Rise of the Instant-Message Generation and the Internet's Impact on Friendships and Family Relationships, 2001, http://www.pewinternet.org/pdfs/PIP_Teens_Report.pdf. Archived at: http://www.webcitation.org/5I8mIrL6f.

39. Rideout, Generation Rx.com.

40. Lenhart, Rainie, and Lewis, Teenage Life Online.

41. See also Lenhart, Madden, and Hitlin, Teens and Technology, for similar findings.

42. Lenhart, Rainie, and Lewis, Teenage Life Online.

43. Ibid.

44. Andrew J. Flanagin and Miriam J. Metzger, The Role of Site Features, User Attributes, and Information Verification Behaviors on the Perceived Credibility of Web-Based Information, *New Media & Society* 9, no. 2 (2007): 319–42.

45. Nicola J. Gray, Jonathan D. Klein, Judith A. Cantrill, and Peter R. Noyce, Adolescent Girls' Use of the Internet for Health Information: Issues Beyond Access, *Journal of Medical Systems* 26 (2002): 545–53.

46. Rideout, Generation Rx.com; Lenhart, Rainie, and Lewis, *Teenage Life Online*; Lenhart, Madden, and Hitlin, *Teens and Technology*; Gray et al., Adolescent Girls' Use of the Internet.

47. Hesse et al., Trust and Sources of Health Information.

48. Eastin, Toward a Cognitive Developmental Approach.

49. See also Stephen Coleman, Doing IT for Themselves: Management Versus Autonomy in Youth E-Citizenship, in *Civic Life Online,* ed. W. Lance Bennett (this series), for a discussion of the shift from managed versus autonomous environments for teens.

50. Andrew J. Flanagin and Miriam J. Metzger, Digital Media and Youth, this volume.

51. Gunther Eysenbach, An Ontology of Quality Initiatives and a Model for Decentralized, Collaborative Quality Management on the (Semantic) World-Wide-Web, *Journal of Medical Internet Research* 3 (2001): E34.

52. Marc Meola, Chucking the Checklist: A Contextual Approach to Teaching Undergraduates Web-Site Evaluation, *Libraries and the Academy* 4 (2004): 331–44.

53. Derek L. Hansen, Holly A. Derry, Paul J. Resnick, and Caroline R. Richardson, Adolescents Searching for Health Information on the Internet: An Observational Study, *Journal of Medical Internet Research* 5 (2003): e25; Skinner, Biscope, and Poland, Quality of Internet Access.

54. Lana Ivanitskaya, Irene O'Boyle, and Anne M. Casey, Health Information Literacy and Competencies of Information Age Students: Results from the Interactive Online Research Readiness Self-Assessment (RRSA), *Journal of Medical Internet Research* 8 (2006): e6.

55. Eysenbach and Diepgen, Patients Looking for Information on the Internet and Seeking Teleadvice.

56. Ibid.; Flanagin and Metzger, The Role of Site Features; Miriam J. Metzger, Andrew J. Flanagin, Keren Eyal, Daisy R. Lemus, and Robert M. McCann, Credibility for the 21st Century: Integrating Perspectives on Source, Message, and Media Credibility in the Contemporary Media Environment, *Communication Yearbook* 27 (2003): 293–335.

57. Eysenbach and Köhler, How Do Consumers Search for and Appraise Health Information on the World-Wide-Web?; John W. Fritch and Robert L. Cromwell, Evaluating Internet Resources: Identity, Affiliation, and Cognitive Authority in a Networked World, *Journal of the American Society of Information Science & Technology* 52 (2001): 499–507; John W. Fritch and Robert L. Cromwell, Delving Deeper into Evaluation: Exploring Cognitive Authority on the Internet, *Reference Services Review* 30, no. 3 (2002): 242–54.

58. Gunther Eysenbach and Thomas L. Diepgen, Towards Quality Management of Medical Information on the Internet: Evaluation, Labelling, and Filtering of Information, *British Medical Journal* 317 (1998): 1496–500.

59. Ibid.

60. See Metzger et al., Credibility for the 21st Century, for a discussion of this issue.

61. Gunther Eysenbach, Towards Ethical Guidelines for E-Health: JMIR Theme Issue on eHealth Ethics, *Journal of Medical Internet Research* 2 (2000): e7.

62. Richard E. Petty and John T. Cacioppo, *Communication and Persuasion: Central and Peripheral Routes to Attitude Change* (New York: Springer, 1986).

63. Elizabeth Murray, Jo Burns, Tai S. See, R. Lai, and Irwin Nazareth, Interactive Health Communication Applications for People with Chronic Disease, *Cochrane Database of Systematic Reviews* (2005).

64. Dean J. Wantland, Carmen J. Portillo, William L. Holzemer, Rob Slaughter, and Eva M. McGhee, The Effectiveness of Web-Based vs. Non-Web-Based Interventions: A Meta-analysis of Behavioral Change Outcomes, *Journal of Medical Internet Research* 6 (2004): e40.

65. See S. Shyam Sundar, this volume.

66. S. Shyam Sundar and Clifford Nass, Conceptualizing Sources in Online News, *Journal of Communication* 51 (2001): 52–72.

67. Gunther Eysenbach, From Intermediation to Disintermediation and Apomediation: New Models for Consumers to Access and Assess the Credibility of Health Information in the Age of Web 2.0., *Medinfo* (in press).

68. Flanagin and Metzger, Digital Media and Youth; R. David Lankes, Trusting the Internet: New Approaches to Credibility Tools, this volume.

69. Gunther Eysenbach and Alejandro R. Jadad, Evidence-Based Patient Choice and Consumer Health Informatics in the Internet Age, *Journal of Medical Internet Research* 3 (2001): e19.

70. Dean F. Sittig, Personal Health Records on the Internet: A Snapshot of the Pioneers at the End of the 20th Century, *International Journal of Medical Informatics* 65 (2002): 1–6.

71. Flanagin and Metzger, Digital Media and Youth; Lankes, Trusting the Internet; Miriam J. Metzger et al., Credibility for the 21st Century.

72. Eysenbach, From Intermediation to Disintermediation and Apomediation.

73. Eysenbach and Diepgen, Towards Quality Management of Medical Information on the Internet.

74. OpenNet Initiative 2004, Internet Filtering in Saudi Arabia in 2004, http://www.opennetinitiative. net/studies/saudi/ONI_Saudi_Arabia_Country_Study.pdf. Archived at: http://www.webcitation.org/ 5Ln6EaupR.

75. Ralph R. Swick and Dan Brickley, PICS Rating Vocabularies in XML/RDF, 2000, http://www. w3.org/TR/rdf-pics. Archived at: http://www.w3.org/TR/rdf-pics.

76. Wikipedia, 2007, Digg. http://en.wikipedia.org/wiki/Digg. Archived at: http://www.webcitation. org/5Ln8MuQ1g.

77. Eysenbach et al., Quality Management, Certification and Rating of Health Information on the Net with MedCERTAIN, 2000; Gunther Eysenbach and Thomas L. Diepgen, Labeling and Filtering of Medical Information on the Internet, *Methods of Information in Medicine* 38 (1999): 80–88.

78. Wikipedia, 2007, Web 2.0. http://en.wikipedia.org/wiki/Web_2.0. Archived at: http://www. webcitation.org/5Lq4p8KBG; Wikipedia, 2007c, Wiki. http://en.wikipedia.org/wiki/Wiki. Archived at: http://www.webcitation.org/5Lq4g3zoO.

79. Richard Ling, Mobile Communications vis-à-vis Teen Emancipation, Peer Group Integration and Deviance, in *The Inside Text: Social Perspectives on SMS in the Mobile Age*, eds. Richard Harper, Leysia Palen, and Alex Taylor (London: Kluwer, 2005), 175–89.

80. Ibid., p. 187.

81. Lankes, Trusting the Internet.

82. Stephen Russell and Rosalie J. Bakken, Development of Autonomy in Adolescence, 2007, http://www.ianrpubs.unl.edu/epublic/live/g1449/build/g1449.pdf. Archived at: http://www.webcitation.org/5LnwnmVGp.

83. Of course, this is provided that the individual has actually a choice, which is not always the case.

84. Cameron D. Norman and Harvey A. Skinner, eHealth Literacy: Essential Skills for Consumer Health in a Networked World, *Journal of Medical Internet Research* 8 (2006): e9.

85. Matthew S. Eastin, Credibility Assessments of Online Health Information: The Effects of Source Expertise and Knowledge of Content, *Journal of Computer-Mediated Communication* 6 (2001).

86. Albert Bandura, Self-efficacy: Toward a Unifying Theory of Behavioral Change, *Psychological Review* 84 (1977): 191–215.

87. Eysenbach and Diepgen, Patients Looking for Information on the Internet and Seeking Teleadvice.

88. James G. Anderson, Michelle R. Rainey, and Gunther Eysenbach, The Impact of CyberHealthcare on the Physician-Patient Relationship, *Journal of Medical Systems* 27 (2003): 67–84; Julia M. Brotherton, Stephen J. Clarke, and Susan Quine, Use of the Internet by Oncology Patients: Its Effect on the Doctor–Patient Relationship, *Medical Journal of Australia* 177 (2002): 395; Eysenbach and Jadad, Evidence-Based Patient Choice and Consumer Health Informatics in the Internet Age; Ben S. Gerber and Arnold R. Eiser, The Patient Physician Relationship in the Internet Age: Future Prospects and the Research Agenda, *Journal of Medical Internet Research* 3 (2001): e15; Angie Hart, Flis Henwood, and Sally Wyatt, The Role of the Internet in Patient-Practitioner Relationships: Findings from a Qualitative Research Study, *Journal of Medical Internet Research* 6 (2004): e36; Elizabeth Murray, Bernard Lo, Lance Pollack, Karen Donelan, Joe Catania, Ken Lee, Kinga Zapert, and Rachel Turner, The Impact of Health Information on the Internet on Health Care and the Physician-Patient Relationship: National U.S. Survey among 1,050 U.S. Physicians, *Journal of Medical Internet Research* 5 (2003): e17; Elizabeth Murray, Bernard Lo, Lance Pollack, Karen Donelan, Joe Catania, Martha White, Kinga Zapert, and Rachel Turner, The Impact of Health Information on the Internet on the Physician-Patient Relationship: Patient Perceptions, *Archives of Internal Medicine* 163 (2003): 1727–34.

89. Murray et al., The Impact of Health Information on the Internet on Health Care and the Physician-Patient Relationship.

90. Eastin, Toward a Cognitive Developmental Approach; Nicola J. Gray, Jonathan D. Klein, Peter R. Noyce, Tracy S. Sesselberg, and Judith A. Cantrill, The Internet: A Window on Adolescent Health Literacy, *Journal of Adolescent Health* 37 (2005): 243.

91. Lenhart, Rainie, and Lewis, Teenage Life Online.

92. Adol Esquivel, Funda Meric-Bernstam, and Elmer V. Bernstam, Accuracy and Self Correction of Information Received from an Internet Breast Cancer List: Content Analysis, *British Medical Journal* 332 (2006): 939–42.

93. Jim Giles, Internet Encyclopaedias Go Head to Head, *Nature* 438 (2005): 900–1.

94. Flanagin and Metzger, The Role of Site Features.

95. John Grohol, Reliability and Validity in a Web 2.0 World, 2007, http://psychcentral.com/lib/2007/01/reliability-and-validity-in-a-web-20-world/. Archived at: http://www.webcitation.org/5LqS6tpoe.

96. B. J. Fogg and Hsiang Tseng, The Elements of Computer Credibility, 1999, http://captology.stanford.edu/pdf/p80-fogg.pdf. Archived at: http://www.webcitation.org/5Lqk5JrrA.

97. Petty and Cacioppo, *Communication and Persuasion*.

98. Fogg and Tseng, The Elements of Computer Credibility.

99. Lila J. Finney Rutten, Neeraj K. Arora, Alexis D. Bakos, Noreen Aziz, and Julia Rowland, Information Needs and Sources of Information among Cancer Patients: A Systematic Review of Research, 1980–2003, *Patient Education Counselor* 57 (2005): 250–61.

100. Randy Dietrich, HCCAP Founder's Story: Randy Dietrich, 2006, http://www.hepcchallenge.org/randy.htm. Archived at: http://www.webcitation.org/5Ls6kCGHn.

101. Albert C. Gunther, Attitude Extremity and Trust in Media, *Journalism Quarterly* 65 (1988): 279–87.

102. Claire Glenton, Elin Nilsen, and Benedicte Carlsen, Lay Perceptions of Evidence-Based Information—A Qualitative Evaluation of a Website for Back Pain Sufferers, *BMC Health Services Research* 6 (2006): 34.

103. Donald A. Redelmeier, Eldar Shafir, and Prince S. Aujla, The Beguiling Pursuit of More Information. *Medical Decision Making* 21 (2001): 376–81.

104. Molly Baldry, Carol Cheal, Brian Fisher, Myra Gillett, and Val Huet, Giving Patients Their Own Records in General Practice: Experience of Patients and Staff, *British Medical Journal (Clinical Research Edition)* 292 (1986): 596–98.

105. Metzger et al., Credibility for the 21st Century.

106. Glenton, Nilsen, and Carlsen, Lay Perceptions of Evidence-Based Information.

107. Experience-based credibility here is different from Tseng and Fogg's (1999) notion of "experienced credibility." Experience-based credibility in this context is earned from someone (a source of some information) having gone through a similar experience as the receiver, and thus possessing a firsthand understanding of what the receiver is going through. Experienced credibility is earned by the receiver having firsthand experience with a particular source of information.

108. Donald R. Atkinson, Ponce Francisco, and Francine Martinez, Effects of Ethnic, Sex, and Attitude Similarity on Counselor Credibility, *Journal of Counseling Psychology* 31(1984): 588–90; Donald R. Atkinson, Stephen Brady, and Jesus M. Casas, Sexual Preference Similarity, Attitude Similarity, and Perceived Counselor Credibility and Attractiveness, *Journal of Counseling Psychology* 28 (1981): 504–9; R. Kelly Aune and Toshiyuki Kichuchi, Effects of Language Intensity Similarity on Perceptions of Credibility, Relational Attributions, and Persuasion, *Journal of Language & Social Psychology* 12 (1993): 224–37; Roger L. Worthington and Donald R. Atkinson, Effects of Perceived Etiology Attribution Similarity on Client Ratings of Counselor Credibility, *Journal of Counseling Psychology* 43 (1996): 423–29.

109. Urban Dictionary 2006. Street Cred. http://www.urbandictionary.com/define.php?term=street+cred. Archived at: http://www.webcitation.org/5KT164TW0.

110. Albert-Lásló Barabasi, *Linked*, 1st ed. (Cambridge, MA: Perseus, 2002).

111. Ibid.

112. S. Shyam Sundar, The MAIN Model: A Heuristic Approach to Understanding Technology Effects on Credibility, this volume.

113. Alison R. Fragale and Chip Heath, Evolving Informational Credentials: The (Mis)attribution of Believable Facts to Credible Sources, *Personality and Social Psychology Bulletin*, 30 (2004): 225–36.

114. Barabasi, *Linked*.

115. Eysenbach, An Ontology of Quality Initiatives.

116. Jennifer A. Goldbeck, Computing and Applying Trust in Web-Based Social Networks (Ph.D. Dissertation, University of Maryland, College Park, 2005), http://trust.mindswap.org/papers/GolbeckDissertation.pdf. Archived at: http://www.webcitation.org/5Lq6IaaFf.

117. Jennifer A. Goldbeck and James Hendler, Inferring Binary Trust Relationships in Web-Based Social Networks, *ACM Transactions on Internet Technology (TOIT)* (2006), preprint at http://trust.mindswap.org/papers/toit.pdf. Archived at: http://www.webcitation.org/5Lq7fbB1u.; Eastin, Credibility Assessments of Online Health Information.

118. Commission of the European Communities, eEurope 2002: Quality Criteria for Health Related Web Sites, *Journal of Medical Internet Research* 4 (2002): e15; Helga Rippen, Criteria for Assessing the Quality of Health Information on the Internet, 1998, http://hitiweb.mitretek.org/docs/policy.pdf. Archived at: http://www.webcitation.org/5LojibKCs.; e-Health Ethics Initiative, e-Health Code of Ethics, *Journal of Medical Internet Research* 2 (2000): e9.

119. Flanagin and Metzger, Digital Media and Youth; Flanagin and Metzger, The Role of Site Features; Metzger et al., Credibility for the 21st Century; Sundar, The MAIN Model.

120. B. J. Fogg, Prominence-Interpretation Theory: Explaining How People Assess Credibility Online, CHI 2003, Ft. Lauderdale, http://credibility.stanford.edu/pdf/PITheory.pdf. Archived at: http://www.webcitation.org/5I4KpdQO6.

121. Arlene Goldbard, Generation D: Global Kids' Digital Media Essay Contest, 2006, http://www.globalkids.org/olp/dmec/DMECReport.pdf. Archived at: http://www.webcitation.org/5Lt3AcpTM, p. 13.

122. Lenhart, Rainie, and Lewis, Teenage Life Online.

123. Eysenbach and Köhler, How Do Consumers Search for and Appraise Health Information on the World-Wide-Web?; B. J. Fogg, Jonathan Marshall, Othman Laraki, Alex Osipovich, Chris Varma, Nicholas Fang, Jyoti Paul, Akshay Rangnekar, John Shon, Preeti Swani, and Marissa Treinen, What Makes Web Sites Credible? A Report on a Large Quantitative Study, in *Proceedings of SIGCHI'01*, March 31–April 4, 2001, Seattle, WA.

124. Gray et al., The Internet.

125. Fogg et al., How Do Users Evaluate the Credibility of Web Sites? A Study with Over 2,500 Participants.

126. Flanagin and Metzger, The Role of Site Features.

127. Meola, Chucking the Checklist.

128. Sundar and Nass, Conceptualizing Sources in Online News.

129. Gunther Eysenbach, John Powell, Oliver Kuss, and Eun-Ryoung Sa, Empirical Studies Assessing the Quality of Health Information for Consumers on the World Wide Web: A Systematic Review, *JAMA: The Journal of the American Medical Association* 287 (2002): 2691–700.

130. Fogg, Prominence-Interpretation Theory.

131. Glenton et al., Lay Perceptions of Evidence-Based Information.

132. Michael Smithson, Conflict Aversion: Preference for Ambiguity vs Conflict in Sources and Evidence, *Organizational Behavior and Human Decision Processes* 79 (1999): 179–98.

133. Fogg and Tseng, The Elements of Computer Credibility.

134. Eysenbach et al., Empirical Studies Assessing the Quality of Health Information.

135. Robert S. Taylor, *Value-Added Processes in Information Systems* (Norwood, NJ: Ablex, 1986).

136. Eysenbach et al., Empirical Studies Assessing the Quality of Health Information.

137. Mohan J. Dutta-Bergman, The Impact of Completeness and Web Use Motivation on the Credibility of e-Health Information, *Journal of Communication* 54 (2004): 253–69.

138. Eysenbach et al., Empirical Studies Assessing the Quality of Health Information.

139. Mitchell D. Wong, Steven M. Asch, Ronald M. Andersen, Ron D. Hays, and Martin F. Shapiro, Racial and Ethnic Differences in Patients' Preferences for Initial Care by Specialists, *American Journal of Medicine* 116 (2004): 613–20.

140. Eysenbach and Köhler, How Do Consumers Search for and Appraise Health Information on the World-Wide-Web?

141. Angela Coulter, Vikki Entwistle, and David Gilbert, Sharing Decisions with Patients: Is the Information Good Enough? *British Medical Journal* 318 (1999): 318–22.

142. Elmer V. Bernstam, Dawn M. Shelton, Muhammad Walji, and Funda Meric-Bernstam, Instruments to Assess the Quality of Health Information on the World Wide Web: What Can Our Patients Actually Use? *International Journal of Medical Informatics* 74 (2005): 13–19.

143. Deborah Charnock, Sasha Shepperd, Gill Needham, and Robert Gann, DISCERN: An Instrument for Judging the Quality of Written Consumer Health Information on Treatment Choices, *Journal of Epidemiological Community Health* 53 (1999): 105–11.

144. Sasha Shepperd, Deborah Charnock, and Adrian Cook, A 5-Star System for Rating the Quality of Information Based on DISCERN. *Health Information Library Journal* 19 (2002): 201–5.

145. The DISCERN questionnaire (http://www.discern.org.uk/) prompts users to rate health-related Web sites by answering focused questions pertaining to the quality of information found on the site(s) they view.

146. Deborah Charnock and Sasha Shepperd, Learning to DISCERN Online: Applying an Appraisal Tool to Health Web Sites in a Workshop Setting, *Health Education Research* 19 (2004): 440–46.

147. Meola, Chucking the Checklist.

148. Gunther Eysenbach and Maria Thomson, The FA4CT Algorithm: A New Model and Tool for Consumers to Assess and Filter Health Information on the Internet, *Medinfo* (in press).

149. Gunther Eysenbach, Infodemiology: The Epidemiology of (Mis)information, *American Journal of Medicine* 113 (2002): 763–65.

150. Eysenbach and Thomson, The FA4CT Algorithm.

151. Matthew Kreuter, David Farrell, Laura Olevitch, and Laura Brennan, *Tailoring Health Messages. Customizing Communication with Computer Technology* (London: LEA, 2000); Matthew W. Kreuter, Fiona C. Bull, Eddie M. Clark, and Debra L. Oswald, Understanding How People Process Health Information: A Comparison of Tailored and Nontailored Weight-Loss Materials, *Health Psychology* 18 (1999): 487–94; Victor Strecher and Melissa McPheeters, The Potential Role of Tailored Messaging, *Behavioral Healthcare* 26 (2006): 24–26.

Challenges to Teaching Credibility Assessment in Contemporary Schooling

Frances Jacobson Harris

University of Illinois at Urbana-Champaign, University Laboratory High School

and University Library

A Call to Arms: Teaching Credibility Assessment

Today's young people have been described as digital natives, fluent in the digital language of computers, video games, and the Internet.[1] Schools, while perhaps not keeping pace with their students' native sensibilities, are much different places than they were ten, or even five years ago. By the fall of 2003, nearly 100 percent of public schools in the United States had access to the Internet, compared with only 35 percent in 1994.[2]

But meaningful access to digital information resources and systems in schools is about much more than a physical connection to the Internet. Digital natives are not necessarily skilled or critical consumers of digital information. Many are still novices when it comes to searching, selecting, and assessing the meaning and value of the information they find.[3]

Indeed, many educators recognize the need for aggressive instructional efforts that will prepare young people to navigate effectively in today's complex media environment and assess the credibility of the information they find there. At the same time, educators face considerable challenges to teaching credibility assessment and its associated concepts. This chapter examines the nature and significance of these challenges, which are both structural and dynamic. *Structural* challenges are institutional, in the form of government regulation, as well as school policies and procedures. *Dynamic* challenges are defined here as the processes and relationships that occur as a consequence of young people's cognitive development and the inherent difficulties of navigating a complex Web environment. In tandem, these challenges limit opportunities for instructional intervention and pose a unique set of problems for educators to solve. The primary focus of this chapter is on adolescents, although much of what is covered may also apply to younger children as well as to young adults.

Background

Teaching credibility assessment is not a new idea. The field of credibility research has produced rich data sets that describe how users *determine* credibility.[4] However, explicit reference to *teaching* credibility assessment in the various "literacies" literatures is scant. This seeming dearth of attention is due to the fact that the concept of credibility is bound up in a wide variety of existing education and library and information science endeavors and is described in the terms and vocabularies of those traditions. In each case, terminology and emphases differ, with the notion of credibility assessment assumed if not explicitly named.

In information science, for example, credibility has been considered an element of the relevance criterion, the ability of an information system to retrieve all documents that a user judges to be relevant for a specific purpose,[5] rather than a separate criterion in its own right.[6] The major information literacy standards documents emphasize such skills as the ability to identify appropriate information, assess relevance, select information, and integrate information, but not the ability to assess credibility per se.[7] However, the theme of information *evaluation*, which incorporates credibility assessment, is a strong thread throughout the information literacy literature.[8] Credibility assessment concepts saturate the textbooks, lessons, and methodologies of information literacy instruction.[9] The education literature, most notably the work on critical thinking, has a great deal to say about concepts surrounding credibility assessment.[10] Judging the credibility of a source is a central tenet of the critical thinking perspective. Credibility assessment themes are also expressed through the related fields of media literacy,[11] information and communication technology (ICT) literacy,[12] reading,[13] and what is becoming known as twenty-first-century literacy.[14] In these discourses, *evaluation* is often the operative term rather than *credibility assessment*, and emphasis on various facets of the process varies. The literature of critical thinking is an exception, with credibility occupying a more central focus and being defined in terms of specific criteria.[15] The perspective of the library and information science community is that the concept of information literacy is broader than, and therefore inclusive of, other domains that have been described in literacy terms, such as media, digital, or technology literacy.[16] Similar claims have been made in reference to media literacy.[17] Tyner promotes a multiliteracies approach[18] and urges researchers to study collaborative literacy models. Ultimately, each of these perspectives points to the pressing need to teach credibility assessment. However, a variety of significant factors inhibits efforts to teach credibility assessment in schools. The next section of this chapter examines some of the major institutional constraints that stand in the way of such endeavors.

Structural Challenges

Structural challenges are those that are built into the political and cultural constructs of contemporary schooling. Public institutions provide stability, continuity, and scalability in our society, but their conservative nature can inhibit growth and development. Schools, like large steamships that maneuver slowly into each turn, set course with great deliberation. Yet they are situated in the midst of a rapidly changing media environment and serve a youth culture that has embraced the new media. It is important for credibility assessment education that suitably addresses the new media to gain a foothold in today's schooling environment. Unfortunately, such a foothold is not so easy to find. External forces—both political and social—are feeding and aggravating schooling's natural tendency toward bureaucracy and inertia.

Three structural factors that present specific challenges to teaching credibility assessment in schools are identified and described in this section of the chapter. The first is the very nature of school governance in the United States, in which curricula and school requirements vary from state to state, and even from district to district within states. The second is an environment of accountability that has resulted in a proliferation of mandated high-stakes testing. The third is legislation and a culture designed to protect children that have had the unintended consequence of limiting their access to digital media—and therefore the opportunity to teach them credibility assessment.

Everyone in Charge, No One in Charge

In the United States, education is locally funded and, in large part, locally controlled. Individual states set graduation requirements and local school districts design curricula to meet them. For good or ill, the United States has no national curriculum. In contrast, curricula, graduation requirements, and sometimes even course sequencing in many other parts of the world are mandated from above. Make no mistake, the U.S. government still leaves its mark on schools across the country by placing conditions on the use of critical federal funds, as will be discussed below. Ironically, however, its power to affect general curriculum design is quite limited. The federal government has no authority to mandate that instruction be given in a particular subject, whether that subject is geometry or credibility assessment of digital media. While this decentralized system of education allows schooling to be relatively responsive to local community needs, it also presents a structural challenge to teaching credibility assessment.

Instead of being subject to federal control, public schools must meet the standards of regional accrediting bodies and the subject-area standards set by state boards of education. Some states address credibility assessment topics within the framework of ICT, media literacy, or information literacy standards. For example, the Missouri "Show-Me" standards include a companion K–12 integrated technology and information literacy curriculum.[19] Its "component checklist" includes such credibility markers as source of information, reliability/authority, bias/prejudice, and fact/opinion. Wisconsin has defined three stages of "Information and Inquiry" performance standards that incorporate evaluation of information and media. By fourth grade, eighth grade, and twelfth grade, students are to have achieved developmentally appropriate benchmarks in such areas as detecting authorship and authoritativeness of information, recognizing point of view or bias, and evaluating graphic images for misleading presentation and manipulated data.[20]

Professional societies also create content-area standards that can have an impact on local curriculum adoption. Most prominent in the area of credibility assessment are the National Educational Technology Standards for Students,[21] the national guidelines and standards for school library media programs from the American Association of School Librarians and the Association for Educational Communications Technology,[22] and the information literacy competencies for higher education from the Association of College and Research Libraries.[23] Subject content standards containing information literacy elements have also been developed by a variety of disciplinary societies.[24] For example, Project 2061, a long-term initiative to improve literacy in science, mathematics, and technology, includes a section in its benchmarks called "critical-response skills" which incorporates credibility assessment concepts.[25] Standard 7 of the "Standards for the English Language Arts" notes:

Students conduct research on issues and interests by generating ideas and questions, and by posing problems. They gather, evaluate, and synthesize data from a variety of sources (e.g., print and non-print texts, artifacts, people) to communicate their discoveries in ways that suit their purpose and audience.[26]

While it is laudable that standards documents of professional societies are beginning to include credibility-assessment elements, nothing requires school districts to adopt them. Compliance with these standards is strictly voluntary and is subject to the priorities of local school boards and the resources that may or may not be available to fund compliance.

High-Stakes Testing

As alluded to earlier, the federal government still wields tremendous influence on American education, despite its decentralized nature. One of the most visible markers of this influence can be seen in the phenomenon of high-stakes testing. Most recently, the No Child Left Behind Act (NCLB), and its attendant dependency on testing, drives curricula and classroom activity across the country.[27] Schools are remarkably closed to new curricula that are not specifically included on mandated tests or reflected in accreditation standards. NCLB considers only two subjects, mathematics and reading. The success or failure of a school rides on student test scores in these two areas, regardless of what students may know about American history, art, or biology, for example. Although nothing stands in the way of schools teaching other subjects, in practice, classroom teachers find themselves spending a disproportionate amount of time teaching the content that will be tested and preparing their students for the standardized testing environment.[28]

Unfortunately, data on the success of NCLB are emerging that reveal that the legislation has not had its intended effect. Recent research reveals that the national average achievement has remained flat in reading and is growing at the same pace in math after NCLB as it was before.[29] High-stakes testing has also spawned a number of unintended side effects, including a tendency to inflate state test results while deflating racial and social achievement gaps, unethical test preparation practices, schools exempting more students from taking the tests, and schools not discouraging low-performing students from dropping out.[30] Unfortunately, children *are* still being left behind. Data from benchmark assessments are used to identify students who are close to passing, identified as "bubble kids."[31] Teachers are encouraged to focus on this group of students rather than help those whose scores are so low that any improvement would still not be at a passing level. High-achieving students who will pass anyway are left to their own devices. If the test scores of bubble kids do not rise, aggregated school scores do not rise and teachers are labeled as failures. In general, low teacher morale and poor retention rates permeate the high-stakes testing landscape.[32]

Critics of high-stakes testing are not against all forms of standardized testing and benchmark assessments. Recommendations for improvement include attention to other subjects, use of multiple methods of assessment when making high-stakes decisions, and authentic assessment that measures critical thinking skills rather than regurgitation of facts.[33] Such improvements would pave the way for testing credibility assessment skills. In fact, the Educational Testing Service, in collaboration with a group of two- and four-year colleges and universities, has developed a scenario-based standardized test to assess ICT literacy at the college level. Among other tasks on this examination, students are required to "judge the quality, relevance, authority, point of view/bias, currency, coverage and accuracy of digital information."[34] Unfortunately, an ICT literacy test that is designed for the K–12 audience is unlikely to be developed and administered without some sort of NCLB-like federal mandate.

Limited Access to Digital Media

The federal government has also left its mark on schooling by attaching strings to funding for Internet access. Public and school libraries that receive "e-rate" discounts for Internet access must comply with the Children's Internet Protection Act (CIPA), which requires the installation of Internet filtering software. Although the law was intended to protect children from pornography and other unsavory material, in practice it has spawned its own impressive set of unintended consequences. Even state-of-the-art filtering software regularly underblocks or overblocks online information, hampering students' efforts to perform legitimate school-related research.[35] In addition, the software is expensive to purchase and requires sophisticated network administration skills to install and maintain. While software filters do not specifically disallow information that is not credible, the ways in which they limit access to information also limits opportunities for young people to learn credibility assessment skills under the guidance of their teachers and librarians. By implication, the task of determining credibility is left to the proprietary practices of filtering companies, who are much more likely to hire technicians and software developers than educators or child development specialists. Numerous nonprofit organizations and public policy groups, such as the American Library Association,[36] the Brennan Center for Justice,[37] and the Electronic Frontier Foundation,[38] have decried the inefficacy of filtering software and its restrictions on access to constitutionally protected speech.

Many schools are guilty of out-of-the-box filtering software installations, not taking advantage of the calibrating options that most software products allow.[39] Even though current federal legislation allows filter settings to be adjusted for specific educational uses, schools rarely take advantage of these options. Customizing, overriding, or disabling filtering settings are time-consuming processes and are generally out of the hands of teachers and librarians. They must rely on instructional technology (IT) support staff, who are often either too busy with basic technology management to spend time tweaking filters or simply do not understand or care about the consequences of leaving a student to wait three days for a site to be unblocked. Sadly, sometimes teachers and librarians are more than willing to honor this status quo, in effect abdicating their instructional responsibilities to the IT staff.

Tech-savvy young people—and even not-so-tech-savvy young people—are able to circumvent filtering software without much trouble. They are aided by activist organizations such as Peacefire (http://www.peacefire.org/), which routinely publishes ways to undermine filtering systems. The 2006 move to enhance CIPA with the Deleting Online Predators Act (DOPA) would have required that schools also block all commercial social networking sites. Such efforts are predicated on what *could* happen and how young people *might* use a tool rather than on the inherent nature of the tool, which is itself neither bad nor good. Ironically, free commercial social networking sites provide an inexpensive and relatively simple method for teachers to use blogging, wikis, and other read/write technology to great effect in their classrooms. However, legislation like CIPA makes it difficult for educators to use, and teach the sound use of, many information and digital learning tools.

Software filtering is only one aspect of how access to digital media in schools is compromised. Teachers themselves introduce filter-style limitations by preselecting Web sites they find credible and appropriate and restricting their students to this prescreened content for Web quests and other activities. The pedagogical goals of some lessons are well served by this type of lesson construction. But if all Internet access is structured in this way, students miss opportunities to learn important searching and evaluation skills.[40] Teachers also differ in their personal understanding of digital information and how it should be evaluated. Many compensate for deficits in their knowledge by limiting the amount of digital information students can use for assignments or, as noted, restricting student use to predetermined resources. Other teachers respond by accepting *any* digital resource that students use without regard to quality or credibility. Such variability in teacher expectations sends mixed messages to students and, in effect, compromises their understanding of credibility assessment.

Local school district Internet access policies and implementation practices also restrict student access to online information. Even as reliable high-speed Internet connections become ubiquitous in American schools, e-mail is still considered off limits in many schools, even for educational purposes. Access is also limited by generic acceptable use policies (AUP) that allow only curriculum-related use. For example, the Chicago Public Schools AUP[41] specifies that the "CPS Network is strictly for educational pursuits" and that noneducational uses are prohibited. The list of prohibited uses includes, but is not limited to, such activities as games, chain letters, jokes, and religious activities. In contrast, the University of Illinois Laboratory High School Computer Usage Agreement[42] specifies acceptable uses in order of priority, starting with academic support, followed by communications, then by general information retrieval, and finally recreation. Users engaged in lower-priority activities are to yield their computers if they are needed for a higher-priority use.

Acceptable use policies codify a prevailing philosophy in contemporary school culture that defines digital media in terms of appropriateness. "Appropriate" content is generally characterized as "educational"—not educational in the broad sense, but educational as the content relates to the specific curriculum a student is studying. Students are commonly directed to preselected and vetted sites, or to recommender sites, where the recommenders are specifically defined. The definition of "inappropriate" includes obvious headline-attracting categories such as pornography. But "inappropriate" may also include social networking sites, blogging sites, and any site accessed for *recreational* purposes. School libraries, however, have long provided recreational material, most notably in their fiction and magazine collections. The availability of such material is considered essential to the promotion of literacy, independent reading, and social and cognitive development. Yet, although high school students are encouraged to read *Seventeen* magazine and *Sports Illustrated* in the school library, they are often not allowed to use the library's computers to read the same articles on the *Seventeen* and *Sports Illustrated* Web sites.

Structural challenges like high-stakes testing and filtered Internet access create false impressions in the public mind. The No Child Left Behind Act leads to a false sense that progress is being made in the improvement of schools. Internet filtering software leads to a false sense that children are safe while online at school. Both initiatives are palliative efforts that help us feel as though we are doing something about difficult and threatening societal problems. Unfortunately, the results are neither substantive nor meaningful. And, as will be discussed in further detail below, they have a detrimental impact on the ability to teach credibility assessment.

Dynamic Challenges

In addition to externally imposed structural challenges, young people engaging in credibility assessment of digital media face dynamic challenges that consist of processes and relationships. These challenges become apparent when young people, with their varying rates of cognitive, social, and emotional development, confront the complex and shifting nature of digital media.

Young people are not "small adults," but an entirely different user population with their own culture, norms, interests, abilities, and information needs.[43] In particular, adolescence is a period of life marked by the need to develop a sense of independence and autonomy.[44] Most parents struggle with this phenomenon, as their formerly affectionate and obedient children begin to prefer peers to family and resent parental attempts at protection and control.

Teenage rebellion can be particularly problematic when juxtaposed with the structural constraints of schooling. The inclination to defy authority is exacerbated when teenagers perceive signs of hypocrisy, double standards, or rules invoked for reasons they deem unfair or lacking in substance. Adolescents easily find evidence of these deficiencies in their schools' technological controls, such as filtering software, or the rule-based controls that prohibit the use of certain digital tools. They observe their teachers' lack of familiarity with digital media and the resulting inconsistent expectations regarding the definition, selection, and use of credible information. Many teens have little compunction about working around systems and rules to gain access to the information and tools they feel are theirs by right. In other words, if teenagers encounter structural barriers, they often will break those barriers.

Adolescent development is one aspect of the dynamic challenges that influence credibility assessment of digital media. The other major piece of this complex picture is the variable nature of information seeking and of information itself in today's constantly evolving digital environment. As young people wrestle with their own development, what happens during the information-seeking process? How do factors like motivation affect their seeking and evaluation skills? Are they able to analyze and deconstruct the credibility cues that populate the new media environment?

Young People and Information Seeking

Despite their reputation as digital natives and Internet gurus,[45] young people's skills in effective navigation of today's information landscape are actually somewhat limited.[46] They always find *something* when searching for information, just not always the *best* thing. A number of factors contribute to these deficits. Although their skills progressively improve with cognitive growth, education, and experience, young people are at a developmental disadvantage when it comes to evaluating digital media.[47] Younger children have difficulty recalling site content when presented with multiple peripheral information objects such as advertising and dynamic features.[48] Older youths may not have the knowledge base to contextualize the digital (or print) information they encounter. They often lack the analytical strategies, such as source corroboration, required to make meaningful assessments of conflicting information sources.[49] To compensate for these deficits, young people tend to employ different evaluation criteria than adults. They are more likely to simplify Web site evaluation tasks and make credibility judgments that rely heavily on design and presentation features rather than content.[50]

Most research on information-seeking behavior starts with the search itself and does not consider the origin and motivation for it.[51] But origin and motivation become very important in the context of credibility assessment. Therefore, it is useful to consider the search task types undertaken by young people through the lens of persuasion theory, such as the Elaboration Likelihood Model (ELM),[52] in which motivation is key. From the ELM perspective, young people evaluate content in a depth equal to their levels of motivation and ability. The more personally important the search task is, the more likely users are to employ a more systematic and effortful "central route" of evaluation of the information. For a task that is perceived as less essential or personally meaningful, young people are more likely to employ a "peripheral route" in their analyses, relying on heuristic judgments that primarily note the superficial or surface characteristics of digital media.[53]

In general, young people engage in two overarching types of information searches—searches that have been imposed on them by others, or imposed queries, and searches they initiate themselves, or self-generated queries.[54] No value judgment is applied to im-posed queries—they are not "bad" simply because they are imposed. But the fact of their imposition means that these queries may be approached differently by information seekers, as may be the manner in which credibility is assessed. A student who is assigned to write a report about the dynasties of ancient Egypt, when she has no intrinsic interest in the topic or the report, is likely to take the peripheral route to credibility assessment. Even within the category of imposed queries, not all are created equal. Some imposed queries are "double" imposed queries, as when a teacher (the imposer) gives a child (the agent) an assignment and the child takes it to a parent (now also an agent) to help resolve. Parents, friends, and others often become agents and collaborators in the information-seeking process, which compli-cates information transactions. Gross also points out the phenomenon of "gift queries,"[55] similar to Twidale, Nichols, and Paice's notion of "serendipitous altruism,"[56] in which indi-viduals *voluntarily* take on the role of agents. In these cases, young people, parents, teachers, or colleagues share information simply because someone they know is interested in it. A "gift agent" is likely to take the central route to credibility assessment, feeling a heightened sense of responsibility for evaluating information credibility precisely because the use of the infor-mation will affect someone else.[57] Because most research on information-seeking behavior starts with the search itself, it tends to neglect the category of self-generated querying or everyday-life information seeking.[58] Everyday-life information seeking (ELIS) is an inciden-tal form of information behavior, a discovery process that often occurs within the context of other activity. It is characterized as a social process rather than a cognitive one that occurs as a purposeful, self-conscious activity.[59] What we do know about everyday-life information seeking and young people suggests that they prefer to seek answers from friends and family rather than libraries.[60] Although very little is known about the ways in which young people assess credibility in these circumstances, it may be safe to assume that motivation is high due to the self-generated nature of the queries.

Information seekers often incorporate a strategy called "satisficing," a decision-making construct that combines the need to both satisfy and suffice.[61] When it is neither reasonable nor practical to consider all existing outcomes and possibilities, people will satisfice rather than optimize, terminating the decision-making process when a goal has been achieved "well enough." In an information-seeking context, particularly when imposed queries are involved, time constraints and information overload are factors that determine individual tolerance for continuing the search and evaluation process. Young people do not necessarily abandon consciousness of credibility assessment and other evaluation criteria, but, in many cases, they are willing to settle for information that is "good enough" in order to complete a task. Satisficing differs from the principle of least effort,[62] which assumes no process at all.

The Web Environment

The complexity of the Web environment produces special challenges for young people as they attempt to determine the credibility of information. Although the need to teach young people to critically appraise information has long been a part of the formal education land-scape, the core skills and issues being essentially the same as they were prior to the current rise in digital technologies, the technologies do present new challenges.[63] Burbules argues that the Web does not lend itself to conventional methods of credibility assessment due to its complex features and structure, lack of standard frames of reference, and its role as both an information archive and a social network.[64] The usual markers of institutional credibility and authority (e.g., publication in a prominent refereed journal, a standard encyclopedia) may not be present, replaced by more distributed credibility markers like hyperlinks, recommender and open authorship opportunities, and other self-referencing schemes. For purposes of credibility assessment, the Web's very strengths are also its weaknesses—its rapid rate of change, the level playing field it provides for all types of information, the hypertextual format that blurs distinctions among documents, and its very size and scope.[65]

The open Web presents many examples of conflicting cues that are difficult for users to identify and analyze. Levine observes that while every Web site looks the same on a list of Google results, a telephone directory at least categorizes listings by type.[66] He goes on to note that a clinic, hospital, or medical lab generally look quite different from a store that sells herbal remedies. But a hospital Web site may not look any different from the herbal remedy store's Web site—or from an accomplished teenager's hobby page. Levine concludes that the Web creates substantial new interpretive burdens even as it provides the opportunity to explore a wider range of ideas. The challenge to educators is to help learners develop strategies for managing and overcoming those interpretive burdens.

For young people, certain visual or contextual cues are particularly problematic:[67] the Web supplies no context for content. It has no fiction section, no nonfiction section, and no biography section. A student looking for information on baseball may stumble on a fantasy baseball team Web site that is populated with real names, places, and events, along with names of the amateurs who created the site and are also named as players. Search engine results do not always link to a site's equivalent of a title page, linking to internal pages instead. So a search on "birth control" may link to information within a church Web site, a political Web site, or a medical Web site. In general, authorship (and the meaning of authorship) can be difficult to determine, particularly as collaboratively developed content proliferates. Wikipedia (http://en.wikipedia.org), the online encyclopedia that anyone can write for or edit, provides many examples of the confusing consequences of distributed authorship. Volunteer editors with competing interests wrestle over individual entries, often "reverting" one another's contributions until the entry is locked or labeled with Wikipedia's disclaimer that the "neutrality" of the entry has been challenged. At any given point in time, what is a young person to make of the content? The teaching challenge here is to engage young people in evaluating source credibility when the source and its intent are elusive.[68]

Relevancy ranking can be another misleading cue. For example, a Google search on "Martin Luther King" currently produces a high-ranked placement for a site operated by a white supremacist organization. This is a "cloaked" Web site, one that disguises its underlying message of racial supremacy through the sophisticated use of domain name registration, graphical design, and text.[69] Its high ranking, derived in large part from numbers of links into the site from other high-ranking sites, implies credibility, as does the ".org" domain in the URL. Ironically, many of the links to this hate site are generated by well-meaning librarians whose Web site evaluation lessons use the King site as an example. Open discussion of ranking algorithms can help demystify the process and perhaps overcome young people's assumptions about the omniscience of search engine relevancy ranking.

Digital content can be intellectually challenging. When students in my classes compare the World Trade Organization Web site (http://www.wto.org) with a spoof site (http://www.gatt.org), they eventually identify the imposter because it currently contains links that lead outside the site or redirect to an e-mail client. But they have great difficulty comprehending the rationale behind the spoof site because they do not understand the satiric context, nor do they have sufficient background knowledge to make sense of the political content. They recognize the errant navigational cues but cannot decode the intellectual cues.

Finally, search engines tell only part of the story. Though used as the default entry point to the Web, they cannot retrieve information from the vast "invisible Web," which lies hidden behind firewalls and databases. As a result, academic subscription databases made available through schools and libraries are often underutilized or poorly understood by students—particularly as sources of credible, vetted information.[70] Other valuable resources are retrievable only by those who already know how to find them. One must know to go to the Library of Congress Web site in order to search the millions of images, song files, maps, texts, and other free resources of the American Memory collections (http://memory.loc.gov). Practically speaking, most young people generally do not find or use the resources of the invisible Web without some sort of formal pedagogical intervention initiated by librarians or teachers.

An Unfortunate Combination

The dynamic challenges just outlined are inextricably confounded with structural challenges. In combination, these two forces have the potential to seriously compromise young people's ability to learn to assess the credibility of digital media. Both types of information seeking— imposed querying and everyday-life information seeking—are affected. In the context of schoolwork, filtering software blocks legitimate information that students need for their assignments. High-stakes testing shrinks the curriculum and leaves less time for teaching process skills like information literacy, which could prepare students to decode the complex cues that permeate the Web environment. Prohibitions against read/write social network technologies like blogs, wikis, instant messaging, social bookmarking sites, and even e-mail, stymie students' collaborative work styles, their potential to communicate with experts, and even their ability to download or exchange information from reputable sources like subscription databases.

In fairness, schools serve many masters. Imagine the potential discomfort of a school administrator leading a group of board members on a tour through a computer lab filled with students browsing eBay, checking sports scores, or downloading music to their MP3 players. But from the student point of view, highly restrictive access policies lump nonacademic Web sites in with the truly odious—the pornographic, the violent, and the hate-filled—hardly a fine-tuned model for credibility assessment.

Structural and dynamic constraints have an even more profound impact on everyday-life information seeking. An argument could be made that school is not the place to solve personal problems or pursue individual interests. Again, the nature of traditional school library collections belies this position. If school is not a place to develop social and emotional skills as well as academic ones, then why do school libraries carry recreational magazines, self-help books, and fiction titles that are not "classics" or assigned reading? Somehow, the education community's shared ethos that the availability of noncurricular print materials promotes literacy and lifelong learning has not transferred to digital media, which is still judged by the "scale of appropriateness" described earlier. The resulting prohibition against using noncurricular online resources at school means that young people are forced to take their self-generated queries to familiar personal sources, often peers, and away from vetted information systems and services.

It may be that schools are reluctant to open the floodgates of Web access because, despite the presence of filtering software, dangerous material may still be only a click away. No trained librarian stands behind collection development on the Web. At a minimum, creating a more open access environment at school would require that credibility assessment instruction be ramped up and recalibrated, as will be discussed below. But in this era of high-stakes testing, school administrators are loathe to add content that does not appear to contribute directly to improving test scores.

Finally, just because teenagers, being teenagers, may ignore or sabotage structural constraints does not mean that such constraints have no place in schools. In cases where rules and security measures have been minimized in favor of an emphasis on education and personal responsibility, schools have run the risk of losing the integrity of their technology systems.[71] Instead, schools are wise to balance three strategies in their implementation of technology—regulatory, technological, and pedagogical.[72] The next section focuses on the pedagogical perspective, with a critique of past models of credibility assessment instruction and a look at how best practices can shape the future of this curriculum.

Beyond the Challenges: Teaching Credibility Assessment

It is clear, despite the many challenges described earlier in this chapter, that credibility assessment of digital media is a skill students (and teachers!) need to learn. However, is credibility assessment being taught in schools? The answer is not simple. Students are certainly learning how to use digital *tools* at school. Tyner distinguishes between "tool literacies"—computer, network, and technology literacies—and "literacies of representation"—information, visual, and media literacies.[73] Tool literacies are concerned with teaching learners to master new technology tools. Literacies of representation build on already-familiar reading and writing literacy foundations in schooling and emphasize the process skills that are needed to analyze information and understand how meaning is created. Often, however, information and communication technology (ICT) skills are taught only as tool literacies, where the technology itself is the object of instruction. This practice has its roots in the traditional business curriculum, in which students are taught the computer applications they need to succeed in the marketplace.[74] In these cases, students are given lessons on such topics as productivity software, Web design software, and audio and video production, but not on "slippery" topics like the ethical use of ICTs or the evaluation of digital media and information.

Perhaps teachers assume that with filtering in place, students do not have access to information that is not credible when they are at school. The fallacy of this assumption is that filtering software is designed to block only certain categories of objectionable content, and does not, indeed cannot, consider content that may "only" lack credibility. The pedagogical argument for teaching the "slippery" topics is that unless educators incorporate purposeful and guided exposure to fallacious online information *during school*, their students may not have the skills to distinguish credible content from that which is not credible when they are *not at school*. Credibility assessment issues rise rapidly to the top of the school radar when public concern demands attention to Web safety. Unfortunately, this particular focus considers credibility assessment only at the gross level of child endangerment. Weingarten describes how a good deal of Internet instruction is cast in the mold of protecting young people from misinformation and online dangers.[75] The emphasis is not on improving critical thinking abilities at a more nuanced and analytical level.

When credibility assessment education does take place in school, who takes responsibility for it? Web site evaluation, which generally includes credibility assessment, is typically taught by the school librarian as part of information literacy instruction. Credibility assessment of broadcast media is covered within the context of media literacy instruction and may be taught by English, reading, speech communications, or journalism teachers. Credibility assessment may or may not be included as a component in computer technology curricula. Finally and ideally, credibility assessment instruction is embedded in content areas of the curriculum, from social studies to science and mathematics. However, it must be emphasized that schools are not generally required to teach "process skills" like information or media literacy that might include credibility assessment components.

What does credibility assessment instruction look like? The predominant method is the checklist model, which focuses on criteria including accuracy, authority, objectivity, currency, and coverage.[76] Students examine Web sites with such checklists in hand, looking for evidence of each element. Some teachers assign checklists as worksheets, requiring students to complete them before proceeding to the next stage of research. The checklist model would be well suited to most types of academic research and imposed query situations—if students employed it when working independently. In practice, users—including young people—rely on other criteria, most notably design and presentation elements.[77] Furthermore, even when Internet users who are skeptical of Web-based information know they should verify the information they get online, they often fail to do so.[78]

Checklist criteria, when used alone, can result in superficial or even false analyses. Noncredible or quasi-credible sites can meet the technical requirements of a checklist. In addition, the reductive nature of many checklists forces students into "yes" or "no" responses, when "yes, but . . . " or "not unless . . . " responses might be more appropriate. Another limitation of the checklist model is that it is not well suited to everyday-life information-seeking needs. Typical academically oriented checklists are ineffective in everyday-life information-seeking contexts because the criteria that would be relevant are not included. The usual checklist-style admonishment to restrict oneself to traditionally defined "authoritative" sources has no meaning for the young person who is looking for relationship advice or music suggestions. Web sites devoted to such topics *do* differ in levels of credibility, and those differences should also be subject to articulation and evaluation. Ultimately, checklists are problematic because the evaluation of information is subjective, relative, and situational rather than objective, absolute, and universally recognizable.[79]

The Millennial Generation

We are teaching a generation of students who have a special relationship with technology and the Internet. In 2005, fully 87 percent of teenagers reported using the Internet, as compared to 66 percent of adults.[80] These students are format agnostic, mixing and matching the communication and information technology functions of their tools to suit their own ends.[81] Eighty-four percent report owning at least one personal media device, including mobile technologies like cell phones and personal digital assistants.[82] This mobility means that students are frequently on their own when it comes time to evaluate credibility. They often start research projects by browsing online, pausing to ping their social network for advice and guidance.[83] They find corroboration in alternative locales—blogs, recommender sites, even within World of Warcraft games.

Although teen use of the Internet at school has increased by 45 percent since 2000,[84] young people perceive a substantial disconnect between how they use the Internet on their own for educational purposes and how they use it during the school day and under teacher direction.[85] Students cite a number of roadblocks that compromise Internet use at school, among them the wide variation in teachers' Internet policies and practices, heavy-handed Web filtering, and uninspired assignments that do not take advantage of the Internet's attributes. It is against this backdrop that educators must examine their attempts to teach credibility assessment. On the one hand, we have an education system that narrowly prescribes how information is to be accessed and what information is considered appropriate, if not credible. On the other hand, we have a generation of learners that has taken matters into its own hands because of access to digital content tools outside of school. However, access to the *technology* tools does not provide them with access to the *intellectual* tools they need. But is it possible to teach students to evaluate digital information when they only see preselected or filtered slices of it? Are we, as educators, credible facilitators or do students perceive us as being hypocritical, or worse, clueless? Indeed, young people may not see most adults as being credible at all when it comes to matters of technology, and that the only real authorities in the digital world are themselves.

Best Practices

Despite the sometimes overwhelming challenges to teaching credibility assessment in today's schooling environment, many teachers and school librarians are finding ways to do so. As intractable as some of the institutional and structural barriers can be, the dynamic challenges are more open to creative pedagogical efforts. Educators are finding ways to accommodate student developmental levels as they design credibility assessment instruction, scaffolding productive explication of the cues that populate a complex media environment. The ultimate goal is to help students develop robust internal heuristics, a personal suite of decision-making strategies that are available for automatic recall during information searching and selection processes.[86]

The development of effective heuristics is more likely to occur during instances of contextual or situated learning. Research in cognitive and educational psychology suggests that knowledge is not an objective artifact but is an entity that is developed and learned within a social context that itself affects or shapes cognition.[87] Therefore, some of the best practices in credibility assessment instruction are those that occur over time, in the context of application, and, in the best cases, provide collaborative and apprenticeship-like opportunities. The various literacy movements concur with this perspective, advocating that such process instruction be integrated across the curriculum and applied in the context of real classroom assignments. For example, the Center for Media Literacy notes that integrating media literacy across the curriculum connects it to national, state, or district educational standards and assessment rubrics.[88] The perspective of Partnership for 21st Century Skills is that integrating 21st century skills into core academic subjects should be the "design specs" for creating effective high schools.[89] And information literacy researchers have long promoted curriculum integration rather than standalone "library skills" instruction.[90]

In addition to recognizing the wisdom of situating credibility assessment activities within broader learning experiences, alternative models of teaching specific credibility assessment skills are now appearing. Meola has developed a contextual model of Web site evaluation that prescribes both steering students to peer and editorially reviewed online resources and having students compare and corroborate information found on one Web site to other Web sites or to print sources.[91] The compare-and-corroborate strategy is a way of triggering the bandwagon heuristic—"if others think this is good information, then I should think so too."[92] Directing students to credible information is reflected in recent thought in exemplary school library Web site design: that subscription databases and librarian-developed research guides be given prominent placement rather than direct links to Google and other search sites that students already access on their own.[93]

Metzger suggests a "sliding scale" approach that is more sensitive to motivation and purpose in information seeking.[94] It allows for a variety of approaches to credibility assessment to accommodate specific search tasks in the context of different situations. In such a model, young people would be taught the checklist and contextual models when their information tasks require high-quality, traditionally defined credible sources. Users who are not very motivated or who are operating under less academically rigorous circumstances could be taught some simple heuristics that would still enable them to assess credibility and, just as important, that they would be likely to use. Part of the educational effort would be to teach students when to use each method.

Another type of checklist model is also emerging, one that adopts a more open-ended and expansive format instead of maneuvering students into yes-and-no checkbox choices. For example, the 21st Century Information Fluency Project offers an online "evaluation wizard" tool.[95] Although strongly oriented to academic information-seeking tasks, it asks the "who, what, where, and why" questions that provoke deeper thinking. The evaluation wizard and its sister tools (which include games and simulations) build on preliminary research findings that suggest students tend to do a better job determining both relevance and reliability if they search for and select information themselves.[96] When Web sites are provided by teachers (as they frequently are), students assume credibility and tend not to employ evaluation heuristics. The teacher endorsement triggers an "authority heuristic"—if an expert (the teacher) believes the information is credible, then it must be.[97] On the other hand, the cognitive effort required by effective searching appears to trigger more effortful credibility assessment heuristics.

Cognitive Flexibility

I have developed a teaching technique that is designed to provoke cognitive dissonance. This approach is influenced by cognitive flexibility theory,[98] which was developed to help people learn important but difficult subject matter. It accomplishes this goal by not oversimplifying complex phenomena, but instead by presenting the material in manageable units through multiple exposures. Ultimately, learners are better equipped to independently navigate ill-structured domains such as the Web. My particular application of the theory follows suit by not presenting "perfect" examples of Web sites to critique. Instead, it provides multiple examples of Web sites that challenge users' initial impressions and force them to look beyond surface assessment criteria and cues. Eighth-grade students are assigned to examine a series of Web sites that present particular interpretive challenges. The students work in pairs or alone, answering a series of prompting questions developed for each site. Then each site is discussed by the class as a whole. The group discourse allows diverse viewpoints to emerge and encourages proximal learning, in which less capable students are able to learn from more capable peers.[99] Finally, students are assigned to take a parent on a "tour" of the Web sites, an activity that requires that they explain their analyses to someone who has no previous knowledge of the sites. By articulating their thinking to an uninitiated outsider, they deepen and internalize their own evaluation heuristics.

A brief analysis of three of these challenging sites illuminates the types of dynamic difficulties the Web can present, as well as the value of presenting multiple, conflicting examples for students to analyze. Two of the sites satisfy surface checklist model standards because they possess traditional cues that trigger authority and accuracy heuristics. The first is a benign example of this phenomenon, a Web page called "The Good News About Chocolate" (http://www.candyusa.org/Media/Nutrition/chocolate_goodnews.asp). Positive markers include a scholarly (if dated) bibliography, a statement of review by a registered dietitian, a professional look, and a ".org" domain name. Students must determine that the page is on the National Confectioners Association Web site, the advocacy agent of the candy industry. While the information on the page is most likely accurate, an inherent conflict of interest exists. The Association is sure to pick and choose the research literature it presents, most likely leaving out unfavorable information. Students need to identify the conflict of interest and, at the very least, recognize that the information should not be used without corroboration from other sources. They should also appreciate that the site may offer other information of value, such as recipes, that could be used for other purposes.

The Web supplies more insidious examples of sites that, at least superficially, appear to meet checklist criteria. A second item from this class exercise is the Web site of the Institute for Historical Review (http://www.ihr.org), a Holocaust denial organization. The site bears traditional credibility cues that are designed to trigger the authority heuristic.[100] The prominently displayed current news and commentary portion of the page is populated with links to articles from mainstream publications such as the *Boston Globe*, the *New York Times*, and the *Miami Herald*, and from Israeli newspapers and Jewish organizations, whose presence conveys an impression of balanced coverage. The piece "A Look at the 'Powerful Jewish Lobby'" (http://www.ihr.org/leaflets/jewishlobby.shtml) cites articles published in the *Jerusalem Post*, *Forward*, the *Guardian*, the *Los Angeles Times*, and books published by the Harvard University Press and the University of Chicago. The context in which these works are cited is where the mischief occurs. Quotes are used as evidence, from Jews themselves, of the existence of an overly powerful Jewish influence on American society and, indeed, on the entire world. Two strategies are available to young people as they study this site. First, they can be alert to the additional cues that should trigger other conflicting credibility assessment heuristics. Second, and less likely to occur given the time investment and the intentionality of such an exercise, they can track down the origins of selected quotes and compare the contexts in which they are used.

The checklist test can go both ways. Sites that, at first examination, "fail" the test can be highly authoritative sources of information. The third example from this lesson is a Web site called The Body (http://thebody.com), an HIV/AIDs information and support resource. The most immediate credibility-damaging indicator on the home page of this site is a prominent display of the logos of the pharmaceutical companies that are its sponsors. Viewers are also confronted by a slick presentation, with images and photos that invite them to "click here to learn more!" Students in my classes are immediately put off by this barrage, assuming the links lead to advertisements. However, most of the links actually lead to other informational parts of the site. The one section of the site that is sponsored by commercial interests is clearly labeled as such.

Even the safety terminology on a consumer medical site like this one can seem suspect. The Body has posted a typical legal disclaimer that warns readers that it is designed for educational purposes only and that the information it provides should not be used for diagnosing or treating a health problem or a disease. My students puzzle about how to interpret this sort of language, which can sound like the organization is trying to hide something. The problem is exacerbated if they click on one of the sponsor links. Each of these pharmaceutical companies is required by law to post a disclaimer that reads "(Name of product) does not cure HIV infection or AIDS and does not reduce the risk of passing HIV to others." The students' confusion deepens further when I ask them to describe what types of people serve on the site's advisory board. They have to look closely to find the fine-print link to "Our Mission and Team," which lists the names and very impressive credentials of the advisory board members. Most are medical professionals at prestigious institutions. In sum, this Web site exercise forces students to reconcile conflicting credibility cues by reading deeply and weighing all the evidence before passing judgment.

In this application of the cognitive flexibility model, the message from teacher to student is, "Here are the general rules for credibility assessment, but you must use them judiciously. Sometimes they apply and sometimes they do not. In the end, it is up to you to determine what is credible and what is not." For teachers, such a teaching approach can be intimidating because it means ceding authority. Students are invited to question what they have been taught, or at least to know when to ignore it. But they are not truly disregarding their lessons. Instead, they are learning when and how to flexibly apply their knowledge in a complex environment that is not suited to simplified analyses.

A similar application of the cognitive flexibility strategy can be used to teach students to "read" sites whose purpose is persuasion or even indoctrination. Careful exposure, during which semantic and visual strategies are deconstructed, can serve as a form of inoculation, particularly against hate sites. A site often used in credibility assessment teaching is the one mentioned earlier titled "Martin Luther King, Jr.—A True Historical Examination" (http://www.martinlutherking.org). I demonstrate this site by conducting a Web search on Martin Luther King and projecting the search results. Students always select this site to look at first, both because of its credible-looking domain name and also because of its invariably high placement ranking. They are then given several minutes to read the screen. It does not take them very long to realize that something is amiss. Although the site looks professional and comprehensive, there is an out-of-context quote that does not fit the tone of the rest of the page.

The students in my classes are probably successful at this detection, in part, because they know they are engaged in a Web site evaluation exercise. They are predisposed to anticipate a "trick." Once they catch on, and after a few other pages on the site are displayed, it is hard for them to imagine that others would be taken in by the deception. The value of the lesson might diminish at this point but then I display other sites, developed by teachers, students, Web portals, news sites, and even libraries, which have linked to the erroneous King site unwittingly. Caught up in the fervor of knowing that they see what others do not see, my students are ready to learn some relatively obscure detection techniques. I show them how to conduct a domain name search, which reveals that the site is owned by the white supremacist organization Stormfront (http://www.stormfront.org). Other hate sites are then displayed and the students are prompted to look for cues that are designed to signify credibility and to evoke positive associations such as patriotism or religious faith.

Changing Institutional Culture

In pursuit of curriculum integration, one of a school librarian's major roles is to collaborate with teachers on resource-based assignments. Evidence of these partnerships is widely available on school library Web sites, which typically link to class project resource guides that build in opportunities for credibility assessment. In 2000, school library media specialist Joyce Valenza institutionalized partnering in her school by instigating a schoolwide research initiative.[101] All research projects are now inquiry-driven, with students tackling compelling research questions that cannot be answered with a simple yes or no. Teachers have been enlisted to communicate high expectations for source credibility. These high expectations, coupled with the more personal investment students make in inquiry-based projects, generally results in students who are intrinsically motivated to find credible sources.

Valenza's school library Web site (http://mciu.k12.pa.us/~spjvweb/) is replete with the kinds of tools that support the development of credibility assessment heuristics. She supplies course-related resource guides and a number of information evaluation guides and exercises that stretch the typical school worksheet or checklist experience. For example, her webquest for evaluating Web sites has students working in groups of four, which distributes the cognitive load by assigning discrete tasks to individuals who then combine their analyses for a final synthesis. She includes a guide to evaluating blogs, which poses clarifying questions such as this set related to a blog's influence: "Does this blogger have influence? Who and how many people link to the blog? Who is commenting? Does this blog appear to be part of a community? The best blogs are likely to be hubs for folks who share interests with the blogger." Valenza's students are also employing metacognitive tools, such as research blogs and annotated bibliographies that include descriptions of their search processes and selection rationales. An analysis of seniors' research experiences indicates that these approaches are assisting students in their development of credibility assessment heuristics.[102]

Going to the Source

Perhaps the richest resource for improving best practices is young people themselves. By incorporating ideas inspired by the millennial generation's behavior, it may be possible to minimize the disconnect that exists between how young people learn while at school and how they learn when they are away from school. If educators can better understand what young people are already doing with digital media and leverage those habits, credibility assessment instruction has a better chance of being situated in a context that is meaningful to them. In addition, digital media tools lend themselves to inquiry-based learning because they can be used to connect students to real-world resources and situations.

What would such an approach look like? To start with, content elements can be made to more closely reflect the digital content that interests students. Teachers might use eBay to teach consumer skills or online sports scores to teach statistics. Students could be assigned to compare the product or media reviews on recommender Web sites to those in traditional consumer print literature. Young people taking political science, civics, or journalism classes might study political blogs, national party Web sites, extremist Web sites, and online news sites, in addition to mainstream newsprint and broadcast media sources. All of these examples are likely to generate interest and motivation for learning in a way that ordinary textbook-based lessons might not. Several of the examples feature what Eysenbach calls "apomediaries"—humans or technology tools that mediate without standing "in between" the consumer and the information (as an intermediary would), and instead "stand by" and provide added value at the will of the consumer.[103] Some of the apomediaries mentioned here are the seller ratings on eBay, the reviews and reviewer ratings on Amazon or epinions.com, the comments posted to political blogs and news site stories, and even the tags and links to the sites that others use in categorizing or evaluating Web sources. In each example, apomediaries offer additional credibility cues and provide metainformation that can help a young person navigate through this complex information environment. It is worth noting that apomediary assistance is not reflected on most traditional checklists, yet is a tool that most users of digital media, including young people, are increasingly relying on for help in credibility assessment.

Finally, new media tools themselves, such as podcasts, Web sites, blogs, videos, and other digital media products, can be employed as tools in direct instruction. Teachers can design the infrastructures or students themselves can become digital media producers, or "prosumers." Such tools and experiences extend the scope of learning beyond the traditional closed conversations with teachers that are so characteristic of formal schooling. In particular, social software tools that promote dialogue can easily be used to enable peer-to-peer as well as other kinds of informal learning. A great deal of learning occurs during such dialogic negotiations, whether students are creating digital media, seeking and evaluating information, or collaborating on a creative endeavor.

Educators can also position themselves within new media environments, carrying credibility-assessment messages to the virtual spaces young people already inhabit. For example, the 3D virtual world Second Life (http://secondlife.com/) now hosts Second Life Library 2.0, developed by the Alliance Library System and OPAL (Online Programming for All Libraries) and staffed by volunteer librarians. A virtual teen library is being developed on the Teen Second Life grid (http://teen.secondlife.com/). Some libraries are establishing a presence within popular social networking services—public libraries typically in MySpace and academic libraries in Facebook. Because of the many restrictions on social networking software in schools, however, school libraries have not ventured much in this direction. A library profile has a name brand advantage that carries implicit credibility associations.

To be truly successful, a social software presence must be much more than a one-way announcement space for a library. It should support two-way communication with users and, most notably, provide a portal to real library services.[104] In other words, what matters is not merely being *where* young people are, but also being *useful* to them by providing library-vetted information. The Brooklyn College Library uses its MySpace site (http://www.myspace.com/brooklyncollegelibrary) to push information to their students who have chosen to be "friended." The Hennepin County Library MySpace profile page (http://www.myspace.com/hennepincountylibrary) features a working search window for the online catalog and a link that allows users to install the online catalog search within their own MySpace profiles. The online catalog itself allows Amazon-like user comments on book records, functioning as an apomediary for assessing book choices.

Conclusion

In the final analysis, we will be more successful teaching credibility assessment by taking advantage of the way young people think and work. If teaching "positive" heuristics is the goal, we should first take a look at the successful models and strategies young people have already developed for themselves. We can accomplish this by allowing and even encouraging the personal connection they feel to digital media. Next, we need to acknowledge and capitalize on young people's collaborative instincts. Before the popularization of social networking software, Twidale et al. wrote about browsing information systems and "serendipitous altruism" as being collaborative processes.[105] Now we have the tools to build in collaborative opportunities for our students as they search for and critically evaluate information using digital media. Finally, we need to understand that young people will continue to use digital media that may not conform to "school standards" of credibility, but which either satisfice or meet their needs in some way. Our endeavors in teaching credibility assessment will also benefit from further research in how credibility-assessment heuristics are learned and how they can be taught.

In a tongue-in-cheek school newspaper editorial summarizing what he had learned during high school, one of our departing seniors had this to say about Wikipedia: "Wikipedia is an essay's best friend. Wikipedia is a bibliography's worst enemy."[106] Educators do not have to compromise their principles regarding source credibility or turn a blind eye to what their students are doing. What they can do is credit students for the search and evaluation *process* and not just the products of their efforts. The Web boards, the recommender sites, and the Wikipedias can have an acknowledged place in the course of learning, but should be accompanied by comparison and corroboration experiences. Students can be taught that credibility criteria differ depending on audience and purpose. By expanding our notions of "appropriateness" in the school setting and exposing students to a fuller range of information to evaluate, our credibility instruction will itself become more credible and, thus, more likely to be successful.

Notes

1. Marc Prensky, Listen to the Natives, *Educational Leadership* 63, no 4 (2005): 8–13.

2. National Center for Education Statistics, Internet Access in U.S. Public Schools and Classrooms 1994–2003, 2005, http://nces.ed.gov/surveys/frss/publications/2005015 (accessed June 4, 2007).

3. Joyce Kasman Valenza, They Might Be Gurus: Teen Information-Seeking Behavior, *Voice of Youth Advocates* 29, no. 1 (2006), http://pdfs.voya.com/VO/YA2/VOYA200604TagTeamTech.pdf (accessed June 4, 2007).

4. Miriam J. Metzger, Making Sense of Credibility on the Web: Models for Evaluating Online Information and Recommendations for Future Research, *Journal of the American Society for Information Science and Technology* 58, no. 10 (2007, in press); Soo Young Rieh and David R. Danielson, Credibility: A Multidisciplinary Framework, in *Annual Review of Information Science and Technology 41*, ed. Blaise Cronin (Medford, NJ: Information Today, 2007): 307–64; C. Nadine Wathen and Jacquelyn Burkell, Believe It or Not: Factors Influencing Credibility on the Web, *Journal of the American Society for Information Science and Technology* 53, no. 2 (2002): 134–44.

5. F. W. Lancaster, Precision and Recall, in *Encyclopedia of Library and Information Science*, Vol. 3, ed. Miriam Drake (New York: Marcel Dekker, 2003), 2346–51.

6. Rieh and Danielson, Credibility: A Multidisciplinary Framework.

7. American Association of School Librarians and Association for Educational Communications and Technology, *Information Power: Building Partnerships for Learning* (Chicago: American Library Association, 1998); Association of College and Research Libraries. *Information Literacy Competency Standards for Higher Education* (Chicago: American Library Association, 2000).

8. Mary Ann Fitzgerald, Evaluating Information: An Information Literacy Challenge, *School Library Media Research* 2 (1999), http://www.ala.org/ala/aasl/aaslpubsandjournals/slmrb/slmrcontents/volume21999/vol2fitzgerald.htm (accessed June 4, 2007); Mary Ann Fitzgerald, Skills for Evaluating Web-Based Information (paper presented at the Internet Credibility and the User Symposium, Seattle, WA, 2005), http://projects.ischool.washington.edu/credibility/Fitzgerald Skills.pdf (accessed June 4, 2007).

9. Marie L. Radford, Susan B. Barnes, and Linda R. Barr, *Web Research: Selecting, Evaluating, and Citing*, 2nd ed. (Boston: Pearson/Allyn and Bacon, 2006).

10. Robert H. Ennis, A Taxonomy of Critical Thinking Dispositions and Abilities, in *Teaching Thinking Skills: Theory and Practice*, ed. Joan Boykoff Baron and Robert J. Sternberg (New York: Freeman, 1987): 9–26; Diane F. Halpern, *Thought & Knowledge: An Introduction to Critical Thinking*, 4th ed. (Mahwah, NJ: Erlbaum, 2003).

11. Elizabeth Thoman and Tessa Jolls, *Literacy for the 21st Century: An Overview and Orientation Guide to Media Literacy Education* (Santa Monica, CA: Center for Media Literacy, 2005); Miriam J. Metzger, Andrew J. Flanagin, Keren Eyal, Daisy R. Lemus, and Robert M. McCann, Credibility for the 21st Century: Integrating Perspectives on Source, Message, and Media Credibility in the Contemporary Media Environment, in *Communication Yearbook*, vol. 27, ed. Pamela J. Kalbfleisch (Mahwah, NJ: Erlbaum, 2003): 293–335.

12. International Society for Technology in Education, *National Educational Technology Standards for Students: Connecting Curriculum and Technology* (Eugene, OR: ISTE, 2000).

13. Bertram C. Bruce, Credibility of the Web: Why We Need Dialectical Reading, *Journal of Philosophy of Education* 34, no. 1 (2000): 97–109.

14. Kathleen R. Tyner, *Literacy in a Digital World: Teaching and Learning in the Age of Information* (Mahwah, NJ: Erlbaum, 1998); North Central Regional Educational Laboratory, enGauge: 21st Century Skills in the Digital Age, 2003, http://www.ncrel.org/engauge/skills/engauge21st.pdf (accessed June 4, 2007); Partnership for 21st Century Skills, Results That Matter: 21st Century Skills and High School Reform, 2006, http://www.21stcenturyskills.org/documents/RTM2006.pdf (accessed June 4, 2007).

15. Ennis, A Taxonomy of Critical Thinking Dispositions and Abilities.

16. Michael Eisenberg, Carrie A. Lowe, and Kathleen L. Spitzer, *Information Literacy: Essential Skills for the Information Age*, 2nd ed. (Westport, CT: Libraries Unlimited, 2004).

17. James W. Potter, *Theory of Media Literacy: A Cognitive Approach* (Thousand Oaks, CA: Sage, 2004).

18. Tyner, *Literacy in a Digital World*.

19. Missouri Department of Elementary and Secondary Education, Information and Technology Literacy: A Companion to the Show-Me Standards, 2002, http://dese.mo.gov/divimprove/curriculum/literacy/ (accessed June 4, 2007).

20. John D. Fortier, Calvin J. Potter, Susan M. Grady, Neah J. Lohr, and Jim Klein, *Wisconsin's Model Academic Standards for Information and Technology Literacy* (Madison: Wisconsin Department of Public Instruction, 1998).

21. International Society for Technology in Education, *National Educational Technology Standards for Students*.

22. American Association of School Librarians and Association for Educational Communications and Technology, *Information Power*.

23. Association of College and Research Libraries, *Information Literacy Competency Standards for Higher Education*.

24. Eisenberg, Lowe, and Spitzer, *Information Literacy*.

25. American Association for the Advancement of Science, Project 2061, (2006), http://www.project2061.org/ (accessed June 4, 2007).

26. National Council of Teachers of English and International Reading Association, Standards for the English Language Arts (2006), http://www.ncte.org/about/over/standards/110846.htm (accessed June 4, 2007).

27. James S. Kim and Gail L. Sunderman, Measuring Academic Proficiency under the No Child Left Behind Act: Implications for Educational Equity, *Educational Researcher* 34, no. 8 (November 2005): 3–13; Gail L. Sunderman, Christopher A. Tracey, Jimmy Kim, and Gary Orfield, *Listening to Teachers: Classroom Realities and No Child Left Behind* (Cambridge, MA: Civil Rights Project, Harvard University, 2004); Eva Zygmunt-Fillwalk and Teresa Evanko Bilello, Parents' Victory in Reclaiming Recess for Their Children, *Childhood Education* 82, no. 1 (2005): 19–23.

28. Center on Education Policy, *From the Capital to the Classroom: Year 4 of the No Child Left Behind Act* (Washington, D.C.: CEP, 2006).

29. Jaekyung Lee, *Tracking Achievement Gaps and Assessing the Impact of NCLB on the Gaps: An In-Depth Look into National and State Reading and Math Outcome Trends* (Cambridge, MA: Civil Rights Project at Harvard University, 2006).

30. Audrey Amrein-Beardsley and David C. Berliner. Re-analysis of NAEP Math and Reading Scores in States with and without High-Stakes Tests: Response to Rosenshine, *Education Policy Analysis Archives* 11, no. 25 (2003); M. Gail Jones, Brett D. Jones, and Tracy Y. Hargrove, *The Unintended Consequences of High-Stakes Testing* (Lanham, MD: Rowman & Littlefield, 2003); Lee, *Tracking Achievement Gaps*; Sharol L. Nichols and David C. Berliner, *The Inevitable Corruption of Indicators and Educators through High-Stakes Testing* (Education Policy Studies Laboratory, Arizona State University, 2005), http://www.asu.edu/educ/epsl/EPRU/documents/EPSL-0503-101-EPRU.pdf (accessed June 4, 2007).

31. Jennifer Booher-Jennings, Rationing Education in an Era of Accountability, *Phi Delta Kappan* 87, no. 10 (2006): 756–61.

32. Jones, Jones, and Hargrove, *The Unintended Consequences of High-Stakes Testing*.

33. Center on Education Policy, *From the Capital to the Classroom: Year 4 of the No Child Left Behind*; Jones, Jones, and Hargrove, *The Unintended Consequences of High-Stakes Testing*.

34. Educational Testing Service, ICT literacy assessment, http://www.ets.org/ictliteracy (accessed June 4, 2007).

35. Nancy Kranich, Why Filters Won't Protect Children or Adults, *Library Administration & Management* 18, no. 1 (2004): 14–18; Lynn Sutton, *Accessed Denied: How Internet Filters Impact Student Learning in High Schools* (Youngstown, NY: Cambria, 2006).

36. American Library Association, Resolution on Opposition to Federally Mandated Filtering, 2001, http://www.ala.org/ala/oif/statementspols/ifresolutions/resolutionopposition.htm (accessed June 4, 2007).

37. Marjorie Heins, Christina Cho, and Ariel Feldman, *Internet Filters: A Public Policy Report*, 2nd ed. (New York: Brennan Center for Justice, 2006).

38. Electronic Frontier Foundation, Internet Blocking and Censorware, n.d., http://www.eff.org/Censorship/Censorware (accessed June 4, 2007).

39. Sutton, *Accessed Denied: How Internet Filters Impact Student Learning in High Schools*.

40. Carl Heine, Credibility in the Context of Searching, unpublished white paper (Aurora, IL: Illinois Mathematics and Science Academy, 2006).

41. Chicago Public Schools, Acceptable Use Policy, n.d., http://policy.cps.k12.il.us/documents/604.2.pdf (accessed June 4, 2007).

42. University of Illinois Laboratory High School, Computer Usage Agreement, Urbana, IL, http://www.uni.uiuc.edu/forms/documents/Computer%20Usage%20Agreement.doc (accessed June 4, 2007).

43. Donna Bilal, Research on Children's Information Seeking on the Web, in *Youth Information-Seeking Behavior: Theories, Models, and Issues*, ed. Mary K. Chelton and Colleen Cool (Lanham, MD: Scarecrow Press, 2004): 271–91; Matthew S. Eastin, Toward a Cognitive Developmental Approach to Youth Perceptions of Credibility, this volume; Sylvia Livingstone, Children's Use of the Internet: Reflections on the Emerging Research Agenda, *New Media and Society* 5, no. 2 (2003): 147–66.

44. Richard M. Lerner and Laurence D. Steinberg, *Handbook of Adolescent Psychology*, 2nd ed. (Hoboken, NJ: Wiley, 2004).

45. Marc Prensky, Listen to the Natives; Paul Hitlin and Lee Rainie, *Teens, Technology, and School* (Washington, DC: Pew Internet & American Life Project, 2005).

46. Andrew K. Shenton and Pat Dixon. Issues Arising From Youngsters' Information-Seeking Behavior, *Library & Information Science Research* 26, no. 2 (2004): 177–200; Valenza, They Might Be Gurus.

47. Fitzgerald, Skills for Evaluating Web-Based Information.

48. Matthew S. Eastin, Mong-Shan Yang, and Amy Nathanson, Children of the Net: An Empirical Exploration into the Evaluation of Internet Content, *Journal of Broadcasting and Electronic Media* 50, no. 2 (2006): 211–30.

49. Frances Jacobson Harris, "There Was a Great Collision in the Stock Market": Middle School Students, Online Primary Sources, and Historical Sense Making, *School Library Media Research* 5, 2002, http://www.ala.org/ala/aasl/aaslpubsandjournals/slmrb/slmrcontents/volume52002/harris.htm (accessed June 4, 2007); Samuel S. Wineburg, Historical Problem Solving: A Study of the Cognitive Processes Used in the Evaluation of Documentary and Pictorial Evidence, *Journal of Educational Psychology* 83 (March 1991): 73–87.

50. Denise E. Agosto, Bounded Rationality and Satisficing in Young People's Web-Based Decision Making, *Journal of the American Society for Information Science and Technology* 53, no. 1 (2002): 16–27; Raya Fidel, Rachel K. Davies, and Mary H. Douglass, A Visit to the Information Mall: Web Searching Behavior of High School Students, *Journal of the American Society for Information Science* 50, no. 1 (1999): 24–37.

51. Melissa Gross, *Studying Children's Questions: Imposed and Self-generated Information Seeking at School* (Lanham, MD: Scarecrow Press, 2006); Soo Young Rieh and Brian Hilligoss, College Students' Credibility Judgments in the Information-Seeking Process, this volume.

52. Richard E. Petty and John T. Cacioppo, *Attitudes and Persuasion: Classic and Contemporary Approaches* (Dubuque, IA: Brown, 1981).

53. Metzger, Making Sense of Credibility on the Web; S. Shyam Sundar, The MAIN Model: A Heuristic Approach to Understanding Technology Effects on Credibility, this volume; Rieh and Hilligoss, College Students' Credibility Judgments in the Information-Seeking Process.

54. Melissa Gross, Imposed Queries in the School Library Media Center: A Descriptive Study, *Library & Information Science Research* 21, no. 4 (1999): 501–21; Gross, *Studying Children's Questions*.

55. Gross, *Studying Children's Questions*.

56. Michael B. Twidale, David M. Nichols, and Chris D. Paice, Browsing Is a Collaborative Process, *Information Processing & Management* 33, no. 6 (1997): 761–83.

57. Rieh and Hilligoss, College Students' Credibility Judgments in the Information-Seeking Process.

58. Amanda Spink and Charles Cole, Introduction to the Special Issue: Everyday Life Information-Seeking Research, *Library & Information Science Research* 23, no. 4 (2001): 301–66; Reijo Savolainen, Everyday Life Information Seeking: Approaching Information Seeking in the Context of "Way of Life," *Library & Information Science Research* 17, no. 3 (1995): 259–94; for recent exceptions,

see Karen E. Fisher, Elizabeth Marcoux, Eric Meyers, and Carol F. Landry, Tweens and Everyday Life Information Behavior: Preliminary Findings from Seattle, in *Youth Information-Seeking Behavior II: Context, Theories, Models, and Issues*, ed. Mary K. Chelton and Colleen Cool (Lanham, MD: Scarecrow Press, 2007), 1–25; Sandra Hughes-Hassell and Denise E. Agosto, Modeling the Everyday Life Information Needs of Urban Teenagers, in *Youth Information-Seeking Behavior II: Context, Theories, Models, and Issues*, ed. Mary K. Chelton and Colleen Cool (Lanham, MD: Scarecrow Press, 2007): 27–61; Bharat Mehra and Donna Braquet, Process of Information Seeking During "Queer" Youth Coming-out Experiences, in *Youth Information-Seeking Behavior II: Context, Theories, Models, and Issues*, ed. Mary K. Chelton and Colleen Cool (Lanham, MD: Scarecrow Press, 2007): 93–131; Rieh and Hilligos, College Students' Credibility Judgments in the Information-Seeking Process.

59. Pamela J. McKenzie, A Model of Information Practices in Accounts of Everyday-Life Information Seeking, *Journal of Documentation* 59, no. 1 (2003): 19–40.

60. Denise E. Agosto and Sandra Hughes-Hassell, People, Places, and Questions: An Investigation of the Everyday Life Information-Seeking Behaviors of Urban Young Adults, *Library & Information Science Research* 27, no. 2 (2005): 141–63.

61. Denise E. Agosto, Bounded Rationality and Satisficing in Young People's Web-Based Decision Making; Herbert Alexander Simon, *Models of Thought* (New Haven, CT: Yale University Press, 1979).

62. George Kingsley Zipf, *Human Behavior and the Principle of Least Effort: An Introduction to Human Ecology* (New York: Addison-Wesley, 1949).

63. Andrew J. Flanagin and Miriam J. Metzger, The Role of Site Features, User Attributes, and Information Verification Behaviors on the Perceived Credibility of Web-Based Information, *New Media and Society*, 9 no. 2 (2007): 319–42.

64. Nicholas C. Burbules, Paradoxes of the Web: The Ethical Dimensions of Credibility, *Library Trends* 49, no. 3 (2001): 441–53.

65. Bruce, Credibility of the Web.

66. Peter Levine, The problem of Online Misinformation and the Role of Schools, *Studies in Media & Information Literacy Education* 5, no. 1 (2005), http://www.utpjournals.com/simile/simile.html (accessed June 4, 2007).

67. See Eastin, Toward a Cognitive Developmental Approach to Youth Perceptions of Credibility.

68. Andrew J. Flanagin and Miriam J. Metzger, Digital Media and Youth: Unparalleled Opportunity and Unprecedented Responsibility, this volume.

69. Jessie Daniels, Race, Civil Rights and Hate Speech in the Digital Era, in *Learning Race and Ethnicity: Youth and Digital Media*, ed. Anna Everett (MacArthur Foundation Initiative on Digital Media and Learning, 2007).

70. Steve Jones and Mary Madden, *The Internet Goes to College: How Students Are Living in the Future With Today's Technology* (Washington, DC: Pew Internet & American Life Project, 2002); Valenza, They Might Be Gurus.

71. Cassandra Van Buren, Teaching Hackers: School Computing Culture and the Future of Cyber-Rights, *Journal of Information Ethics* 10, no. 1 (2001): 51–72.

72. Frances Jacobson Harris, *I Found It on the Internet: Coming of Age Online* (Chicago: American Library Association, 2005).

73. Tyner, *Literacy in a Digital World*.

74. Eisenberg, Lowe, and Spitzer, *Information Literacy*.

75. Fred W. Weingarten, Credibility, Politics, and Public Policy, this volume.

76. Metzger, Making Sense of Credibility on the Web.

77. B. J. Fogg, Cathy Soohoo, David R. Danielson, Leslie Marable, Julianne Stanford, and Ellen R. Tauber, How Do Users Evaluate the Credibility of Web Sites? A Study with Over 2,500 Participants (paper presented at the Designing for User Experiences Conference, San Francisco, CA, 2003), http://portal.acm.org/citation.cfm?doid=997078.997097 (accessed June 4, 2007); Agosto, Bounded Rationality and Satisficing in Young People's Web-Based Decision Making.

78. Flanagin and Metzger, The Role of Site Features, User Attributes, and Information Verification Behaviors.

79. Soo Young Rieh, Judgment of Information Quality and Cognitive Authority in the Web, *Journal of the American Society for Information Science and Technology* 53, no. 2 (2002): 145–61; Rieh and Danielson, Credibility.

80. Amanda Lenhart, Mary Madden, and Paul Hitlin, *Teens and Technology: Teens Are Leading the Transition to a Fully Wired and Mobile Nation* (Washington, DC: Pew Internet & American Life Project, 2005).

81. Stephen Abram and Judy Luther, Born with the Chip, *Library Journal* 129, no. 8 (2004): 34–37; Harris, *I Found It on the Internet: Coming of Age Online.*

82. Lenhart, Madden, and Hitlin, *Teens and Technology.*

83. Lee Rainie, Life Online: Teens and Technology and the World to Come (paper presented at Public Library Association National Conference, Boston, MA, 2006).

84. Hitlin and Rainie, *Teens, Technology, and School.*

85. Doug Levin, Sousan Arafeh, Amanda Lenhart, and Lee Rainie, *The Digital Disconnect: The Widening Gap Between Internet-Savvy Students and Their Schools* (Washington, DC: Pew Internet & American Life Project, 2002).

86. Sundar, The MAIN Model.

87. John Seely Brown, Allan Collins, and Paul Duguid, Situated Cognition and the Culture of Learning, *Educational Researcher* 18, no. 1 (1989): 32–42.

88. Center for Media Literacy.

89. Partnership for 21st Century Skills.

90. Eisenberg, Lowe, and Spitzer, *Information Literacy*; Ross J. Todd, Integrated Information Skills Instruction: Does It Make a Difference? *School Library Media Quarterly* 23 (Winter 1995): 133–38.

91. Marc Meola, Chucking the Checklist: A Contextual Approach to Teaching Undergraduates Web-Site Evaluation, *portal*: *Libraries and the Academy* 4, no. 3 (2004): 331–44.

92. Sundar, The MAIN Model.

93. Walter Minkel, Going Gaga over Google, *School Library Journal* 49, no. 9 (2003): 37; Joyce Kasman Valenza, Discovering a Descriptive Taxonomy of Attributes of Exemplary School Library Websites, Paper presentation at the American Library Association Annual Conference, New Orleans, LA, 2006, http://mciu.org/~spjvweb/highsmith.ppt (accessed June 4, 2007).

94. Metzger, Making Sense of Credibility on the Web.

95. 21st Century Information Fluency Project, "Evaluation Wizard," Illinois Mathematics and Science Academy, http://21cif.imsa.edu/tools/evaluate (accessed June 4, 2007).

96. Heine, *Credibility in the Context of Searching.*

97. Sundar, The MAIN Model.

98. Rand J. Spiro, Brian P. Collins, and Jose Jagadish Thota, Cognitive Flexibility Theory: Hyperme-dia for Complex Learning, Adaptive Knowledge Application, and Experience Acceleration, *Educational Technology* 43, no. 5 (2003): 5–10.

99. Lev S. Vygotsky, *Mind in Society: The Development of Higher Psychological Processes* (Cambridge, MA: Harvard University Press, 1978).

100. Sundar, The MAIN Model.

101. Debra Lau Whelan, Making Research Count, *School Library Journal* 48, no. 11 (November 2002): 48–51.

102. Joyce Kasman Valenza, "It'd Be Really Dumb Not To Use it": Virtual Libraries and High School Stu-dents' Information Seeking and Use—A Focus Group Investigation, in *Youth Information-Seeking Behavior II: Context, Theories, Models, and Issues,* ed. Mary K. Chelton and Colleen Cool (Lanham, MD: Scarecrow Press, 2007): 207–55.

103. Gunther Eysenbach, Credibility of Health Information in Digital Media: New Perspectives and Implications for Youth, this volume.

104. Meridith Farkas, *Libraries in Social Networking Software,* Information Wants To Be Free, 2006, http://meredith.wolfwater.com/wordpress/index.php/2006/05/10/libraries-in-social-networking-software (ac-cessed June 4, 2007).

105. Twidale, Nichols, and Paice, Browsing Is a Collaborative Process.

106. Max Goldberg, What I Learned at Uni High, University Laboratory High School, University of Illinois at Urbana-Champaign, 2006, http://www.uni.uiuc.edu/gargoyle/2006/06/column_what_i_learned_at_uni_h.htm (accessed June 4, 2007).

Credibility, Politics, and Public Policy

Fred W. Weingarten

American Library Association, Office for Information Technology Policy

The previous chapters have implicitly or explicitly raised serious concerns and issues about Web credibility, particularly with respect to young people. Does government at any level have a role to play in addressing these issues? Should it intervene? To the extent there is a public policy reason to act, what tools are available? This chapter will examine these and related questions about the potential roles of government at all levels in dealing with issues of the credibility of Web-based information.

Ensuring the credibility of speech on the Internet is certainly not a political issue that usually garners headlines or generates much political heat. Policy makers use the term credibility rarely if at all. In fact, the idea of government interposing itself in the exchange of information among parties, even if for the best of reasons, makes many people uncomfortable, given that we live in a country with a written constitution that, among other protections, forbids government from "abridging the freedom of speech."

However, in actuality, courts have always granted government leeway by allowing it to intervene in and even abridge speech in certain instances. This leeway is not unrestricted; government faces hurdles, sometimes very high hurdles, requiring it to demonstrate a substantial public interest to justify such action. Nonetheless, government clears those hurdles with sufficient frequency to give free speech proponents no small degree of heartburn. Furthermore, and particularly important for this volume given its emphasis on children and the media, those hurdles nearly always are lower with regard to potential restrictions on access by children to certain forms of speech, especially speech deemed "harmful" to them in some way.

Government has also enjoyed a longstanding responsibility for education, on the assumption that an educated, literate public is vital to democracy, economic strength, and social stability. States and local governments operate schools. In 1862, the Morrill Act established the land grant colleges as institutions to educate the rural population, and through later extensions of the program to conduct research and disseminate new knowledge about agricultural practice. Public libraries were established by government to provide the populace with increased access to the information they might need in their lives. Furthermore, from the earliest days, government has had responsibilities to collect and disseminate information. The constitution directed government to conduct the census, but at least in the English-speaking world, government's taste for collecting statistical information dates back to the Doomsday Book commissioned by William the Conqueror so he could collect taxes more efficiently. Thus, we can think of government interventions in Internet credibility as falling into three categories:

- *Government as Censor*—government restricts speech and/or access to speech it considers "questionable" (typically the category that makes people most uneasy since it seems most in contradiction to the First Amendment prohibition).

- *Government as Educator*—government directly instructs, develops, and promotes curricula, and sets educational standards aimed at teaching people how to distinguish among credible and noncredible information and information sources.

- *Government as Trusted Source*—government exercises its traditional and important role as collector and disseminator of information in ways that help people find credible information directly from its own resources and indirectly by using its expertise to identify other credible sources.

Throughout this chapter, policies reflecting the first role, government-as-censor, will generally be referred to as "restrictive" policies, and policies that reflect the second two categories will be referred to as "supportive" policies.

The chapter postulates that (1) credibility in digital media is an important political issue that will continue to receive significant public policy attention; (2) in the political debate, credibility is usually embedded in broader social concerns such as financial fraud, protecting children from sexual predators, regulating the marketplace, protecting public health, and so on; (3) to date the potential for effective educational policies has been generally overlooked by government in favor of less effective restrictive policies; and (4) in order to achieve the full social benefits of the Internet, government and the commercial and nonprofit sectors need to pay serious attention to approaches such as information literacy, the development of more sophisticated tools to help users assess the credibility of information, intermediary services to identify credible sources of information, and the assurance of credible government information sources. Such an approach is not only aligned with democratic views about information access but, in most cases, it is more likely to be effective in achieving the desired goals than attempts to censor or restrict speech. Finally, to the extent that those concerned with fully exploiting the potential that digital media offer for learning have their own policy agenda, this chapter will suggest how and why that agenda needs to be injected into a broader public debate in order to have influence.

Some Credibility Scenarios

But, how does the issue of credibility relate to government policy in the first place? To start discussion, consider the following three fictitious, but not implausible, scenarios:

First, suppose that a large U.S.-based pharmaceutical firm places information on its Web site that makes erroneous claims about a drug that it manufactures. And, assume that a doctor acting on that information could cause serious harm to a patient. Few would argue that there is a not a compelling necessity, in the name of preserving public health, for the Food and Drug Administration (FDA) to require that firm to withdraw the false information and possibly even issue a public retraction and correction. It would need to do so both to protect against individual harm and, more generally, to maintain public trust in the integrity of the medical system.

As a second case, assume that an individual in a foreign country anonymously posts a Web site arguing that the world is shaped like a doughnut. To most observers, there would seem to be an insignificant public interest here to motivate direct government intervention resulting in restrictions on the speaker or barring access to the site. The speaker could be difficult, if not impossible, to identify and find; and even if he or she were found, the ability of U.S. law to influence the speaker's behavior is questionable. Of course, for a scholar looking for examples of aberrant belief systems, the doughnut earth site might be a useful resource; for an uncritical geography student it would be considered highly misleading and consequential in terms of academic performance. On the other hand, let's assume that an elementary school geography student working on an assignment comes across the site in a Google search and submits a paper asserting that the earth is, in fact, doughnut-shaped. This then becomes a compelling example to educators and librarians of the need to help students in their information seeking to evaluate critically what they find, to distinguish good from bad, useless from useful.

Third, let's consider that a midlevel employee of a federal science agency puts information on its Web site claiming that an unmanned satellite had just returned proof that the moon was made of green cheese. (Rather than assume that the employee is either dumb or malicious, let's just say he does it as an ill-considered April Fool's joke or a prank.) When the site is discovered, the horrified agency director has the site taken down and, furthermore, establishes a new policy requiring that all postings to the agency site be approved by an appropriate high-level agency manager. She would certainly have the authority to do so. Presumably, a major reason for such an action would be to preserve the agency's reputation as a source of credible science information. We can dig into these scenarios just a little deeper to tease out some issues that will be discussed later in this chapter.

Pharmaceutical Example

First, let's consider *why* the government (specifically, the FDA) intervenes to restrict fraudulent speech. The motivation that comes first to mind, of course, is to prevent direct or indirect damage to the health of an individual as a consequence of a physician acting on the erroneous information on the Web site. Clearly, there is a strong policy interest in protecting the public from such harm.

A second, broader and perhaps less apparent reason is to protect the integrity of a formal public policy process. The FDA is charged with approving the sale and use of new drugs, and it does so through an open, public consideration of the safety and efficacy of the drug. That consideration is based in large part on the results of an elaborate program of mandated scientific research studying the effectiveness and safety of the drug, and the pharmaceutical firms are usually the principal performers and/or sponsors of that research. To ensure the integrity of its regulatory decision making, the agency needs to be assured that it has in hand all available accurate data, and, because it performed or funded the research, the drug manufacturer is a major source of those data. In other words, for this regulatory process to work, the pharmaceutical firm must be a trusted source of information about its product. From a credibility policy perspective, then, we have the interesting case that, beyond simply banning the publication of erroneous information, government more broadly is insisting that a private corporation be a fully and publicly credible source of information about its products.

We can also ask in this scenario under what *authority* government is acting. In this case, the FDA's broad and powerful authority to regulate speech by pharmaceutical companies comes from a set of laws empowering government to regulate aspects of health care, an area of concern that is deemed particularly important to the public interest. This illustrates a key point about credibility policy: government interest and authority is very much domain specific. Its authority to control and even compel speech is thus quite limited to a few specific policy arenas in which it has been legislatively granted such authority—such as drugs, protecting the stability of financial markets, and, perhaps to a somewhat lesser extent, encouraging truth in advertising, restricting tobacco and alcohol promotion, and so on.

Finally, let's look at the *enforcement* question. We have painted a picture of a potentially uncomfortable, adversarial relationship between the FDA and the companies it regulates. But, from an Internet perspective, the FDA has some advantages in this relationship that may not always be present in other policy domains. Specifically, it has an identifiable and locatable firm it is dealing with, and the agency has something the firm ultimately wants: permission to sell its product. Thus, the FDA has a powerful means to enforce its decision beyond the mere threat of fines or court orders. Assuming the firm is well established with a physical presence and major markets in the United States, it presumably would have a strong incentive to comply.

Individual Web Site Example

Several important ideas emerge out of this example. In the first place, look at the question of *why* government intervention is appropriate or desirable. There have been many reasons advanced over the centuries for government involvement in education. In the contemporary political debate in the United States, of course, economic competitiveness, both for the individual and for the nation as a whole, is thought to rest on an educated workforce.[1] This forms a powerful political argument for government policies that encourage education. In particular, assuming that digital technologies have become major sources of knowledge, information literacy needs to encompass the ability to assess the credibility of new media. There are other arguments for information literacy education, of course. For instance, the civic engagement volume of this series discusses the uses of new media to enhance democratic participation. And, of course, as the world becomes more complex and as people confront personal decisions about health care, insurance, personal finances, and so on, they need basic skills in finding and evaluating the information they need to make those decisions. A key point raised in the chapters by Eysenbach, Flanagin and Metzger, Harris, and Lankes[2] is that the nature of the emerging digital media, specifically the tendency to disintermediate user access to information sources while we at the same time grow increasingly dependent on them in our daily lives, raises the stakes, making it even more important that people be able to distinguish credible information and information sources online. This, in turn, creates an even greater public policy incentive for government intervention at the federal and local level.

A second lesson we can draw from this example is that differently informed or motivated information seekers might assess the utility of a site differently, depending on their interests and purposes. To a scientist, the doughnut earth site would be useless, certain to be ignored and left off any recommended list of instructional sites. However, an anthropologist studying odd belief systems might find the site to contain interesting and even valid information. Furthermore, as Harris points out,[3] even noncredible sites have their purposes in literacy instruction. This is one practical reason, beyond the powerful civil liberties arguments, that we must approach the government-as-censor model with much caution.

Science Agency Example

Finally, the government science agency example poses an interesting credibility dilemma. In the first place, it can be assumed from the start that, in general, government not only has the ability, but is bound by the duty, to be a trusted source of information it provides directly. If this is so, the agency administrator was correct to be concerned about erroneous information on the agency's Web site. One might also argue that it was a sensible policy to push approval of Web content up the chain of command. But, does this really improve the trustworthiness of information on the site?

Government agencies have two basic sets of forces acting on them, and these forces often conflict. In the first place, agencies have a legal mandate and a public constituency and, for the most part, serving that mandate and constituency requires that they act as a trustworthy source of information. On the other hand, they can also be exposed to powerful political pressures, both from the executive side and from their congressional overseers. Suppose information on an agency's Web site contradicts or undermines in some way particular political positions. This not only can, but actually does, often happen with economic data, scientific research results, health statistics, demographic data, environmental information, and so on. Pressures on the agency to suppress or edit the data can be severe, potentially enforced by political power over the agency's budgets and appropriations. Yet, ironically, the examples listed above are areas for which the public most looks to government for accurate and complete reporting. Perhaps, to go back to our scenario, a policy of centralized, high-level approval, rather than improving the quality of information, could make it easier to insert political judgment into the process. As such, the scenario raises a host of very important credibility questions: can we trust the government as information provider? Does our response to that question vary by agency, by type of information, or even as administrations change? Are local governments more or less trustworthy than the federal government? And so on. The bottom-line credibility policy question is: should we, and if so how can we, ensure that government agencies at all levels are trustworthy sources of information?

Of course, government agencies are not just sources of information about themselves and their activities. They may direct users to other sources. They may link to other information sites from their own Web pages, for example. In the case of public libraries and schools, they may provide materials and steer their constituents to information services and resources that are not created by themselves. One could see how the same issues of trust and credibility raised in this scenario would be extended in these cases. When an agency links to another site from its pages, is it endorsing the linked content? Is it compromising its own status as a credible source?

Rather than striving to answer the specific issues raised in these scenarios, this chapter will look at the underlying political dynamics that shape both the decisions to intervene and the methods of doing so. It will argue that Internet public policy has been, and will continue to be, a political negotiation between a positive vision of the Internet as crucial to education and the nation's economic and social well-being, and a negative vision of an unregulated Internet as a hostile and dangerous environment, particularly for children. Each of these views has helped to shape the policies and policy proposals that have been put forth regarding the Internet in recent years.

Politics, Public Policy, and the Internet

"Policy" is one of those common words that is used frequently but that eludes clear definition, and there are as many meanings of public policy as there are writers on the subject. In general, "public policy" refers to laws, regulations, and other formal or informal rules governing individual or institutional behavior. The rules are established by some government authority (legislature, regulatory or executive agency, or court) at the federal, state, or local level; they cover some specific population of people or institutions; and they are usually accompanied by some form of sanctions—official consequences for subjects that do not obey the rules. Two points need to be emphasized.

First, the boundaries between what we would call public policy (laws, regulations, and rules promulgated by government) and private policy (rules promulgated by private organizations) are not always well defined. They blend and blur at the edges. A private organization's information policies may be influenced by government regulation or law. It also may be influenced by its own sense of public responsibility. This is a particularly important interface to keep in mind in the area of information policy, including credibility. Government's role in regulating the flow of and access to information is necessarily constrained, and we depend greatly (if sometimes to our peril) on the reliability of private institutions,[4] be they search engines, software and content providers, information services, publishers, or even television networks.

Second, institutions like public libraries and public schools are instruments of government. Their policies are government policies. The decision of a public library board to offer Internet access or information literacy instruction is a public policy decision in the sense of the term used here. So is the acceptable-use policy posted above the public terminal stating what it may or may not be used for and who may use it.

People often talk about policy at a very general level, referring to the broad principles, philosophies, and goals behind specific rules. We speak of "foreign policy," "economic policy," even "Internet policy." But, the reality is that most public policy is not developed in the top-down, rational, and consensual manner that is suggested by this use of the term. Instead, public policy is much more often the product of intense and often messy conflicts over specific issues that take place among multiple stakeholders with opposing ideologies, values, and self-interests. Internet policy is no different. In fact, this model of "policy making as conflict" is particularly useful to understand how political concerns about the way young people experience the Internet may, or may not, result in laws that attempt to govern that experience.

Some technologies (e.g., telephones, automobiles, aircraft) have been around long enough to be well integrated into the social fabric, and one could argue that the public has developed a general, albeit unarticulated consensus that at least bounds and guides policy discussions about them. For good or for bad, lawmakers and regulators stray outside those bounds at their own risk. The Internet, however, has not yet achieved that status. The Internet as a public infrastructure is only twenty-five years old, and it is still evolving rapidly. Industry is still experimenting with business models and structural questions, and new applications continue to appear that challenge assumptions and raise new social questions. This book, and indeed this series, is predicated on the assumption that digital media, including the Internet, pose deep and important social questions that we have only begun to address.

Internet policy making is, and likely will be for some time, a clash of sharply opposing views and values. The political response to the Internet as it has moved rapidly into popular culture over the last two decades is a story of intense conflicts among social attitudes, values, and expectations. Over time, a more general social consensus may emerge from this clash, but it does not seem to have happened yet. But, even in the absence of such consensus, rules are being set. These rules will, in turn, shape future changes in the technical, business, and social structure of the Internet. For example, they will determine who gets to use it, how they get to use it, who pays for it (and how much), and even who gets to monitor use and under what terms they can do so.

Underlying all these decisions is a fundamental question: assuming the Internet and all newly emerging digital media are in fact becoming the powerful global economic and socially transformational forces that they appear to be, who will benefit from them and who will be left behind? It may not be immediately obvious that public policy with respect to credibility can bear such a heavy analytical burden, but laws and regulations tend to be crude instruments. To the extent that policy makers, in the name of credibility, restrict access to sites, restrict available content, or, on the positive side, mandate education or serve as trusted information sources, their decisions will undoubtedly have broader and longer-term consequences for Internet users, whether intended or unintended. In any case, the policy research community needs to be made aware of these effects.

Different issues may lead to different restrictive or supportive policy approaches. Consider the scenarios presented at the outset of this chapter. These examples raise an important issue of how credibility is viewed in the policy world. In the pharmaceutical case, the policy concern generally turns on two factors: (1) the veracity, truthfulness, or quality of the information on the Web site or in the message, measured in this case by the potential for harm from acting on it, and (2) the assumption—even the insistence—that the firm's site should be a trusted source, and will be thought so by physicians and patients who refer to it. The persuasiveness of the site is of much less importance.

As such, the FDA would not be less concerned about the site if it were poorly designed, sloppy, or had other characteristics that may lead people to question it. The example of the science agency illustrates a similar intertwining of policy concerns about the validity of the information on the site and the presumption that the site itself must be a trusted source. It wouldn't matter if the prankster imbedded clear clues that would signal to an information-literate viewer that the posting was a joke because some people still might take it seriously simply because the site was a government agency, and that would undermine the agency's trustworthiness.

On the other hand, the education example, because of its attention to the user rather than to the content provider, has a much different and broader concern. As Harris discusses,[5] students need to learn to approach an information source with a critical eye and employ a variety of tools to assess its credibility. One cannot, for instance, assume that all commercial sites are subject to the same scrutiny and restrictions as those encountered by the pharmaceutical industry. In fact, a user is always well served to approach all sources, even regulated or government sites, with a critical perspective, which brings to the fore policy questions surrounding information literacy education.

Social Images of the Internet and Policy Making

Most significant government policy arises from the need to resolve social conflicts in some form. Some individuals, organizations, or government agencies decide that something is broken and needs to be fixed by law or regulation. Alternatively, someone decides that an opportunity exists for public benefit that requires policy action in order to fully realize the benefit. Very rarely, no one disagrees with the issue or the proposed solution, and a policy adjustment is made without much debate. Usually, instead some individuals or groups disagree. They may disagree about the existence, nature, or severity of the issue, or they may disagree about the desirability of the proposed new policies. Often, the proposed policies benefit some at the expense of others. As a result, debate ensues.

Of course, the mere existence of debate among some stakeholders does not guarantee that an issue will gain the attention of policy makers. A myriad of postulated problems and proposed solutions are raised every day. Few of them attract serious attention, and fewer still actually result in a law, court decision, or regulation. Only a few issues are on the public agenda at any time. How and why a particular issue gets on the policy agenda is a complex and subtle process that is, itself, the subject of a great deal of study. At minimum, though, for an issue to garner public attention, it must contain a basic conflict and the stakeholders in the debate must expand the conflict to touch broader concerns in the public mind.[6]

Given this limited space for public attention, it may be surprising that Internet policy seems to have received more than its fair share of political attention in recent years. But conflicts abound within this domain, as will be discussed later, and the parties to the conflicts have been very successful in linking these conflicts to deeper public attitudes and values. Those who want to see legislation have three basic tasks just to get it on the agenda.[7]

First, they need to tie the problem to an issue of broad national concern. Is this the sort of thing that people expect their legislators to deal with? Second, and perhaps more difficult, proponents need to generalize the debate, arguing that this single incident is illustrative of a broad trend by convincing the American public, or a significant portion of it, that they or their children are also at risk. Finally, proponents need to argue that the Internet poses specific new and different threats to young people that require new legislation specifically tailored to the digital infrastructure. After all, children are vulnerable in many environments, and there are countless laws in existence that are intended to protect them. Such assertions about the Internet tend to be broad and general, and are often lacking specificity or, for that matter, much serious analytical or research basis. Nonetheless, over time, when they are made in enough political contexts to support a variety of proposals addressing a variety of presumed problems, they begin to create an enduring image in the public's mind that can be tapped repeatedly in the political debate.

The political image of the Internet as a haven for dangerous and offensive material, beginning with concerns about online pornography, started in the mid-1990s and had its first legislative culmination in the Communications Decency Act (CDA).[8] The CDA was intended to restrict sexually explicit content on the Internet for fear that minors would have access to such material. After the CDA was declared unconstitutional by the U.S. Supreme Court in 1997,[9] there has been a long line of proposed and enacted legislation predicated on the same political narrative of a treacherous Internet, particularly for minors. For example, the Child Online Protection Act (COPA) in 1998[10] and more recently, in 2000, the Children's Internet Protection Act (CIPA) and Neighborhood Children's Internet Protection Act (NCIPA),[11] which required Internet filtering in libraries and schools that accept some forms of federal funding. In a complicated and contentious decision, the U.S. Supreme Court upheld CIPA and NCIPA with some limitations. This decision set a precedent in terms of government requirements for limiting access to online content for reasons that could likely stretch beyond the specific concerns of pornography to broader concerns of trust on the Internet.[12] And, as Harris points out in this volume, filtering in schools and libraries poses difficulties for teaching information literacy.

Perhaps not surprisingly, the unveiling of the Internet followed a typical pattern in which new communication technologies always seem to raise social and psychological fears about the dangers of uncontrolled access. During the introduction of the telephone, for example, alarm was expressed in the popular press that young people, particularly young women, were using this new technology to expand their social circle dangerously beyond the direct observation and control of parents.[13] Similarly, the dangers of unfettered use of radio came to the fore after the Titanic disaster with widespread reports, mostly unsubstantiated, of false distress signals and radio calls leading rescuers to the wrong location or blocking the real distress signals from the ship itself.[14]

It is notable that both radio and telephony have been very heavily regulated almost from their beginnings. In most countries, the telecommunications companies grew up as regulated monopolies, and in many countries they were government owned and controlled monopolies. Although the path each communication industry took to regulation and monopoly status was different, there is no doubt that part of the public tolerance or even encouragement of government intervention stemmed from a general sense that new communication technologies create dangerous new environments that require control. Along these lines, it was perhaps predictable that the Internet's capacity to open new virtual spaces for communications that seem beyond traditional modes of social control would similarly lead to calls for restriction and regulation.[15] Opponents and supporters of the Internet both invoked images of the old west, a frontier devoid of government control.[16] Interestingly, it is this openness and apparent resistance to control (i.e., anyone can publish on the Web) that also generates the very issues of credibility that concern this volume.[17] In the case of the Internet, an alternative, positive image has also driven public policy for many years. From its earliest days, the Internet has been viewed as an instrument of learning and scholarship, and much government research and development policy is, and has been, driven by that vision. The Internet was originally created by government science agencies, at first purely as a Department of Defense experiment, but almost immediately, this experimental network developed into an infrastructure supporting government-funded researchers. In the early to mid-1990s, the Internet began to emerge from the academic laboratory to appear in schools, libraries, and even the home and at work. It was predicted to become a major new environment for education and democratic access to public information.

This expansion of mission was even apparent in the evolution of the names for the network as it moved out of the science agencies. At the National Science Foundation (NSF), one of the principal drivers in the commercialization of the Internet, the names and visions evolved and expanded quite rapidly: at first it was the NSFNet, a network to serve NSF-funded researchers; next it became the National Science Network (NSN), a network to serve all federally funded or affiliated researchers; it was later renamed the National Research Network (NRN), a network to serve the entire academic and industrial research community; which then again became the National Research and Educational Network (NREN), a network to serve all scholarly research and education.

Each change reflected a major expansion of the perceived community to be served by the network and, most important for this volume, an expansion of the number and variety of persons who not only used the Internet as a source of information, but as a publishing medium.[18] In the second half of the 1990s, with the development of the World Wide Web, the democratization of the Web was completed. The broad public value of the Internet came to the fore, and the Internet was transformed from a government funded and operated infrastructure to a privately operated and publicly accessible infrastructure. Everyone could post information on the Internet, and many did. As more people had access to the Internet and its rapidly expanding collection of information, political attention inevitably shifted to the nature of the content that the public, and particularly children, could access.

In sum, since the pioneering days of the early 1990s and the dot-com enthusiasm of the late 1990s, two conflicting visions of the Internet have taken hold in the public mind and political debate: one view holds the Internet as the indispensable foundation for the new knowledge society and economy of the twenty-first century, while the other views the

Internet as a dangerous, threatening environment, especially, although not exclusively, for children. The history of Internet public policy for the last twenty years or so since it first began to move out of the laboratory and into the public sphere has been shaped by the growing conflict between these two social constructs. Each oversimplifies, and yet each also contains a sufficient core of legitimacy to drive the debate. No discussion of public policy and the Internet, particularly in the context of credibility and learning, can ignore the power of these two visions to both motivate and limit possibilities for government action.

A striking example of the apparent cognitive dissonance resulting from this conflict can be seen in portions of the Telecommunications Act of 1996 mentioned above. In that Act, Congress established the "e-rate" program that provides discounts on telecommunication services for K–12 schools and libraries under one explicit goal: providing Internet access to every library and classroom in the United States. Yet, at the same time, Congress included in the same act the CDA, a law that placed the burden on schools and libraries, along with other public access providers, to block student, faculty, and patron access to a wide range of educationally and socially useful materials. Arguably, certainly in the eyes of the education and library communities, the two sections sent totally contradictory signals: encouraging making Internet access available to people, while drastically limiting their ability to use it. As pointed out above, although the CDA was eventually deemed unconstitutional, subsequent legislation requires libraries and schools receiving e-rate support to filter access to online content.

Technology, Social Response, and Public Policy

So, does this example simply reflect business as usual as Congress searched for something, anything, to do about the Internet? How and why does a new technology become an intense lightning rod for legislation and regulation by policy makers who often don't even know what it is or how it works? If, to rise to national attention, political issues need to be linked with broader public concerns, the answers to these and similar questions must relate to the way that the public adapts and reacts to new technologies, and how these reactions result in heated policy debates.

The questions are, of course, complex and are the source of intense scholarly study. For the purposes of this chapter, three fundamental processes that seem to be at work in the case of the Internet are identified: (1) technology as a social practice, (2) unintended social consequences, and (3) conflicting social values of information.

Technology as a Social Practice

In its pure form, technology does not affect society or public policy. It is the way technology is shaped, adopted, and used and the way people and cultures respond to those uses that create social tensions and policy issues. There are three key factors that shape how technology and society intersect. First, there are *technological factors*, which include the basic knowledge, tools, and techniques required to create, for example, a computer or a communications network and the intrinsic characteristics of the technology itself. Second, *organizational factors* are the choices organizations make that turn the technology into useable products and infrastructures. Finally, *cultural factors* include the values, ideologies, and attitudes of people toward these new technologies. Technology as we experience it in the real world becomes adopted by society as the result of a three-way negotiation among these factors.

From a policy perspective, it is the conflicts between values and technology practices that create the most intense policy debates. From the perspective of this volume, the desire for more communication, information, and voices and sources of information inevitably conflicts with concerns about the quality and trustworthiness of information and the resulting harm that could potentially arise, especially for children, who access digital media. That said, credibility is not the sole focus of these intense conflicts. Concerns in areas like privacy, intellectual property, freedom of speech and censorship, and equity are also claiming public policy attention.

Each technology also brings new capabilities, and eventually new, unexpected uses depending on social choices and creativity. These new capabilities, in turn, can create stresses both on the institutions that created and adopted it and on the public at large. The automobile replaced the horse-drawn carriage. However, since automobiles could go much farther and faster, they also created new opportunities for use. In the long run, they fundamentally changed transportation patterns and the movement of people and goods. The cycle completed itself as these social choices and institutional changes in turn shaped the design and engineering of next-generation automobiles.

People react to new uses of technology according to their own cultural norms and expectations, and as we see in the case of the Internet, that reaction may be very diverse. Some may become early adopters; some may resist. Interestingly, some seem to do both. Some people complain about the increasing demands that instant access through cell phones and wireless e-mail place on their lives, while making sure that they have the latest wireless technology available at a touch. This ambivalence about the effects of wireless communication in the face of rapidly growing adoption results in barring cell phone use in "quiet cars" on trains, restrictions on cell phone use while driving, and banning the use of wireless technology by students in schools. These are policy responses of society to technologies that are becoming commonplace, and are therefore fulfilling some social need, and yet are also, in the public's mind, creating new problems.

As institutional roles change in response to new technology, private and public organizations also look to legislation or regulation to clarify or renegotiate boundaries. The structure of the telecommunications industry has changed dramatically over the last twenty years. This change has played out in a very active marketplace, with mergers and restructuring of firms, and the rapid introduction of new information devices and services. It has also resulted in numerous legislative initiatives and regulatory challenges with Congress, the FCC, and even the courts being called upon to decide who can offer what service in competition with whom, or who can merge with whom and under what conditions. Now, the growth of the Internet is being blamed for the fact that, after passing in 1996 a comprehensive reform of telecommunications regulation, Congress has already begun considering another major overhaul of telecommunication regulation.

Many people still look uncomfortably at telecommunications, especially when it is directed into the home. This was illustrated recently by congressional and FCC swift and strong response to the Janet Jackson Superbowl incident in January 2005.[19] It reflects concern about lack of control over content that streams into the home via the media, particularly content that may be accessible to young people. Indeed, the fallout of the incident was striking—a rash of new FCC restrictions, a series of fines of the networks not only for that "infraction" but for many others. Finally, Congress passed a new law increasing the fines the FCC could levy in indecency cases.

Of course, such social and political ambivalence about the benefits of communication technology in the face of rapid adoption is not new. In discussing the early social reactions a century ago to telephony, Marvin wrote, "the picture. . . is one of the bourgeois family under attack. New forms of communication put. . . families under stress by making contacts between its members and outsiders difficult to supervise. They permitted the circulation of intimate secrets and fostered irregular association with little chance of community intervention."[20] This description of public attitudes a century ago could easily be mistaken as a reaction not only to radio and television broadcast content, but to cell phones, text messaging, social networking, and the many ways young people are now using digital technologies to create new patterns of social interaction.

Although none of this concern slowed the adoption of the telephone 100 years ago in the slightest, this is not to say that there was no validity to those concerns. The societal effects of the telephone have been widespread, profound, well documented, and disruptive to some values and ways of life. Similarly, concerns over the implications of the new media for credibility also are well founded. Disintermediation between writer and reader promises to vastly increase the amount and variety of information available, and to decrease the delay in making it available. But, in so doing, it also clearly presents new challenges to deal with the removal of the editorial roles those intermediaries played in validating the content they provided.[21]

Unintended Consequences of Technology

Another underlying driver of public policy conflicts is the unintended consequences of technological adoption. That is, when we as a society—as a consequence of the three-way dialogue described above—decide to massively adopt some technology, the automobile, television, the cell phone, and the Internet, we are almost always in for some surprises.[22]

We can see this clearly in the history of communication technologies. The inventor of radio, Guglielmo Marconi, considered the principal use of the technology to be point-to-point communication. Mass media broadcasting did not enter his mind. At least in part, this was because a key institutional demand (and market) he saw his technology fulfilling was for a means to communicate with ships at sea. Similarly, Alexander Graham Bell thought the telephone would be very useful in broadcast mode—for one speaker to many listeners applications, not switched point-to-point communication as it actually developed.[23]

Some surprises, of course, can be most unpleasant. The automobile may contribute to global warming; television may have deleterious effects on the cognitive development of young children; cell phone use may contribute to traffic accidents, and so on. The Internet is no exception, and we are beginning to experience some of those effects, whether it be the propagation of viruses and other so-called malware, spam, and fraud on the Web. It is hard to picture the inventors of the Internet in their laboratories imagining these phenomena, or at least imagining that they would occur at a scale sufficient to provoke serious public concern.

Several reasons may account for technology's tendency to surprise us. One reason is the unexpected second-generation application. In this view, technology is invented to serve an immediate, perceived social need. Thus, in its first manifestation, it is mainly a substitution for a previous mode of doing something. Later, when the new technology has been accepted more widely, someone figures out how to use it in new ways for some other purpose than originally intended or even foreseen by the inventor. The Internet is replete with such examples; the World Wide Web is a classic next-generation application that was unforeseen by Internet developers, but that has totally transformed the use and user population of the Internet. The evolution of the networked personal computer in the office as a substitute for the typewriter is another example. It has transformed work patterns; it has changed the skills demanded of clerical workers; and, even more fundamentally, it has transformed information flows inside and outside organizations. And, in terms of credibility, e-mail has created new avenues for fraud and crime, and annoyance in the form of spam, phishing,[24] and other forms of misuse.

A second source of unexpected impacts is scale. A single car doesn't pollute significantly; but millions of cars can transform the atmosphere. An Internet that served a dozen or so research labs was unnoticeable as a source of public policy issues; but an Internet that touches most people in some way and that has become a crucial source of information for our society becomes a major source of public policy conflicts. So deeply embedded and broad have the Internet and Web become, that political concern about social equity—about the need to assist those who do not have immediate access to the Internet—is, itself, a major public policy debate.

Certainly much of the credibility debate is driven by scale, in that most people get their information from the Internet, that anyone can put information on the Internet, and consequently, that it is virtually impossible to view all content or "supervise" all content producers. These are all issues created by scale.[25]

Conflicting Information Values

The final underlying force driving public policy that must be discussed is specific to communication and information technology. People have inconsistent, often conflicting values regarding information and society, and much of what we might call "information policy" represents attempts to resolve or balance tensions among these values. Some of these balances are so fundamental to our society that they are rooted in the Constitution.

For example, to the extent that we consider ourselves independent, autonomous people, we value privacy—our control over the intrusiveness of government or even private entities in our lives. As computers and communication technologies have grown more central to society, attention has focused on the privacy of information. Our basic instinct is to say "Mind your own business!" to intruders, including government. On the other hand, we do want law enforcement to catch criminals and protect us from threats, both domestic and international. But, to do so, law enforcement asks for greater and easier access to our telephone conversations, to our Internet use, and to the myriad databases that organizations hold about us. This presents us with a fundamental conflict. How do we balance the needs of government to protect us with our expectations of privacy? In this example, the Constitution provides guidance in the form of the Fourth Amendment, which affirms neither privacy nor government's need for information as the dominant interest, but prescribes a method for balancing between them—in this case, by requiring government to convince a judge that their need for access is sufficiently strong. Privacy concerns conflict with proposals to address Internet credibility, since identifying and authenticating a content producer on a Web site or in an e-mail could help a user assess the credibility of messages. On the other hand, it challenges traditional and strong privacy and freedom of speech values about protecting anonymity in speech.

Another such tension lies in the domain of intellectual property, where the belief that writings, compositions, or works of art are, in some sense, the property of their creators who should be allowed to profit from them is balanced against the belief that a society can only function and grow when information flows freely and is easily accessible to all. Again, that balance is expressed in the Constitution, which in Article 1 Section 8 directs Congress to establish intellectual property protection as a limited and balanced set of creator rights that are established for the purpose of promoting education and innovation.

Perhaps most relevant to a discussion of digital media and credibility is the area of speech. Although in this case, the First Amendment may appear to reject balance in favor of flatly restricting government's right to restrict speech, there are many reasons for which speech is restricted, and which the courts have tolerated as permissible. For example, national security and other critical public interests allow the government to control access to certain types of information. Criminal laws restrict pornographic speech; civil law sanctions libel and slander. Even copyright law restricts speech in that it forbids, with some exceptions, the republishing or performance of a work without permission. In all of these examples, the courts, however reluctantly and, in many cases, with severe limitations, have found there to be acceptable reasons for government restriction of speech.

Why Does (or Should) Government Intervene in Speech?

We generally assume that in a democracy, government should not restrict communication. The expectation expressed by many early "cybercitizens" that government would always keep its hands entirely off the Internet has always been overly optimistic. In fact, government has offered, with some success, many reasons to regulate, monitor, or prescribe speech, and these reasons pre-date the Internet by decades, if not centuries. These reasons include protecting individuals from harm, protecting the integrity of important social institutions and infrastructures, developing human capacity, and ensuring the provenance and authority of information. Each will be considered in turn, along with their implications for credibility.

First, the government enacts laws and regulations to *protect individuals from harm*. This category includes laws protecting people from misleading medical advertising, for example. Legislative initiatives such as DOPA intended to protect children from being misled into dangerous situations fall into this category as well. These laws are often all about credibility although the word is seldom if ever used. They inevitably address concerns related to fraudulent or misleading speech, whether the speech is intended to lure children into dangerous or inappropriate situations, to get people to use products that may be harmful to their health, or to prevent fraud, identity theft, or larceny.

The government also strives to *protect the integrity of important social institutions and infrastructures* by ensuring the credibility and trustworthiness of the information they produce and disseminate. For instance, the government has regulations that govern the transparency and legitimacy of corporate speech. These rules provide protection for individual investors, but, more generally, the real reason behind these extensive and restrictive regulations is to preserve societal trust in financial markets. Similarly, government science agencies have strict rules with strong sanctions that are intended to prevent fraud in the reporting of scientific research. A researcher transgresses at the risk of his or her career. The main purpose of these regulations is to preserve the integrity of the entire institution of scientific research by protecting the credibility of scholarly communication, and it is predicated on the belief in the vital importance of the research establishment to the national interest.

Government interest in *developing human capacity* goes back centuries, and this includes government interest in education and the content of instruction. This interest extends to both prescriptions and proscriptions on the content of instruction. But, beyond narrow concerns with content, educators have always been concerned with teaching the cognitive skills required to judge the utility and credibility of information from whatever source. The assumption that an informed public is critical to democracy and to economic competitiveness has underpinned efforts to create literacy programs and to develop curriculum in critical thinking. The ability to assess the credibility of information has been an important part of literacy instruction and will be even more so in the future.

The government also seeks to *ensure the provenance and authority of information*. The most direct example of this is the requirement that government itself ensures the accuracy of its own record. Government has an obligation to ensure that its laws, regulations, and other formal and informal policy statements are clear, consistent, and accurate. Unless it has been formally changed in some regular process, the version of a law one reads today in a library in Maryland should be identical to the version of the same law one reads tomorrow in a library in New York. And, this responsibility extends through time. Society has an interest in seeing that the historical record of government decisions is accurate. This interest extends beyond government, of course, to the entire cultural record of a nation.

Beyond responsibility for the accuracy and trustworthiness of its own records, government also has several statistical data collection and publication responsibilities. It collects statistics on economic production, agriculture, energy production, and education. And, of course, the U.S. Census Department hosts an enormously large statistical database on the U.S. population. Most of these data must be made available to the public, and it must be credible as critically important decisions rest on it.

Credibility, Policy, and Digital Media

The community concerned with the numerous issues raised in these volumes about digital media, learning, and youth will need to deal with two different types of questions about public policy. First, what are the processes that could lead a government concerned about credibility in new media to impose policy on the media, and what kinds of policies are those likely to be? Second, to the extent that there is some consensus in the community that some policies are desirable, how could they be realized? The answers to both questions lie in the deeper political process described in this chapter.

It is doubtful that any government lawmaker or regulator has ever used the word *credibility* in public to label a law, explain a proposal, or justify a vote. Nor is it likely to be used that way in the future because, as pointed out earlier, in the process of raising an issue to an active public debate, the issue must be framed in terms of broader public concerns. Nevertheless, however the issue is labeled, the credibility of information on the Internet lurks just beneath the surface of a number of issues currently under debate in Washington. That is because, in terms of the two-step framework described above, concerns about credibility create contentious policy debates that, in turn, are rather easily generalized to broader social concerns.

For example, in the ongoing policy debate about the use of social networking applications by sexual predators to identify and connect with young people, the argument has been that predators are able to falsify their identities, pretending to be peers of the young people on the site, and thereby establish a relationship with a potential victim. One interesting aspect of this example as a credibility issue is that it is the identity and intent of the speaker, rather than the specific content of the messages themselves, that are the focus of attention. Even if the content of every message sent by a perpetrator were "true" in a technical sense (an unlikely case), if the identity of the speaker were false, the communication itself would lack credibility; thus, this example constitutes a credibility issue. On the other hand, it reaches the level of congressional attention because the issue is defined as protecting children from sexual abuse.

Spam is another example of a public policy issue that is related to credibility, although it is not framed in those terms. In 2003 Congress enacted antispam legislation.[26] In it, the Federal Trade Commission was directed to establish rules and regulations to deter mass e-mail solicitations. By any measure, spam is a major annoyance to anyone dependent on e-mail. It takes time to deal with spam, it uses computing resources, and it can be just plain offensive to see in one's mailbox. But, beyond annoyance, spam is often used for more nefarious purposes. It may be used to transmit computer viruses or "worms" and to commit fraud. And, it is in that realm of concern that credibility becomes an issue. Unsolicited e-advertising from a known party is annoying, but somewhat manageable. A message from a bank purporting to be a legitimate transaction but that is, in fact, an attempt to obtain a bank account number and identification information is quite another. Fraudulent messages from other countries with pathetic pleas asking for help and offering riches to the recipient have become so common as to seem patently unbelievable, yet they still attract the gullible. On the other hand, despite several attempts, creating policy or technology that effectively separates these sorts of fraudulent messages from legitimate and credible messages has eluded policy makers.

Modes of Government Intervention in the Credibility Domain

As the examples throughout this chapter indicate, there is a range of ways in which governments intervene to affect Internet content or the use of content on the Internet. It is useful to examine them briefly in an orderly way as they relate specifically to the problem of Internet credibility. In general, government policy in this area can be divided into two categories—restrictive and supportive.

Restrictive Policies

Policies that restrict speech are intended to either control or limit information put on the Internet or to control or limit access to it. They are usually focused on information providers and/or intermediaries such as schools, libraries, or ISPs. Many are not specific to the Internet, but are policies that apply to a broader range of speech, including that which occurs on the Internet. These include policies that restrict content on Web sites; policies that require the content provider to control and/or authenticate access to its content; policies that require public access providers such as schools, libraries, and community centers to restrict access to digital information, principally by the use of filters or other technological measures; and policies that attempt to restrict what individuals can do or access on their own systems.

Policies That Restrict Content on Web Sites   In many instances, certain types of content are prohibited. Few such instances are purely directed at Internet publishing, but a general rule of thumb is that if false or misleading content is prohibited in print, the prohibition likely extends to the Internet. Fraudulent statements about a corporation's financial condition, libel, or false claims about the efficacy of drugs, are some examples. Because these policies step closest to the line drawn by the First Amendment, the purpose of these policies, whether online or off, is nearly always to protect people from serious harm by ensuring they have access to credible information, a purpose that can presumably stand up to constitutional scrutiny.

Policies That Require the Content Provider to Control and/or Authenticate Access to Its Content This has been tried or suggested as policy for preventing young people from accessing sites that offer adult-oriented content or liquor advertising, or for authenticating participants on social networking sites. As we have pointed out above, authentication of source is also a way of encouraging access to credible information. It gives the user more cues as to the credibility of information and, in some cases, may be an incentive for content providers to be more careful.

Authentication is an extremely difficult technical problem on the Internet. The old *New Yorker* cartoon captioned "On the Internet, no one knows you're a dog" still holds true, and technologists have yet to invent an effective remote canine detector. The most popular approach has been to require the use of credit cards, relying on the financial industry's self-interest in validating the identities of their cardholders. Beyond technical problems, there is a First Amendment interest in protecting anonymous speech. Thus, as with policies that restrict Web site content, the aim of policies that require content providers to control or authenticate access to their content stem from the government's motivation to protect individuals, particularly children, from physical, psychological, or financial harm from accessing inappropriate, misleading, or fraudulent content.

Policies That Require Public Access Providers such as Schools, Libraries, and Community Centers, to Restrict Access to Digital Information, Principally by the Use of Filters or Other Technological Measures The filtering requirements placed on schools and libraries by the Children's Internet Protection Act are an example. This law requires all schools and libraries that accept certain forms of federal funding to use filters on terminals used to provide public Internet access.[27] The impetus for these types of policies reflects the tension described earlier between competing views of the Internet as a critical source of information and, thus, education and the Internet as a dangerous and threatening environment. Although these policies recognize the Internet's potential for important educational and learning goals through providing access to information technology freely to all citizens, especially those unable to purchase their own computers, they are at the same time designed to protect children from accessing "harmful" information.

Policies That Attempt to Restrict What Individuals Can Do or Access on Their Own Systems These policies are usually associated with certain technological measures that are built into devices or into the content itself. For example, Congress has mandated that new television sets must all incorporate V-chips that allow parents to block violent or suggestive programming. Digital Rights Management (DRM) technology is being built into digital devices of all kinds to control the use of copyrighted content, and federal law makes it illegal to circumvent these measures. As the need to validate digital documents increases, we can expect laws that mandate and protect the use of such imbedded technologies. The intent of these laws is not only to protect the public or individual users from harm but also to both protect the integrity of information policies, such as copyright law, and to ensure the provenance and authority of electronic documents, such as contracts. In so doing, they implicate credibility.

Supportive Policies

Supportive policies focus on the users and the intermediaries that serve them. Rather than attempt to restrict or control access to "bad" information, these policies are intended to help users find or use credible sources. Supportive policies include policies that use intermediary services to provide access to digital media, policies that promote education and literacy, the development of navigation and search tools, and government as a source of reliable information.

Policies That Employ Intermediaries to Access   Public institutions such as libraries, schools, community centers, senior services, and so on have become important sources of access to the Internet and digital content. Many of these organizations invest considerable resources in providing advice, training, and support—helping users find good and credible information appropriate for their needs. As mentioned before, these policies stem from the government's interest in promoting the development of human capacity. At the federal level, an example would be the so-called e-rate described earlier. The purpose of providing e-rate discounts for telecommunication services is to strengthen the ability of libraries and schools to provide public Internet access. Of course, over the last decade, public funding at all levels—local, state, and federal—has greatly expanded their roles in providing Internet access to their constituencies.

Policies That Promote Education and Literacy   Many of the intermediary institutions mentioned above are also providing information literacy instruction—teaching users how to search for information they need, how to use tools in ways that identify credible sources, and how to critically assess information they find on the Web. The motivation is, here again, developing human capacity. Libraries, in particular, have been central in developing instructional programs in Internet use and information literacy for the public, and thus have played a major role in educating the public about issues of credibility and digital media.

The Development of Navigation and Search Tools   There is significant potential for research on search tools designed to assist users in identifying and locating credible sources of information, or that signal the possible credibility values of sites that are found. Under the rubric of developing human capacity, government is a major supporter and consumer of research in the computer and information sciences, and many popular search engines currently used are based on research work begun in university research laboratories.

Government as an Information Source   Finally, as suggested much earlier in this chapter, government can be a direct and authoritative source for information, putting its imprimatur on the site. For many kinds of information, it is in fact *the* principal source of authority and credible information.[28] This includes information about government, statements of policy, documentation of decisions, and the like, as well as the presentation of information collected and generated by government in its research labs and numerous statistical collection and analysis activities.

To understand how various issues may lead to either restrictive or supportive policy approaches, consider the three scenarios presented at the outset of this chapter. In the case of the pharmaceutical company disseminating erroneous claims about a drug, government has a clear incentive to act to protect its citizens from harm. Second, as pointed out above, government also has both the authority and the means to actually restrict content on the site. Given the combination of strong public policy incentive and the government's technical and legal ability to restrict content, it will likely do so.

In the case of the geography student being duped by a legitimate-appearing, but non-credible Web site, it would be hard to convincingly argue the existence of some clear and present danger to a child's mind from visiting that particular site. Furthermore, as discussed earlier, government lacks both the technical and legal means to restrict the site. On the other hand, as pointed out before, there is a legitimate concern about the broader context that the site exemplifies. The bewildering array of falsehoods, truths, and just plain goofiness on the Internet can, in its totality, present a serious impediment to learning. Also mentioned before, scale itself can present social issues. These considerations point to the importance of teaching children how to evaluate the credibility of information rather than direct government intervention or restriction of speech.

The third scenario, concerning information on a government agency Web site, reflected the need for the agency to present authoritative content. As in the second example, it would be hard to argue that any serious harm would come to an individual who stumbled on the false information, in fact it would be difficult to argue that anyone would even believe it. On the other hand, harm to the overall reputation and image of the site (and its sponsor) as an authoritative source of scientific information would, indeed, be a matter of concern to agency administrators, perhaps serious enough to motivate action and policy. Furthermore, the agency unquestionably has the means and the authority to set and enforce policies about content on its own site.

These three examples show a clear relationship between problem and policy response. However, in many cases, it is not so clear. Take the examples of the sexual predator or fraudulent spammer. In these cases, there certainly are dangers of harm. Policy makers can argue about the degree of threat, how many are out there, and how many succeed. Statistics are notoriously difficult to collect in this area. But, no one can argue that fraud or preying on children is not a matter of legitimate and serious concern to government, nor that the government ought to take steps to protect people, especially children. So, having established the existence of harm, should government respond with restrictive policies? Not necessarily. In the first case, the government had not only harm but the authority and the ability to restrict content. Authority and ability are not so clear in this case. In the first place, the First Amendment throws up hurdles—not absolute barriers, but definite hurdles—to government attempts to restrict speech. Second, government's technical ability to restrict general speech on the global Internet is limited at best. So, this consideration suggests that restrictive policies are not the best choice, even if they make favorable headlines or campaign ads. And therein lies the debate. Those looking most closely at harm stress restrictive policies, while those looking at authority and technical limitations stress education and a more technically sophisticated and effective law enforcement system.

Conclusion

Extrapolating from history, one can conclude that credibility has been and will continue to be a key underlying political issue with digital media. In part, this is because media never stop evolving and the evolution is taking place so rapidly that we hardly have time to digest the last new application before a new one comes along to replace it.

These changes have also been fundamental. Thirty years ago, the Internet was a restricted communications system intended to seamlessly share among a small group of researchers access to geographically dispersed computers. About fifteen years ago, with the invention of the World Wide Web, the Internet became a system to share files of electronic information among millions of people distributed all over the world. Now, we are embarking on another transformation, as the Internet is becoming a participatory social technology for creating diverse, geographically dispersed virtual communities for work, play, political deliberation, and learning.

It is hard for politicians and, indeed, for many of their constituents to make sense out of what is happening. Change always seems to bring both threats and promises, along with an intense dialog among those who focus on one or the other. And, as discussed in this chapter, those dialogues invite policy making to resolve the tensions.

But, it should not be assumed that only those who see evil in change are the source of policy. As was said earlier, those concerned with exploiting the full potential that new digital media have for a learning society also have a policy agenda. Jenkins lays out three concerns that in his view may call for policy intervention.[29] In his words, these are *the participation gap*, which refers to the unequal access to the opportunities, skills, and knowledge that will prepare youth for full participation in the world of tomorrow; *the transparency problem*, which consists of the challenges young people face in learning to see clearly the ways that media shape perceptions of the world; and *the ethics challenge*, or the breakdown of traditional forms of professional training and socialization that might prepare young people for their increasingly public roles as media makers and community participants.

It is not hard to see significant public policy challenges in all of these areas. It is equally easy to see how the unanticipated consequences of uninformed policy making regarding the Internet and new digital media, particularly restrictive policies, could exacerbate all of these problems. Public institutions like schools and libraries, which are in a position to address all three of these areas of concern, could be prevented from doing so. In fact, as Harris argues,[30] school literacy programs are already hindered by restrictive filtering requirements. Nearly all public libraries provide public access to computing and the Internet, and for many populations, they are crucial for providing equitable access. Yet, for a variety of reasons, they are struggling to stay ahead of the technological curve.

The message to be gained from this chapter is clear. To be dealt with effectively, policy needs must overcome several challenges to capture the benefits of the digital media revolution. There is no strict formula for success, but this chapter suggests the following first steps:

1   Define a clear and understandable set of policy needs.

2   Frame those needs in the broader terms of political debate—for instance, security, fairness, economic success, democracy, and so on.

3   Find allies in such sectors as industry, academia, community leadership, and the public sector.

4   Above all, take the debate public. Engage society in a discussion that aims to deflect the simplistic good-versus-evil dichotomy that so often creeps into Internet policy debates and seek to find a middle ground where a careful, thoughtful assessment of the opportunities and dangers can be made.

If, as Jenkins argues,[31] we are in the early stages of yet another significant technological and social change, we are also in for a prolonged policy debate as society decides how to negotiate that change. Furthermore, we can assume that problems of identifying credible information and sources in this environment will be a continuing source of public anxiety and, hence, will be triggering underlying factors for this debate. As this volume documents well, we are starting to know a lot about how people, and particularly young people, can be taught to deal with the problems of identifying credible information. Our challenge now is to inject this knowledge effectively into the policy debate.

Notes

1. See, e.g., the Web site of the Partnership for 21st Century Skills, http://www.21stcenturyskills.org/, an influential coalition of the high-tech industry focused on this issue (accessed June 4, 2007).

2. Gunther Eysenbach, Credibility of Health Information and Digital Media: New Perspectives and Implications for Youth, this volume; Andrew J. Flanagin and Miriam J. Metzger, Digital Media and Youth: Unparalleled Opportunity and Unprecedented Responsibility, this volume; Frances Jacobson Harris, Challenges to Teaching Credibility Assessment in Contemporary Schooling, this volume; and R. David Lankes, Trusting the Internet: New Approaches to Credibility Tools, this volume.

3. Harris, Challenges to Teaching Credibility Assessment, this volume.

4. See Lankes, Trusting the Internet, this volume.

5. Harris, Challenges to Teaching Credibility Assessment, this volume.

6. This is not an idiosyncratic view of policy making. See, e.g., Elmer E. Schattschneider, *The Semisovereign People: A Realist's View of Democracy in America* (Hinsdale: Dryden, 1975).

7. This discussion oversimplifies a whole field of political science investigation. For instance, it ignores the role of Congress itself in searching for issues and illustrative examples, the role of the press in raising attention to a particular incident and the presumed causes of it, the roles of issue advocacy organizations, and so on. See John W. Kingdon, *Agendas, Alternatives, and Public Policies*, 2nd ed. (New York: Addison-Wesley, 1995).

8. Communications Decency Act of 1996, 47 U.S.C. 223 (a) (1) (B) (ii).

9. Reno et al. v. American Civil Liberties Union, 1997. No. 96-511 (decided June 26, 1997).

10. Child Online Protection Act, 47 U.S.C. 231. COPA is still under court challenge at the time of this writing, but the government is currently enjoined from enforcing it until a final decision is made.

11. Children's Internet Protection Act, PL 106-554.

12. United States et al. v. American Library Association, Inc., et al., No. 02-361 (decided June 23, 2003).

13. Carolyn Marvin, *When Old Technologies Were New* (Oxford: Oxford University Press, 1988).

14. Susan Douglas, *Inventing American Broadcasting: 1899-1922* (Baltimore: Johns Hopkins University Press, 1987).

15. Of course, if a technology were to hold real or perceived dangers that appeared to heavily outweigh any conceivable benefits, there would be little political debate about its regulation. If necessary, the technology would be banned; but more likely, the market would not even sustain its development and deployment. This, however, is a rare case. More often, a countervailing benefit is also seen, and that is when the battle begins.

16. One of the most influential public interest organizations formed at that time, and one that still has a major voice in Internet policy, is the Electronic Frontier Foundation.

17. See Flanagin and Metzger, Digital Media and Youth, this volume.

18. We should note that this repeated expansion by government of the Internet user community was less a deliberate conscious policy than it was simply a recognition of reality. From its inception, the

Internet seems to have grown on its own, unimpressed by bureaucratic attempts to limit and define its roles and users, but continually reshaped by the desires and visions of those users.

19. Frederick Lane, *The Decency Wars: The Campaign to Cleanse American Culture* (Amherst: Prometheus Books, 2006).

20. Marvin, *When Old Technologies Were New*, 69.

21. See Flanagin and Metzger, Digital Media and Youth, this volume.

22. See Edward Tenner, *Why Things Bite Back: Technology and the Revenge of Unintended Consequences* (New York: Knopf, 1996), for a fascinating and detailed examination of the nature and causes of this phenomenon; for a more general discussion of unintended consequences for digital media, see *Digital Youth, Innovation, and the Unexpected* (ed. Tara McPherson) in this series.

23. In another more recent reversal showing such patterns are not necessarily permanent, radio has become a major telephonic communication medium in the form of cellular technology, and television is increasingly delivered over very high capacity lines owned by cable and telephone companies. After a century, Marconi and Bell turned out to be right after all!

24. *Phishing* is a term applied to unsolicited e-mails that purport to be from legitimate institutions such as banks, eBay, or even the IRS. Their intent is to persuade a user to click on an apparently legitimate Web site that is intended to collect sensitive personal information for illegitimate purposes.

25. See Flanagin and Metzger, Digital Media and Youth, this volume, for a discussion of these and related issues.

26. Controlling the Assault of Non-Solicited Pornography and Marketing Act of 2003, PL 108-187.

27. The link to federal funding helps the law to pass constitutional scrutiny.

28. I must digress here to point out that from a democratic policy perspective, although supportive policies may seem to be, and in fact may well be, more benign than restrictive policies, a grain of caution is still required. Although restrictive policies are more directly intrusive and redolent of government as "Big Brother," it is important to recall that some of the images of state control in Orwell's book *1984* were of government as a source of information: e.g., the ever-present television screen and the carefully edited and retroactively rewritten news archives. While we do not tend to think of teachers and librarians as propagandists, even though they are employees of the state, government agencies have nevertheless been accused of distorting or altering information on their Web sites; commercial search engines can be used to steer users to certain sites or even block access to sites; filters can and do block political content; and so on. The fact is that any of the restrictive or supportive policy approaches discussed in this chapter can potentially be subverted to the political interests of the state. The more pertinent that information becomes to a political issue, the more one person's falsehood becomes another's truth. And, it is not always clear when information assumes political content. Even scientific information may suddenly and unexpectedly become pertinent to a political debate over environmental, energy, or health policy issues. This is not to say that government policy should not touch the issue of information credibility. There are too many important reasons for it to do so and, in any case, the political forces will encourage it to do so. That said, we must be sensitive to the potential for misuse of any policy approach.

29. Henry Jenkins et al., Confronting the Challenges of Participatory Culture: Media Education for the 21st Century, 68 (The John D. and Catherine T. MacArthur Foundation, 2006).

30. Harris, Challenges to Teaching Credibility Assessment, this volume.

31. Jenkins et al., Confronting the Challenges of Participatory Culture.